Winning Speech Moments

Winning Speech Moments

How to Achieve Your Objective with Anyone, Anytime, Anywhere

by

JAY OZA

5ToolGroup.com

42 Village Court, Hazlet, NJ 07730

ISBN 978-0-999-30940-7 (softcover)

ISBN 978-0-999-30941-4 (ebook)

Printed in the United States of America

Book and cover design by bookclaw.com

ATTN: QUANTITY DISCOUNTS ARE AVAILABLE TO YOUR COMPANY, EDUCATIONAL INSTITUTION, PROFESSIONAL ORGANIZATION, OR CLUBS for reselling, educational purposes, subscription incentives, gifts, fundraising campaigns, or any other ideas you may have.

For more information, please contact the publisher at 5ToolGroup.com, 42 Village Court, Hazlet, New Jersey 07730, 732-547-3624, joza@5toolgroup.com or joza@winningspeechmoments.com.

DEDICATION

To my late in-laws, Ghanshyam and Usha Trivedi, who taught me and others about generosity with love.

All great speakers were bad speakers at first.

— *Ralph Waldo Emerson*

Contents

PREFACE

The only reason to give a speech is to change the world.

— John F. Kennedy

As you are about to read this book, you are probably asking, "Does the stuff in this book work, or is it going to be a big waste of my time?" It works. I use it, and I have seen it work for the clients I have coached for job interviews, business meetings, and speeches. I also provide many examples of how others do it effectively, including politicians, business leaders, and celebrities in general. Since great speakers rarely write a how-to book on how they became great speakers, I have written this book so *you* can become a good-to-great speaker. So get ready. On your mark, get set...

Congratulations!

You don't need anyone's permission to start your journey to become a good-to-great speaker, a journey that has the potential to change your life. You rarely ever find a successful person who does not speak well. You just started, and only you can end it (that is, if you get tired of winning). Where will it lead you? Only you can answer that. I am just here to guide you through this journey. So let's get to it.

During the past twenty-four hours, a week, a month, or perhaps even a year, you spoke to quite a few people, who probably included colleagues, clients, prospects, friends, acquaintances, family members, other relatives, and strangers. Did anyone create a speech moment that you remember? Did you create one that others would remember? If so, was it a winning speech moment? What was your "win"?

So, what is a winning speech moment? Was it when Martin Luther King Jr. used "I have a dream"? Or when John F. Kennedy said in his famous phrase during his 1960 inauguration speech: "Ask not what your country can do for you, ask what you can do for your country"? These were winning speech moments. Why? We still remember them today. They influenced an entire generation and even changed history. That is the power of winning speech moments.

But such power is something you can create when you are speaking, too. And you must speak if you want to win. Of course, listening is important in helping you better understand others' viewpoints so you can support your points with winning speech moments, but you can score points and win only when you are speaking.

Now that you know a little about what a winning speech moment is, how far back do you have to go before you can remember creating a winning speech moment? If you are not creating a winning speech moment often, or if you have to go far back in time to remember one, then this book is for you. Unless you are creating winning speech moments, it is highly unlikely that people are going to remember much about your speech and help you win—that is, help you achieve your overall objective.

Winning speech moments aren't created only by great speakers anymore. Today, with social media, anyone can create a speaking moment that results in a win. Danielle Bregoli appeared on an episode of *The Dr. Phil Show* that focused on mothers dealing with unruly daughters. She certainly lived up to her billing when, at one point during the show, she became irritated at the audience laughing at her poor use of the English language and yelled, "Cash me ousside. Howbow dah?" Many laughed, but that speaking moment soon went viral and made her an instant YouTube star. She has since parlayed her one defining winning speech moment on TV into making up to $40K per appearance. She may even get her reality TV show depicting her life.[1] That is the power of a winning speech moment today. Now there are a lot of unruly daughters out there, so why is Danielle the one who captured people's attention? She created the right moment at the right time, at the right place, on the right show, reaching the right audience. She got lucky; we have to work hard at it.

Before you get angry, go to Amazon, and give me a one-star review, here is the fact that I simply can't ignore. I have hundreds of videos on YouTube and have had about 0.01 percent of Danielle's YouTube views. Now, you are probably not going to say in a high-stakes business presentation, "Cash me ousside. Howbow dah?" But you'd better come up with something that is acceptable and catchy if you want to win. Like Danielle, you'd better create a winning speech moment.

People are so overwhelmed with information today that they have mostly outsourced their thinking to others. Unless you can cut through the noise with something that sticks, what you say will not resonate with people. Your speech will be remembered only if it has a "sticky" winning speech moment.

In this book, I don't focus on giving a speech for the sake of giving one. I focus on giving a speech to win. And I believe you are more likely to win if you can create winning speech moments every time you speak, whether it is in public or private.

Is creating a winning speech moment hard? Yes. Can you do it? Absolutely. Will you do it? I believe so if you enjoy winning in life, whether at work or just for fun.

Speaking has always, through the ages, been important for success in both life and work, but today people's attention span has become shorter because of all kinds of distractions. Often, you have only one opportunity and very little time for your speech to win over an audience of one or many. Therefore, to win—whether in a job interview, with project funding, with a business deal, in an election, in a relationship, or just to persuade with your idea—you *must* create a winning speech moment. Why? As I pointed out, that is what people remember. According to cognitive scientist Carmen Simon, "people act on what they remember, not on what they forget."[2] To achieve your objective, what do you want people to remember?

Winning speech moments compel people to tell others, and their spreading your message helps you win. Winning in anything is a team sport. A good-to-great speech not only motivates others to get on your team, but it helps you grow the team quickly. A good-to-great speech makes you look like a winner, and people tend to gravitate toward those who look like winners.

We saw an excellent example of someone who won because he created many winning speech moments. Donald Trump won the 2016 presidential election with no political experience. Whether you like Trump or not, he certainly knew better than his opponent how to win the votes from people in key areas, enabling him to win the most important job in the world. So, what was his secret?

He had no secret. There are many theories on why he won. You don't have to think too hard; just go with your observation. During the campaign, he simply outcommunicated—in his unique way—everyone he faced. I am not going to make you speak like

Donald Trump and win, but I will show you how to develop and master high-stakes speaking skills so you too can succeed by creating winning speech moments.

I will not place any wager that you can give a speech. I know you can. But you and I both observed in the 2016 presidential election that the difference between giving speeches and giving winning speeches is that Donald Trump is the president and Hillary Clinton, though she won the popular vote by approximately three million, is not. Both knew the rules of the game. Trump played the communication game better and won. You must learn to play the communication game like Trump did if you want to win in anything. And that is what this book is all about. Again, this book is not about giving speeches; it is about winning by giving speeches.

Note: In this book, I write about politicians, both present and past, as examples for teaching purposes only. I do not endorse them, their political views, or their policies. I am using politicians' speeches because they are more transparent compared with speeches given by people in business or other professions.

"The more words you use, the more people you lose."

Does this quote, which I often cite, by itself do anything for you? It shouldn't. It lacks a context for it to be memorable. But suppose I use this same quote at the end of a short speech on what I do for a living—that is, speak, teach, and coach people on how to deliver winning high-stakes speeches. Now the quote may be memorable to you; perhaps it may even be a winning speech moment in helping you remember me, recommend my book or coaching service, or become my client. I have infected you with my message, so you want to get more information from my website, and hopefully, you will spread my message or even take action.

However, creating a winning speech moment takes some work. You must first craft content, develop a message, and deliver a performance. Only by integrating these three parts (content, message, and performance) are you more likely to create winning speech moments. Trying to create a winning speech moment without all three parts is like looking at a beautiful picture of a beach resort on the Internet. The resort looks great, but you won't feel anything unless you visit the resort and experience it yourself. And when you do visit the resort, and if it lives up to your expectations, then not only are you going to remember it, but you will tell others and perhaps even visit it again. Similarly, when you are speaking one on one, in a small group, or before a large audience, you must strive to integrate the three parts to create winning speech moments.

In a nutshell, the Big Idea of this book is the following: **To master the art of creating winning speech moments, you need to integrate the three parts with the intention of winning—that is, with the intention of achieving your overall objective. You need to change your mindset from just giving speeches to giving winning speeches.**

I will show you how to craft and deliver winning speech moments incrementally and iteratively. You need to start today (if you haven't already) and stay the course by making tweaks as needed. On the other hand, if you are looking for a heroic approach to making you a good-to-great high-stakes speaker, then this book is not for you.

I want you to become a good-to-great speaker every day; therefore, you must turn what I am teaching into a daily habit. Knowledge will make you smart, practice will help you develop skills, and deliberate practice—over time—will give you mastery. I wrote this book because I believe anyone—that is, *you*—can achieve mastery of this skill if you are committed, if you are willing to work hard, and if you stay committed for the long term. It's not that complicated.

My approach is practical, simple, and easy to integrate into your speech-giving goals. All I am asking from you is to give this method ninety days. After practicing for ninety days, not only are you going to improve, but you will start winning when you are speaking and, most important, you will look forward to giving high-stakes speeches.

What makes this book different from others is that I treat every speech as being high-stakes. Before you ever get a chance to give a speech in front of key decision makers of an organization, or deliver a keynote or a TED Talk, you need to give a boatload of high-stakes speeches, including introduction speeches, impromptu speeches, pitches, short speeches, and long speeches. For example, before Martin Luther King Jr. gave his famous "I Have a Dream" speech, he had given close to two thousand formal speeches. If he had not been winning the audience with less-publicized speeches, he would not have had the opportunity to give a historic speech in front of close to three hundred thousand people on the steps of the Lincoln Memorial.

So, will this book make you like such past great speakers as John F. Kennedy, Martin Luther King Jr., Ronald Reagan, Bill Clinton, Barack Obama, or like some outstanding contemporary speakers from business and academia, such as Seth Godin (entrepreneur and author), Neil deGrasse Tyson (astrophysicist and author), Sheryl Sandberg (COO of Facebook and author), or Amy Cuddy (Harvard Business School professor, author, and one of the most popular TED Talk speakers, with more than forty million views as of this writing)?

No.

And you don't want to. However, you *do* want to become who you have the potential to be: **a great high-stakes speaker**. Look, I continuously keep working hard to become Jay Oza, a great high-stakes speaker. And what's wrong with that?

You own your success. Now go tackle this book. Not just with one speech on one day… but *every* time you speak!

Good luck!

Jay Oza

Hazlet, New Jersey

September 2017

INTRODUCTION:

Speak to Win!

*We don't rise to the level of our expectations, we fall
to the level of our training.*

— Archilochus, a Greek lyric poet

Who was the greatest high-stakes speaker of all time? I believe it was the legendary queen and storyteller in the famous saga *The Arabian Nights*: Scheherazade.[1]

In the story, King Shahryár, a pagan Persian, married a beautiful queen but became enraged when he found out that she was unfaithful. Not only did he have the queen executed, but to seek revenge on womankind in general, he made a vow to marry a woman every night and kill her the next morning. The vengeance of Shahryár lasted for three years, until there were only two women of marriageable age left in the kingdom: Scheherazade and her sister, Dunyazad.

Scheherazade decided to marry the king, but she had devised a clever plan. She would have her sister visit her that night and beg her to tell a story. The story Scheherazade would tell would be so captivating that she would end it on a cliffhanger when the morning arrived so she could finish it the next night. Shahryár was so intrigued by the story that he let Scheherazade live. Next night, Scheherazade would tell another captivating story, and again she left it on a cliffhanger when dawn arrived to finish it the next night, thus living another day. Scheherazade did this for one thousand and one nights before finally prevailing on King Shahryár to abandon his vow and not kill his queen.

The book *The Arabian Nights* (also known as the *One Thousand and One Nights*) is one of the greatest pieces of fiction in world literature. Look at what Scheherazade accomplished: She was not the queen of high-stakes speaking; more accurately, she was the queen of *high-wire speaking*! If she had told even a single story that Shahryár disliked, she would have been killed.

Fortunately, when you speak, the consequences are not life or death. But if you want to get ahead and stay ahead, you must be good at crafting and delivering high-stakes speeches, where you will either win or lose. You must give a speech performance as if you were a "speakerazade," speaking before a Shahryár-like audience that you must win over. If you want to keep winning, you'd better make the audience want to listen to you again and again, until you achieve your objective.

When was the last time you delivered a high-stakes speech? I ask this question because many people who speak, even those who speak often, rarely deliver high-stakes speeches or even give much thought to the potential stakes involved when they are speaking. In a sense, for many of them, speaking is like breathing; they just do it. Now, Nike's popular "Just Do It" slogan is great for exercising but not for speaking, especially when the stakes are high. You need to do it right and well the first time you are speaking before an audience, since you may not get a second chance with that same audience.

* * *

I wish I had come across a book like this right after I graduated from college and started my first job. A month into my job, my boss, Dave, informed me that it was my turn to give the engineering update to the leadership team at the next weekly status meeting. Naturally, I was excited but also a little anxious. I said to myself, "How tough can this be?" My update was going to take only a couple of minutes. Hence, I did not think I had to prepare much. All I did was gather information from the engineering team; I felt I was ready to provide the update.

At the meeting, my boss called my name to provide the leadership team my engineering update. *I heard my name, and I was immediately gripped with anxiety and couldn't utter a word.* I completely lost track of time. My boss must have signaled to my colleague Chris, who was sitting next to me, to take over. Chris then took the notes I had prepared and provided the update. He later told me (as a comfort, I believe) that I had put together an excellent status update. I thanked him, and I never discussed that incident with anyone inside or outside the company. I ignored it afterward, thinking that my fear of speaking in public would somehow magically disappear.

Was giving a status update a high-stakes activity? Absolutely. You don't get many opportunities to gain visibility among your peers, superiors, and other department heads at work, especially when you are just starting your career. People make decisions quickly, and it is difficult to change their initial, overall perception.

You have to make each opportunity count if you want to get ahead. Unfortunately, I didn't look at it that way then, and eventually I got bored with my job; I ended up leaving the company in eighteen months. Meanwhile, my colleague Chris, who had joined a few months before me, was being groomed to become the manager of the engineering department. Chris and I were both excellent software engineers, but the difference was that he was a better communicator than I was.

I should have learned a valuable lesson at my first job, but I didn't: **Often the difference between success and failure comes down to your communication skills.** Unfortunately, as with bad breath, no one dares tell you that you stink at public speaking. You'd better take stock of this skill yourself and take immediate action. It will pay off. Don't make the same mistake I made!

I did not learn this lesson, and I didn't take corrective action immediately. As a result, I lost a lot of precious time developing my public speaking skills. Yes, I kept advancing in my career by being technically competent. But I eventually hit the proverbial brick wall at a mid-level management position in my mid-forties, and I left the corporate world to start my consulting company. I am sure some of you can relate to this, and others, sadly, will find out a little too late. My advice to all who aspire to get to the top is to not delay like I did in developing this skill. I recommend that you get proactive so you can master this skill over time and thrive. Your future success depends on it.

Giving a high-stakes speech gets you noticed no matter whether you are a man or a woman, young or old, short or tall, white or black, good-looking or average-looking—whatever. You must "grab the mike" and make it count, fast. Today, speaking to just communicate is no longer sufficient to get ahead. The bar has been raised. Today you have to speak to win—*all the time*. One of the main reasons why 1 percent in any field thrive, and 0.1 percent in any field rule, is because they all are very comfortable giving high-stakes speeches, and they enjoy it. You just can't get ahead today without having the superpower of high-stakes speaking skills.

Take the Shots

I have written this book to share my method and practices, which are based on my research, teaching, mentoring, coaching, practicing, and experience giving speeches. Since I am very passionate about this topic, I will try to motivate you to start your public speaking journey. However, no matter what I write to motivate you to develop and master this skill, only you can make yourself do the deliberate practice necessary to get better at it. You have the book. What are you going to do with it? Nothing? Or "all in," right now?

The rule to get ahead and stay ahead in both life and at work is simple: **You have to be good to great at giving a high-stakes speech.** When there are no stakes attached to it, a speech is not that important. When you break it down at the top level, a speech comes down to three things: **building, delivering, and winning**. Winning is the most important of the three, but it is often neglected. Many people are so exhausted from putting in the work for a speech that they are just happy to be done with it. You should not be one of them.

One thing I have to make clear: When I say you will become a good-to-great high-stakes speaker, I do not mean that you are always going to wow people with your speaking skills. Is it important to wow your audience? Not always. If you are good to great, you are more likely to achieve your overall objective. If achieving your objective means wowing your audience with your excellent speaking skills, then that's all well and good. Unfortunately, however, a lot of speakers focus too much on wowing their audience at the expense of achieving their overall objective. Such excessive focus on wowing is a waste of a speech. You are never going to win all your audience. Focus on the ones you are more likely to win over. To win, to ensure success, you need to iteratively and incrementally build and test your content, your message, and your performance.

If your speech did not help you achieve some specific victory, then all you did was make some noise that no one will remember. Unfortunately, most speeches, to put it bluntly, are just noise. The audience is often left wondering what the speaker was trying to achieve. In contrast, you are going to make every speech count.

Michael Jordan, one of the greatest professional basketball players of all time, exemplified performing well in high-stakes situations on a basketball court in front of tens of thousands of spectators and millions of television viewers. He once said,

> I've missed more than nine thousand shots in my career. I've lost almost three hundred games. Twenty-six times, I've been trusted to take the game-winning shot and missed. I've failed over and over and over again in my life. And that is why I succeed.[2]

Michael Jordan remembers the stats of his failures, because he put himself in a position to take and miss many shots, which eventually helped him become a great basketball player.

This applies to public speaking skills, too. When you lack competence, you will also lack the confidence to take big or even small shots. If you are not good at public speaking, you are not going to put yourself in a position to take many shots in life or at work. Subsequently, unlike Michael Jordan, you will not have the stats of missed shots to brag about. Life is not that different from being on a basketball court, or at home plate on a baseball field, or even on a golf course ready to hit your next shot. Sometimes, you will miss. The only thing professional athletes control is that they make sure they are well prepared to keep shooting, to keep swinging, to keep practicing, so that eventually, they will put themselves in a position so they can win. You control your speaking success, and you must also put yourself often in a position to win, too.

Before you move on, I want you to think more about this metaphor of taking shots, since my writing this book comes down to helping you develop competence, so you will become sufficiently confident to take many high-stakes shots in life, business, relationships, or just about anything. If you do that, then you, too, can "be like Mike"[3] and brag about your many missed shots in both life and work.

Fear

True success is overcoming the fear of being unsuccessful.

— Paul Sweeney, Irish economist

This book does not focus much on how to overcome the fear of public speaking, but in this section I do discuss fear a bit. If you have fear of public speaking, the best place to turn to is your local Toastmasters International club. I joined one, and it helped me immensely; I highly recommend it. After I joined, it took me a few speeches before I started feeling comfortable speaking in front of people. That said, this section discusses some useful things to understand about fear.

Fear is the number-one reason cited why people find public speaking difficult. Many people are terrified to speak in front of an audience. And it gets even worse when the stakes are high. Many believe that there is not much they can do to overcome their anxiety of public speaking; hence, they avoid giving a speech altogether, or they try to do just about anything to get out of giving a speech.

According to many surveys, fear of public speaking ranks somewhere just above the fear of death. Given a choice between the two, I am sure people would somehow muster some courage to give a speech. But the surveys point to how much we hate being judged by others when we are speaking. Jerry Seinfeld, an American comedian, joked about public speaking in his stand-up routine, asserting that many who are at the funeral would prefer to be in the casket instead of giving a eulogy. No matter how bad you may think you are as a public speaker, I can assure you that you are not going to die giving a speech—at least not from stage fright!

No one is immune from the fear of public speaking. James Rosebush, former chief of staff for Nancy Reagan, writes about the conversation he had with Margaret Thatcher, former prime minister of Great Britain, about her being such an outstanding speaker.[4] Here's what she told Rosebush:

> You never completely lose the fear, no, never. Sometimes when I reach the podium I have to say to myself, "Come on, old gal, you can do it." But that little bit of fear always sticks with you, and the energy you derive from it gives you more courage to press onward with what you have to say.

Even the "Iron Lady," as she was nicknamed by a Soviet journalist for her tough leadership style, had to overcome the fear of public speaking every time she gave a speech.

According to Gregory Berns, professor of Neuroeconomics at Emory University, there are three biological reasons for the fear of public speaking: social intelligence, fear response, and perception.[5] Public speaking brings all three to the forefront. The social intelligence requires you to connect with the audience, inform them on a topic that they will find interesting, and then persuade them. Doing all three social intelligence requirements is hard—and your brain is not wired for that. The fear response has to do with the fact that you probably don't like attention focused on you; your brain is wired to sense harm when people are staring at you. Perception has to do with the fact that you are exposing yourself to the audience, and they may not see things the way you see them and are presenting them; you want to be accepted and not judged or rejected, and your heightened anxiety can result in a poor speech performance.

It is typical to experience some element of fear when you are speaking. If you didn't, then either you don't care about the speech you are giving, or there are little to no stakes in how well you perform. You rarely fear talking to your family members, friends, and colleagues, since the stakes are usually low to none. But when you have to give a speech and the stakes are high, you can become gripped with fear. You start thinking that you'd better do a great job, because you are not going to get a second chance. You might also fear being exposed as a fraud or an impostor. Your brain begins to overthink and not focus on delivering your message in a plain, simple, and direct manner.

One thing that can help you overcome fear is to reframe how you feel when you start speaking. You may have been told that what will help is to take a deep breath and relax. But that technique is not so effective, according to the research conducted by Allison Wood Brooks, assistant professor at Harvard University, research explained by author Adam Grant.[6] Brooks had students give an extemporaneous three-minute persuasive speech in front of a class on why they would make good collaborators at work. All the speeches were videotaped to be rated by a committee of peers later.

Brooks asked half the speakers to say, "I am calm," and the other half to say, "I am excited." What the research showed was that those who said, "I am excited," were judged 17 percent more persuasive and 15 percent more confident. Furthermore, the "excited" group spoke 29 percent longer. The reason why excitement works better than being relaxed is that fear is a strong emotion. You can't just apply brakes and expect to stop it. It is better to step on the gas and transfer that emotion to a different place.

Brooks conducted another study where she made students sing the first few verse of rock group Journey's "Don't Stop Believin'." The students were measured by a software program that gauged pitch, volume, and rhythm. She then reframed their thought by a simple statement. Those who were asked to say, "I am excited," scored 81 percent accurate. Those who were asked to say, "I am anxious," scored 69 percent accurate. Those who were asked to say, "I am calm," scored 53 percent. The main takeaway from the research was that focusing on the positive outcomes makes you far more confident.

Once you have learned to manage your fear and want to speak confidently with people both formally and informally, I recommend you take the courses on public speaking offered by the leading online education company, Coursera.

Is This Book for You?

I have written this book for people who want to give more high-stakes speeches and create more winning speech moments so they succeed in both life and at work.

I have been mentoring students from all over the world, including students who want to improve their public speaking skills, advance in their careers, give speeches in academic settings, and give speeches at their religious places, clubs, schools, and so on. I teach worldwide audiences by hosting a weekly YouTube show called *Speech Talk Live*,[7] where guests and I offer tips, techniques, and insights on improving a student's public speaking skills.

Once you lay the foundation of public speaking skills and develop confidence, you will be ready to start giving high-stakes speeches. And this book will focus specifically on high-stakes speaking, since this is the kind of speaking that results in success that is seldom adequately covered in many public speaking books. After reading these books, people are left disappointed when they don't see tangible results within sixty to ninety days. Hence, I am once again making it very clear that this is not a book for those who are interested in simply giving a speech; this book is for those who want to win with their speech.

Another reader who will find this book valuable is the professional who gives a lot of speeches at work. With some tweaking, you can easily take your speaking to the next level. You will find this book very helpful no matter what stage you are in your career. However, as you raise the stakes, you do need to practice regularly to be effective. Pablo Casals, one of the world's greatest cellists, at the age of ninety-three was asked why he practiced three hours a day, to which he replied, "I'm beginning to notice some improvement." Similarly, public speaking is a skill you can improve as long as you are breathing. If you follow my method for ninety days, I am confident that you will start noticing some improvement in your high-stakes speaking skills, too.

Hacks

To show you how to craft and deliver high-stakes speeches, I cover three *hacks*: **content hack, message hack,** and **performance hack.**

I define the word *hack* as a method to craft a speech that is fast, minimally tested, yet impactful. The purpose of a hack is to get the job done with your speech when you are time constrained. If, like a TED speaker, you have plenty of time to give a speech, one that is close to perfect, then hacks may not deliver the perfection of speeches that you see at TED Talk events.

With a hack, you start a speech that is "quick and dirty," and through iteration, you keep improving the speech—as necessary—based on the feedback you receive. Through testing your speech with others or by yourself, you will get a better idea on whether you are likely to achieve your objective when you deliver the speech to your target audience. The purpose of using a hack is to do what's necessary quickly to achieve your objective: to win.

Hacking, in the context of software development, is widely used by such companies as Facebook, Google, General Electric, and many others to develop products that customers want, can afford to buy, and then cannot stop telling others about. Hence, I believe hacking can also be used effectively to build your most important product: your speech. Yes, your speech should be viewed as a product you are building. You can't achieve anything without building this product first.

Working toward Mastery

Here's a powerful, practical tip—a simple sentence—that can guide you toward giving successful high-stakes speeches:

Record your speeches using your smartphone; then review them to see what you did well and what you need to improve—and keep doing it.

That's it. If you stop reading further and go do this one, simple thing, you are going to be more successful than someone reading this entire book but who does nothing. But as you can see, becoming a confident high-stakes speaker is mostly about self-discipline and practice. You will find that all great speakers struggled when they started giving speeches.

One of the greatest speakers of the twentieth century, Winston Churchill, struggled as a speaker when he was starting his political career. Boris Johnson, former mayor of London and current secretary of state for foreign and Commonwealth affairs for Great Britain, wrote[8] that at the age of twenty-nine, on April 22, 1904, Churchill had a meltdown when he was giving a speech before Parliament. Churchill was making a case for striking workers, arguing that they should be allowed to use bully tactics to encourage nonstriking workers to join them and that they should not go to jail or pay fines.

After speaking for approximately forty minutes, Churchill suddenly stopped after saying, "And it rests with those who…" He froze. He stood there for several minutes, trying to regain his thoughts. He could not regain them, so he said, "I thank the House for having listened to me," and he sat down. It was an embarrassing moment for Churchill. He had to work hard to become a great speaker; according to Johnson, "Churchill's speeches were a triumph of effort, and preparation, in which phrases were revised and licked into shape as a she-bear licks her cubs."

* * *

In this book, I use the word *speaking* interchangeably with *public speaking*; actually, I believe there is no such thing as "public speaking." There is only good speaking, bad speaking, and no speaking.

Today, you can't hide—or survive—for long being a bad speaker. You are going to be judged on how well you speak, whether it is live or on video. If you embarrass yourself on video today, you don't get to have a good laugh like you would have in the old days if you were on the TV show *Candid Camera*. Because of YouTube and various other live-streaming video applications, your video will be available forever, for all to see—and there is nothing you can do about it. People will judge the way you appear on video. Whether we like it or not, we are all "public" figures today. Rather than trying to fight it, why not just invest some time in becoming a confident speaker and capitalize on this new reality?

The point is that you must be very careful when you speak today, whether you're speaking publicly or privately. You have to assume that every time you are speaking, you are speaking in public and are being recorded. If you are not careful, you could pay a big price. My common rule of thumb is this: View everything you say as being public and of high-stakes. This will save you a lot of grief later.

Lastly, remember this: You simply can't get too far in life or in business without mastering high-stakes speaking skills. The reason for this is that people's attention span keeps getting shorter, so you must communicate in a way that not only captures people's attention quickly but *maintains* it. **Attention is today's currency.**

Simple, Memorable, and Repeatable

The shortest path to your speech success is appealing to people's gut. It is much easier to win if you appeal to someone's "feel-good" state, making them feel good about themselves. Whoever captures someone's "feel-good" state usually wins.

For example, Donald Trump, with his "Make America Great Again" slogan, made people feel good about the future, just like the way President Ronald Reagan did with the slogan "Morning in America" in his 1984 reelection campaign. A simple, memorable, and repeatable message gives people reasons for supporting a particular candidate or for taking any action. You can test this out: Examine just about anyone or anything that wins, and you will see that it usually meets these three attributes: simple, memorable, and repeatable. Hence, to have a lasting effect, your speech needs to be simple, memorable, and repeatable.

Life Is Like a Beauty Pageant

One of the things I love about watching the Miss Universe beauty pageant is the final question. It all comes down to answering this same final question by the final three contestants that will determine who gets crowned Miss Universe. Beauty, talent, grit, and hard work may have gotten them to be one of the three finalists, but it is not going to help them win. It will come down to answering that final question in less than thirty seconds, which will change the life of one young woman. The hard truth is this: No one will remember the names of the runners-up. The difference between winning and losing is often so close that it often comes down to the one who can give the best speech that influences the people who will make the final decision.

In the 2015 Miss Universe pageant, Miss Colombia, Miss Philippines, and Miss USA were asked this question: "Why do you think you deserve to win the Miss Universe crown?"

Miss Philippines won with the following answer:[9]

> To be a Miss Universe is both an honor and responsibility. I will use my voice to influence the youth. I would shed light on causes like HIV. Show the world that I am confidently beautiful with a heart.

Now, if you are cynical, you may be saying that this is just entertainment. But you nonetheless face some kind of "beauty pageant" in whatever you do, though obviously not on live TV before tens of millions of viewers. My point is this: The way you speak has the potential of changing your life—whether it is in a job interview, an informal meeting, or a formal address. The only thing you control is whether you are well prepared, so that you are confident and can deliver a good-to-great speech when it matters.

You may make it on the stage because you know how to market and sell yourself well, but you are not likely to win often if you are not prepared to engage, connect, inform, influence, and persuade. If you develop the speaker's mindset, convinced that every speech you give matters, you are more likely to win with anyone, anytime, anywhere.

One of my clients whom I coached, John, was going through a real-life "beauty pageant." He wanted to get accepted into a medical residency program that he had selected. As in a beauty pageant, he was competing against dozens, if not hundreds, of other candidates vying for a handful of coveted positions in the top residency programs throughout the country. My client's acceptance into a top residency program depended on how well he answered questions during his brief interview with key decision makers. The stakes were very high, and there were no "right" answers, unlike in the many tests and exams he had taken in schools over the years to get where he was.

Here is an example of a question that John was asked during his interview by a director of the anesthesiology department at a major teaching hospital in New Jersey: "You are in an operating room, and there is a scrub technician, a circulating nurse, a surgeon, a surgery resident, an anesthesiologist, and you, the anesthesia resident. Who is the most important person in the room?" He thought for a couple of seconds and confidently said, "The patient." He told me that the director nodded in approval and moved to the next question. After that, he was on "offense" for the rest of the interview, and he immediately knew he had scored points that would likely put him high in their ranking.

John's hunch was correct. Based on his academic credentials and interview performance, he was indeed ranked high by the program and was accepted. He is now pursuing his dream of becoming an anesthesiologist. He aced many tests and exams, but he also had to ace the final test—the interview—to gain admission into the anesthesia residency program. Acing the final test came down to his ability to speak well when the stakes were high.

Life is not fair, but you can at least level the playing field by being prepared to win. To succeed in life, you must interview well. Life is a long interview. Eric Schmidt, executive chairman of Alphabet, and Jonathan Rosenberg, former senior vice president of products at Google, believe that interviewing is so important for businesspeople that they have a subchapter titled "Interviewing is the most important skill."[10] The one thing such top companies as Amazon, Google, and Facebook spare no expenses for is in hiring. They know that everything can be copied except their human talent. They have a rigorous interview process to ensure that they are hiring the right candidate who will help keep them at the top. To stay at the top, they work hard at improving their interviewing skill. So if you want to get into one of these tier-one companies, or in anything, you must learn to interview well.

To interview well, you have to prepare and be able to give answers in thoughtful, organized, impactful short speeches. If you can do that, not only will you create a memorable winning speech moment, but likely you will walk away with a job offer. I have coached people who have done that, so I know it is a must-have skill for success today.

The Gettysburg Standard

Because of people's short attention span, today you have between 1 and 272 words to make a difference in someone's life or even to change the world. Why 1 to 272 words? Two hundred and seventy-two is the number of words Abraham Lincoln used to reframe the nation with his Gettysburg Address. What's your excuse for not being able to meet Lincoln's lofty communication standard? There isn't one!

If you can't get your message across in 272 words, then you better be highly entertaining in order to keep your audience's attention. How much do you remember of the last speech you heard? And were you moved to action after listening to the speech? If you are like most people, you probably don't remember much of the last speech you heard—and you probably were not moved to action afterward.

Many communications you have with people are a total waste of time, whether they're one on one, in a small group, or before a large audience. They achieve nothing. Then there are the high-stakes speeches, where you will either win or lose something.

A memorable winning speech moment is not just an event but an experience. This simple insight took me a while to figure out, and I will explain in this book how you can go from crafting content quickly to raising the stakes by developing a compelling message and delivering memorable moments during your performance, thereby creating an unforgettable experience. If you develop this speech mindset, you are more likely to achieve your overall objective.

You picked up this book because you want to get ahead and stay ahead in anything you pursue. But it's hard to achieve that objective without giving a lot of high-stakes speeches—and giving them well and often. If you get into a simple habit of recording your thoughts on video and posting them on YouTube, you will be far ahead of many in becoming a good speaker. I have a motto (adapted from a famous baseball quote by Earl Weaver, Hall of Fame Major League baseball manager of the Baltimore Orioles): **Motivation is the next day's deliberate practice.** You must put in the work to become a good-to-great high-stakes speaker, so let's get started—right here, right now.

How This Book Is Organized

I have organized this book in four parts.

In Part One, I go over the basics of public speaking, so you understand why this is such a critical skill for your success and what causes many speeches to fail. I discuss the most important speech you ever give. (If you mess this up, you may not get to give any more speeches.) I end this part with the steps you need to take to become a high-stakes speaker.

In Part Two, I introduce the method—in particular, the content hack. I discuss the steps for becoming a confident speaker.

In Part Three, I continue to present the method, now describing the other two hacks: the message hack and the performance hack. I discuss the steps for becoming a good-to-great high-stakes speaker. By practicing the three hacks (including the content hack, described in Part Two) and by integrating them, you can deliver a great experience to your audience.

Note: You often don't have time to craft and deliver a speech using all three hacks, so they are in order of importance based on the time constraints you are likely to encounter when you have to give a high-stakes speech.

In Part Four, I go over the speech you are going to give soon. I include a chapter on how to assess your progress, how to give and receive feedback, and how I coach myself to develop my public speaking skills. I conclude with the key three moments of a speech that lead to success, and I make the bold claim—and the promise!—that we are all professional speakers today.

So, let's get right to it.

PART ONE:

The Basics

CHAPTER 1

Why Master High-Stakes Public Speaking Skills?

Speech is power: speech is to persuade, to convert, to compel.

— Ralph Waldo Emerson

When I was in seventh grade, a nurse called several of us students to her office for an eye test. When we arrived at the nurse's office, I was lucky that I was not first in line. I felt lucky, because when I looked at the eye chart, I knew I was in deep trouble. I could not clearly read the 20/20 row or even the 20/25 row. The nurse did not hide the chart, since she did not think any student would cheat on an eye test. After all, she was probably thinking, "What does one have to gain by cheating on something that's going to benefit them?"

Evidently, the nurse did not know how scary it can be for a young boy to realize, like I did at that moment, that his life was about to change—for the worse. I panicked. I did not want the nurse to confirm my poor eyesight by sending a note to my parents, asking them to take me to an eye doctor for a thorough eye examination. My big break came when the nurse was busy writing a note for the student before me, which gave me enough time to slowly edge forward, squint a little, and quickly memorize the 20/20 and the 20/25 rows. Having memorized the two rows, I was suddenly imbued with a newfound confidence that I was going to ace the eye test.

When my turn came, I was convinced that with heroic efforts, I could reverse my poor eyesight by eating more almonds and carrots and even by curtailing the amount of television I watched. This was what was going through my head as I stepped up to the line.

The nurse started with 20/50 row. No problem. She then went to the 20/40 row. Again, I aced it. Next, she wanted me to read the 20/30 row. My immediate thought after taking a quick peek was "Houston, we have a problem." I could not read several letters, and my confidence quickly sank. The nurse, sensing trouble, asked me to repeat it, but again I could not read several of the letters. To my horror, she abruptly ended the test.

I pleaded with her to let me read the 20/25 and the 20/20 rows, but she was not persuaded, and she wrote out a note that I was to take to my parents. I had never been so sad in my life as I was on that day, especially since it was now official that I needed glasses. My dream of being a New York Knicks guard was officially over. When you're young, this is as close to the end of the world as it gets. As I was leaving the nurse's office, I remember feeling angry at myself for not memorizing the 20/30 row. But the good thing that did come out of this mini-tragedy was that my grades suddenly improved. Perhaps it was a divine intervention, and divine wisdom as well: "The Lord giveth, and the Lord taketh away." But I also learned a valuable life lesson that cheating isn't worth the effort.

What does this sad story have to do with speaking well? The point I am making is that you will likely struggle to succeed in relationships, jobs, and business unless you can speak well first. Corrected vision was fundamental to my success in school, and my cheating could only sabotage that success. Speaking well is a fundamental skill, and without it, or by trying to compensate for its absence with other, less-fundamental skills, you will likely flounder in your efforts to succeed.

It helps a lot to develop this fundamental skill early and then to work hard to master it, thereby increasing your chances of success in just about anything. It is never too late to start, since you still have a lot of speaking left to do.

Warren Buffett, American business magnate, investor and philanthropist, said to students at Columbia Business School that to be successful you have to master public speaking skills. He said that you have to "get very comfortable—it may take a while—with public speaking… That's an asset that will last for fifty to sixty years."[1] In fact, Buffett attributes his confidence as an excellent public speaker to attending Dale Carnegie courses on public speaking when he was young. Buffett and his long-time business partner, Charlie Munger, are still actively speaking in their late eighties and early nineties, respectively. If you want to see both of them in action on YouTube, besides watching them do many interviews on television, check out the duo conducting a marathon Q&A session (lasting over five hours) at their Berkshire Hathaway annual shareholder meeting in May each year. They are both excellent examples of the importance of public speaking at any age. And when these two businessmen talk, people listen, spread their message, and act on their business or personal advice.

Other skills may help you in the short term, but for the long term, I believe, no skill is as critical to your success as the ability to speak clearly, directly, and purposefully, especially as the stakes increase. And it is becoming even more important as the world gets more complex. Speaking well is like having "complexity insurance." For example, in a job interview, it is difficult, if not impossible, to sell your talent and competence without having good speaking skills. During a job interview, you don't get to do the job; you get to *speak* the job, hopefully well, so the interviewer will feel confident that you indeed can do the job.

Effective verbal communication is not a one-day thing; it is an everyday occurrence. Unless you view speaking as high-stakes, you are more likely to make speaking mistakes. In each and every situation, before you open your mouth, you need to become conscious of the high-stakes significance of what you are going to say. The reason for this is very simple: people judge you by the way you speak. And you know very well that first impressions are very hard, if not impossible, to change. You have to be on your game at all times. In daily life, it's *always* high-stakes speech time.

The Public Speaking Skill as a Keystone Habit

Pulitzer Prize–winning journalist and author Charles Duhigg explains the concept of the *keystone habit* with an excellent story about Paul O'Neill, former CEO of Alcoa and later George W. Bush's treasury secretary. After being hired as the CEO of Alcoa, in his first speech to the media, he started with the following statement: "I want to talk to you about worker safety… I intend to make Alcoa the safest company in America."[2]

Media were dumbfounded, since they had expected O'Neill to talk about improving the company's financial performance. But O'Neill knew what he was doing. Within one year, Alcoa not only had improved its safety record but had realized record-high profits, a record that continued when he left the company in 2000. By getting the entire company to focus on safety, by making safety a keystone habit at Alcoa, O'Neill improved the company's financial performance.

In the same way, you can make public speaking your keystone habit to improve your performance. Your doing that will result in good things happening, such as getting a good date, making new friends, enhancing your image, securing new business, or simply enjoying life's pleasures. Such is the transformative power of a right keystone habit. Aristotle said it best: **"We are what we repeatedly do. Excellence, then, is not an act, but a habit."**

Return on Investment (ROI)

Now, some of you may be asking, "Why should I spend time on developing a skill when I don't know its ROI?" It's a fair question to ask, especially before you decide to devote money, time, and energy on improving your public speaking skills. I have used the method I teach in this book with clients I coach, clients who don't have ninety days to develop this skill on their own for their specific high-stakes situation.

Note: There are no quick fixes to developing and mastering this skill. I am here to guide you, so you succeed and so you look forward to giving high-stakes speeches.

I once coached a woman named Kathy, who had many years of experience in marketing and was starting her own business in how companies can discover what their customers really think about their products, using metaphors instead of using focus groups. She submitted a proposal to speak at a marketing conference, and to her surprise, it was accepted. That was the good news. The bad news was that she had not given a speech in front of a large audience in a very long time. Kathy reached out to me for help. Even though we worked together for only two weeks (rather than ninety days), she still delivered an effective speech at the marketing conference. She was so emboldened from that experience that she is now pursuing more speaking opportunities to corporations and marketing events. Kathy now has a mission to educate people on her expertise, and she plans to leave her job and start her own company, where she can consult and do more speaking. She feels rejuvenated.

I coached another woman, Sarah, who was looking to change a job. She wanted to go from an established company in the educational field to a small company. I had to help her with her message development, so she could effectively answer questions from key executives at her job interview. We collaborated on developing and communicating a solid message. After she was offered the job, we tweaked the message a little to help her negotiate a higher salary. I give her all the credit, but she did say to me that our coaching sessions helped her become more confident. She increased her salary from $85,000 to $130,000. When I spoke to her recently, she had received a raise of $10,000 and was very happy at the company where she is working. Most important of all, Sarah exuded the confidence of someone looking to create more opportunities for herself.

I worked with a military veteran of thirty years, Victor, who was making a transition from military service to the corporate world. It is difficult to make a transition, especially when you have given so much to a single institution. In preparing for his first interview with the company's COO, I asked Victor to focus on three things that were important for the job he was pursuing, such as leadership, problem solving, and teamwork. For each one, I asked him to elaborate in the interview by describing a specific problem he had faced, the solution that he had come up with, and the outcome he had delivered. If it had been a group effort, I told him that he should certainly mention that fact. He followed my guidance, and the COO was so impressed with his qualifications and how well he communicated that he was asked to meet with the CEO next. For that meeting, I coached Victor to focus on strategy, vision, and growth. He did as we had discussed, and the CEO was so impressed that he offered him the job at the end of the interview.

Victor beat out ten others who were vying for the same job. With some negotiation, he accepted the job offer and decided to make the transition. This took only one week, so it is highly likely that I may have worked with an exceptional veteran out of many that the military seems to produce. Victor said that without my help, he would not have been well prepared. I got him to come up with short speeches that mapped what he had done to what was important to the company. And it worked. He got the good high-paying job that he wanted.

The last one was a medical doctor, Rohan, who wanted to leave a small practice to join a large medical group. Since he had not interviewed for a while, I had to work with him to ensure he was being authentic about why he became a doctor in the first place and why he wanted to join a large medical group. I helped him create a vision on the different ways he could make the group grow their practice in rehab care.

Rohan gave a presentation to a group of physicians who would make the hiring decision. They were very impressed with him, and they made him an offer where he would become a partner in three years. Working with me on getting the job and negotiating the salary helped Rohan make over $250,000 by becoming a partner in only eighteen months.

So, the payoff for having excellent public speaking skills is important in many situations, not just in speaking in front of a large audience. You see the fast payoff when you are interviewing for a job or speaking at business meetings. You know quickly whether you have won or lost. But the payoff for the longer term is incalculable and cannot always be defined in a monetary sense.

It's often hard to quantify the ROI of any skill that you may capitalize on in the future. You must trust the process and bet on yourself. To do that, you have to think of a future skill like an investment and then work backward so you are focused in the present on what will help you achieve your future goals. *Harvard Business Review* blogger Peter Bregman says it well: "You need to spend time on the future even when there are more important things to do in the present and even when there is no immediately apparent return to your efforts."[3]

Visibility Is Everything

According to author Sally Hogshead, "You will not win by being invisible. Today, you win by being seen and remembered."[4]

Public speaking skills make you visible. And unless you are visible, it is hard to be successful, especially in the attention-deficit world in which we live. You are simply "Mr. Cellophane," as far as others are concerned, as Amos Hart sings in that famous song from the great Broadway musical *Chicago*. To them, you are "Invisible, inconsequential… Cellophane, Mister Cellophane." Developing public speaking skills has the potential to transform you from Mr. Cellophane to Mr. Charisma. And you don't have to be James Bond to be charismatic. All you need to do is be on top of your game when you are speaking, which you will learn how to do later in this book.

Robert Moses, who was the master builder of New York for four decades in the twentieth century, wielded a tremendous amount of power without ever being elected to a political office. How is that even possible? He did it by being a parks commissioner. Moses knew how to wield power through building parks.[5] Moses understood that if you build parks, you get support from the people of all classes and the print media who love programs that improve the quality of life.

Because of this groundswell of public support, the wealthy and influential could not stop Moses from implementing his vision of building parks, as well as roads and bridges so that common people could easily get to the parks he built. But why parks? Simply because they are visible—people can see them, people can feel them, and people can enjoy them. Moses knew the importance of visibility and how important it is to succeed, and this vision helped him gain more and more power.

The other person who knows something about visibility is Senator Chuck Schumer, Democrat from New York. He is very media savvy and has been known for holding press conferences on Sunday mornings ever since he's been a politician to bring visibility to obscure yet important issues. He did these press conferences on Sundays, because it is a slow news day, and he knew that on this day he would get more visibility than on any other day. By appearing on the news, Schumer was showing his constituents that he was working hard on their behalf and thus could easily keep getting reelected. As of this writing, Schumer has leveraged his media exposure skill to become the Senate minority leader.

The last one, of course, is Donald Trump. He has always been in the news since the early 1980s, and until the early summer of 2015, he was famous for being a TV celebrity. But after he announced his candidacy for the presidency, he kept himself visible by giving speeches to huge rallies, doing plenty of interviews on both radio talk shows and cable news networks, and using social media effectively and strategically. Trump won the Republican nomination because among the Republican candidates, no one was more visible than he. Trump knows that to get people's attention, you must be visible, either through a TV appearance or by sending a tweet. Visibility is everything to

Trump, and it has paid off "bigly." And it can pay off for you, too, if you speak a lot and well.

Today, if you are not visible, you don't exist. Why? People face so many distractions that they can't focus on any one thing for too long. And that applies to what you are saying, and even to what you are doing. Take for example a famous experiment conducted by the *Washington Post*.[6] They had the world-famous classical violinist Joshua Bell play incognito at a busy Washington, DC, Metro station.

If you search a YouTube of Bell playing at the station, you will see that most people just rushed past him to get to their destination during the morning rush time. They did not pay attention to the once-in-a-lifetime virtuoso performance—for free!—at a Metro station. Bell collected just $32.12, not his usual $45,000 per performance he receives playing at famous concert halls around the world.

If Joshua Bell can't capture attention, then you can see how much harder it is for everyone else to get attention. Today, time may still be money, but I think attention is wealth. Whoever can capture attention is going to wield a lot of power and become both successful and wealthy.

Insurance against Machines

Machines are getting smarter, better, faster, and cheaper every day. How can you compete against this onslaught? You will have to do it with your communication skills, especially your speaking skills. If you don't, then you are not going to be gainfully employed for long. I am basing this blunt assessment on the trends that I see around me and read about in the news every day.

People are getting very anxious today when they read about jobs being taken over by intelligent technology. Companies no longer need to hire a lot of people to get the work done, as they did in the old days. Now companies are productive hiring fewer employees, who can work with machines. But one area where the machines have not made tremendous inroads is with interpersonal skills. I don't want to say that machines never will acquire such skills, but let's just say it is not happening that fast—not yet anyway. I often joke that we are safe as long as machines don't learn how to gossip.

Humans do hold a big advantage, obviously, with the speaking skill; hence, this skill is highly valued. You'd better develop this skill fast, since, as the authors of an award-winning paper titled "Racing with and against the Machine: Changes in Occupational Skill Composition in an Era of Rapid Technological Advance" assert, "For any given skill one can think of, some computer scientist may already be trying to develop an algorithm to do it."[7] The authors conclude that those who have many years left in their career had better find a new job or complementary skills where humans are needed.

Your only job security is to adapt and develop skills that complement the machines. Many experts think it will take another decade before we start seeing many jobs being replaced by machines. Based on how fast the technology is advancing, I would not be surprised if that time frame is much shorter. I would not bet against technological progress. Mark Cuban, an American businessman, investor, author, and television personality, tweeted on February 19, 2017, that "automation is going to cause unemployment and we need to prepare for it."[8] Bill Gates and Elon Musk have also raised similar concerns that jobs are going to disappear because of technology, especially with artificial intelligence.

Machines are now doing things that we used to think only humans could do, such as writing a political speech. Valentin

Kassarnig of the University of Massachusetts, Amherst, has developed a machine that can do just that.[9]

But one thing machines are a long way from doing is to speak well to engage, connect, inform, influence, and persuade. Until that happens, we humans are still going to be indispensable. Speaking well is probably your last key differentiator in this competitive landscape to not only survive but thrive.

I don't want to scare you about the future, but at the same time, I don't want to act like a member of that quartet on the deck in the movie *Titanic* playing "Nearer My God to Thee" while the ship was sinking. Skills, where we outperform machines, are disappearing at a faster rate than imagined. For example, Google has developed a computer program called AlphaGo, which defeated the world's top ranked Go player, Lee Se-dol, in March 2016.[10] According to artificial intelligence experts, the game of Go is more difficult than chess for an intelligent computer program to be able to defeat a human being. But what is so interesting about this achievement was not that a computer program beat a top player but how it did it. Unlike in 1997, when Deep Blue from IBM beat Gary Kasparov at chess using a brute-force method of looking at moves ahead, AlphaGo could triumph because of a factor beyond just its computational speed.

We humans who are experts in something are not good at explaining what makes us so good, which is referred to as Polanyi's Paradox, after Michael Polanyi, who briefly summarized that "we know more than we can tell." The paradox poses a huge challenge when it comes to programming computers to beat humans. To overcome the paradox, AlphaGo first had to learn from past examples and experience playing humans using a method called "deep learning," or *reinforcement learning*—that is, using algorithms (sets of instructions) and computational power to mimic how our brains work to learn.

To beat humans, AlphaGo had to play millions of games against itself, using reinforcement learning, and keep track of the strategies that worked and those that didn't work. It amassed a vast amount of knowledge that is simply not possible for humans, and it beat the best player, Lee Se-dol, by a score of four games to one.[11] "We still have a long way to go, but the implications are profound," wrote Andrew McAfee and Erik Brynjolfsson in their *New York Times* article.[12]

You think you can beat a machine at what you do? You'd better face the new reality and develop a skill that machines can't do better than you. And the only skill I can think of that the machines are not going to do better than you is your ability to speak in order to engage, connect, inform, influence, and persuade. According to Geoff Colvin, an editor for *Fortune* magazine and an author of *Humans Are Underrated: What High Achievers Know That Brilliant Machines Never Will*,[13]

> Advancing technology will profoundly change the nature of high-value human skills, and that is threatening, but we aren't doomed. The skills of deep human interaction, the abilities to manage the exchanges that occur only between people, will only become more valuable.[14]

Unfortunately, most people neglect to develop their "soft skills," or interpersonal skills, since these are difficult to measure. But lacking soft skills cost companies a lot of money and time, even though you never see this on a company's ledger, either positive or negative.

Money can eventually be made up, but time cannot. Companies that I have worked for never measured time wasted and money lost because of poor communication at work. Today, some forward-looking companies, however, such as Google, McKinsey & Company, and Goldman Sachs, are putting a very high premium on soft skills, since they want their employees to do a lot more with a lot less. It is not possible to do that without excellent communication and collaboration, especially as technology keeps advancing at a rapid pace.

People judge companies on how well their people—from executives to junior-level staff members—communicate. Companies that have people who can communicate well have a clear and distinct competitive advantage over their competitors.

According to a famous Chinese proverb, "The best time to plant a tree was twenty years ago. The second best time is now." If you are reading this book, then you have already started, or you want to start now, since not only will you enjoy life more by engaging and connecting with people, but it is likely that such engaging and connecting will open new opportunities for you.

Speak Your Way to the Top

I used to think that one needed three skills to be highly successful today: data, decision making, and communication. But in 2016, Donald Trump won the presidency with one key attribute: excellent communication skills. He did not use data, political consultants, or pollsters to help him make decisions on whom to target or what to say. He relied on four skills he had honed over the years: intuition, marketing, salesmanship, and communication. He had a skeleton staff and spent the least amount of money among the major candidates. Trump proved that communication with a solid message "trumps" financial and other advantages.

According to *New York Times* columnist Anand Giridharadas,

> More than any other candidate, Mr. Trump embodies the evolving norms of communication that are being enabled and encouraged by technology and the matrix of connectivity that

defines modern life: authenticity over authority, surprise over consistency, celebrity over experience.[15]

Trump spoke directly to people at political rallies and through utilizing both traditional and social media. He demonstrated that the power of communication, especially the power of public speaking, can catapult anyone, anytime, anywhere. Trump showed that even with technological advancement, communication skills will always remain a powerful way of succeeding in just about anything you do, whether it is personal, professional, or political. As president, Trump will continue to take his message directly to people, especially to those who support him and his policies.

Regardless of what you may think of Trump's politics, he has shown that the most important title today that you can own is the title of chief communication officer (CCO) for yourself. You can't outsource this important job to anyone. And it is unlikely that Trump will ever give this up to anyone. Trump believes that any communication, even negative communication, is better than no communication. And you must admit that it has worked like a charm for him. In fact, he may have changed the way leaders will communicate from now on.

Lloyd Blankfein, chairman and CEO of Goldman Sachs, realized that he also had to be the chief communication officer too. He said on Jim Cramer's *Mad Money* show on CNBC that it is no longer enough to get the word out to just your institutional customers. You must get the word out to the people through social media like Twitter. If you don't do it, then others are going to define you and hurt your reputation.[16]

You may not be the president of the United States or the CEO of a major corporation, but you own your message, and you need to take it to the people through any media—but especially social media. You want people to receive your message unedited and unfiltered.

To capture and keep people's attention, strive to capture the three most important real estate properties that people own: their short-term memory, their long-term memory, and social media. The short-term memory can store only a limited amount of information, so you want people to remember the slogan, which often is the signature of your speech. From the slogan or signature, you can help unlock the information that resides in people's long-term memory. From the long-term memory, people can access additional information on social media or the Internet so they can easily spread the message to others and also take action. Whoever understands this and exploits this well not only will win but will dominate.

Get Good Jobs

Companies today do not provide training to make you a confident speaker. You have to do it. Many companies prefer to wait and hire a "perfect" candidate, who has both the hard skills and the soft skills they are looking for. Jeff Bezos, CEO of Amazon, once said: "I'd rather interview fifty people and not hire anyone than hire the wrong person." In other words, not only must you be better than the people who are interviewing you, you must be able to demonstrate that during the interview so the interviewers feel comfortable and confident that you are the "A" player they are looking for.

If you are a student, understand that good grades no longer guarantee a good job. According to an article in the *New York Post*, skills that make you successful in school are not necessarily going to make you successful in the workforce.[17] Though some schools are trying to integrate developing soft skills into their curriculum, most leave it up to the students to develop these skills by participating in different activities. And, according to a Bloomberg report, the number-one skill that many industry recruiters look for in MBA graduates is communication skill.[18]

Recently, we have seen some people in industrialized countries express their anger at the ballot box because of what globalization has done to their economic conditions; this is especially true for people who don't possess marketable skills to get good jobs. I know it's hard for many to make a change through lifelong learning, especially as you get older. But today you must be in a constant change mode and be able to handle the speed of today's economy. If you can't handle the speed, you are going to be left behind.

Let me explain how this works: To watch high school football costs very little. The young men who play football may get some status in school, but they don't get paid. Those good enough to play in college often receive athletic scholarships, but still, they don't get paid. Those who excel in college may make it to the NFL and get paid depending on their skill set. It's a long path, and very few make it. The difference at each level is the speed of the game. The speed of the game is much faster in the NFL than it is in college. And the speed of the game in college is much faster than it is in high school. And that is why professional players are so well paid.

The same idea applies today in the workforce. You have to work at a higher speed to make good wages. Those who can't do so get left behind. MIT professor Erik Brynjolfsson and MIT scientist Andrew McAfee assert that "social skills are increasing in demand."[19] You must learn something new quickly, collaborate with different people, and get the job done faster, cheaper, better, and smarter. This is the new reality, which is not likely to change. The only thing you can do to manage the technological acceleration is to learn fast and well. According to *New York Times* columnist Tom Friedman,

The notion that we can go to college for four years and then spend that knowledge for the next 30 is over. If you want to be a lifelong employee anywhere today, you have to be a lifelong learner.[20]

Avoid Career Stagnation

You may be asking yourself why it's important to spend so much time learning this skill right now when you have a good-paying job and probably have other priorities to deal with. Eventually you hope to get around to develop this skill. Unfortunately, that would be taking a big risk. You probably see the need to develop public speaking skills based on the trends you are seeing; however, if you wait too long, it will be too late to do anything about it. Here is how author Ernest Hemingway described how bankruptcy takes place: "Two ways: Gradually, then suddenly."[21] In the same way, hitting a proverbial wall in your career happens just like that. I know this well, since it happened to me.

A recent Pew Research Center report stated that "the vast majority of U.S. workers say that new skills and training may hold the key to their future job success."[22] Eighty-five percent said that training in writing and communications is important to their success.

According to regular *New Yorker* contributor Mark Gimein, "The experience of job loss in late middle age is a common one, and often difficult to recover from."[23] If you are lucky enough to reinvent yourself and get a job, your salary is likely to be less than what you were earning before. If you can speak well, however, you are more likely to be in big demand, even if you're middle age and beyond. You have to take public speaking skills seriously, so you maintain control over your career at any age.

Gain Power to Make a Difference

Speaking well will put you in a power position, but that does not mean you will be powerful. You still have to earn it. When people see the word *power*, they generally think of force, fraud, and manipulation. Though that form of power still exists in the marketplace, power there today resides with those who can make a difference in people's life. According to author Dacher Keltner, "Power lies in altering the tastes, preferences, and opinions of others."[24]

Social media today has made it easier to reach people all over the world; hence, anyone realistically has the power to make a difference. I see that with the videos I post on YouTube on public speaking. I get e-mails from people all over the world asking me for advice on how they can become more confident speakers. Having the power to help others in this way is extremely gratifying.

If someone stumbled across one of my videos and then was motivated to send me a constructive note, I have to reply to that person. Power is not about what I do. It is about how I can help. If you look at history, many who gained power have fallen into "helping others" category, including Mahatma Gandhi, Mother Teresa, Bill Gates, and Oprah Winfrey. You have to start with making a difference for one person first.

Become Comfortable in the Connection Economy

David Brooks, author and political commentator, writes about a woman whom he met in West Virginia during his travels through some of the most-stressed parts of the country. Brooks was struck when the woman said to him that that she felt relieved that she did not have to speak at her church service, and he quotes her saying, "We're not word people."[25] Brooks makes a good observation that many people are getting left behind because they are not comfortable in the modern economy. Brooks adds that "it's hard to thrive in the information age if you don't feel comfortable with verbal communication."

I do most of my shopping from just two places: Costco and Amazon. And I don't remember if I had any interaction with any of their employees in the last year. I shop there, since they provide a good experience, but I have no loyalty toward them, since I don't know anyone there. For me to keep doing business with them, they'd better be faster, smarter, cheaper, and better than their competitors.

On the other hand, I look forward to visiting my barber, Tamara. Why? I enjoy talking to my barber for the short time it takes to get my hair cut. She is very engaging, and I find talking to her just as valuable as the money I pay for my haircut. Though there are other barbers nearby who are probably just as good and perhaps even cheaper, but I have yet to go to a different barber in over two decades. The point of this is that if you are not able to engage, connect, and inform at a basic human level, you are going to have a difficult time thriving in the service economy.

New York Times columnist Tom Friedman and Johns Hopkins University Professor Michael Mandelbaum write that just doing one's job, even doing it well, makes you average today.[26] They write that you now need to ask the following question: "What is it about how I do my job that is going to differentiate me?"

What makes people like Tamara special is that besides cutting hair, she has created a welcoming place where I don't mind waiting to get a haircut. And when my turn comes, I get not only Tamara's superb haircutting talent but also her excellent conversation skills that make me feel smarter. Afterward, I feel good, not only because I look presentable but also for having had a good conversation with someone who was attentive. The "extras" she provides is what gives her a competitive advantage and makes her hard to copy.

When you add up all the extras Tamara provides, the price of a haircut becomes a bargain, and in return her customers remain loyal. Sounds simple? But it isn't. Otherwise, everyone would be acting like Tamara. But everyone had better start acting like her soon. You need to find "extras" to add value to your clients and customers, so they don't even dare consider visiting a competitor's physical location, website, or Facebook page.

No business and country is immune to this new reality. And this applies especially to such countries as China, India, Mexico, and others who have grown their economy rapidly through manufacturing. However, manufacturing is going the way of agriculture, where we can produce a lot with fewer people. The people in those countries will have to develop skills that are important in the service economy, which includes communication.

Harvard Business Review bloggers David De Cremer and Jason D. Shaw write that

> a manufacturing economy has different requirements than a service economy. To deal with this challenge, one important focus for Chinese companies will be to train, educate, and incentivize their work force in ways that develop a pro-active attitude motivated by an intrinsic desire to create long-term customer value.[27]

One tool to do this is to enhance employees' communication skills, so they understand customer needs and can then teach the value that the company's product brings to the customers.

Employees who can speak well will be gainfully employed, and the companies who foster that culture will thrive.

"Get in Their Face" and Win People Over

During his 2008 presidential campaign, then Senator Barack Obama urged his supporters to persuade their friends and neighbors to vote for him in order to enable the change they could believe in for once in their life. Here is what he said to the audience at his rally in Elko, Nevada:

> I need you to go out and talk to your friends and talk to your neighbors. I want you to talk to them whether they are independent or whether they are Republican. I want you to argue with them and get in their face.[28]

It sounds crude and overly aggressive—the idea of getting in someone's face. But I have to say that Obama was right. Nothing is as impactful as getting in someone's face and politely arguing with them to persuade them. Hence, you never want to pass up an opportunity to get in someone's face if you want to achieve your objective and win. Why do you think politicians participate in rallies and town hall meetings? They know that when you connect with one, it has a multiplier effect in people spreading the message.

When you are talking to someone, you are not just talking to persuade that one person, but to provide a sound bite and talking points so that one person can then use what you said to persuade others. And that is what Obama did in his rallies, and it worked. Obama knew that he alone couldn't change people. He did not know other people well, nor did he have the time to persuade other people. He had to enlist help from other to help spread his message. Obama proved to be very effective in getting others' support, which helped him win the presidency. But remember, before you try to persuade others, you must know what to say, how to say it, and, most important, why you are saying it. If you have that covered, then take Obama's advice to get in people's face and win them over.

One of the reasons why *New York Times* best-selling author Michael Lewis is such a great writer is because he can explain complex things in a book or a speech. In his book *Flash Boys: A Wall Street Revolt*, Lewis writes about someone else who has this ability. Though many have worked on Wall Street, he writes, only a handful knew the inner workings of a stock trade.[29] One of those person who learned how a stock trade moves through the intricate stock trading systems was Brad Katsuyama, CEO and cofounder of IEX.

During one meeting Katsuyama had with an investor, the investor said,

> All of a sudden the market is all about algos [algorithms] and routers. It's hard to figure this stuff out. There is no book you can read. It's calling up people and talking to them…. The first time I talked to Brad and he was telling me how it all actually worked, my jaw must have hit the floor.

As the world keeps getting more and more complex, it is good to know how things work, but what's even better is if you can explain it to others. Katsuyama did that and is the main hero of Michael Lewis's book. He saw a problem with the stock market, he came up with a solution, and he created an outcome where there was transparency when you traded stock that had never existed before, since no one knew how it worked, nor even cared to ask why it worked the way it did. You can't change anything whether it is political, social, economic, or financial unless you, first, can understand the complexity and, second, even more important, can make others understand it. Later in the book, Lewis writes,

> That is why Brad Katsuyama's most distinctive trait—his desire to explain things not so he would be understood but so that others would understand—was so seditious.

Today, if you want to be powerful, then you'd better be able to simplify things so others can understand it and view you as a valuable resource. The reason for this is that we are overloaded with information, and the overloading is going to be on steroids starting in 2020, according to Dr. Carmen Simon, a cognitive scientist. At the HubSpot's INBOUND I&E 2015 conference,[30] she said that starting in 2020, the information will double every seventy-two days. If we want to add value, we have to become "Explainer-in-Chief" in our field.

Develop a Good Long-Term Relationship

Many single people want to have a good romantic relationship but are frustrated when they can't find an attractive partner. Many are attracted initially by the prospective partner's looks, but soon that is not sufficient to sustain the relationship, which soon ends. Social media have made it easier to get into a relationship but not to stay in a relationship. The only proven way to stay in a relationship is through communication, especially through one's ability to have good conversations.

If you can speak well, then you are going to become attractive and stay attractive to your partner. Looks will get you attention, but if you can't have intelligent conversations, then your relationship is going to become static very quickly. You are not going to be successful in attracting smart, interesting people if you can't have intelligent conversations. The good news is that you don't have to go to an Ivy League school to talk as though you did. You just have to read books and start turning what you read into short speeches. What I teach in this book, especially with the introduction speech and the impromptu speech, will help you meet people and have good intelligent conversations that can help you develop a long-lasting relationship.

A Forever Skill to Have a Good Life

I know you are constantly working hard to acquire yet another skill to get ahead and stay ahead in this hypercompetitive world you live in. Though you do need to acquire hard skills today with the way the technology is advancing, do not neglect soft skills, especially public speaking skills. To have long-term success, you need to think like Jeff Bezos, founder and CEO of Amazon, before you spend more time and money acquiring new hard skills, diplomas, degrees, and certificates. The question Bezos asks before going into business is, **What is not likely to change in a year, five years, and even ten years from now?** You may call pondering this question risk-averse, but it has made him very successful and wealthy. Similarly, the question you have to ask is similar:

What is one skill that I will need that is not going to change in five, ten, and twenty-five years from now?

Public speaking is that skill. In case you are not convinced, *Forbes* blogger Keld Jensen cites research conducted by the Carnegie Institute of Technology that discovered that

> 85 percent of your financial success is due to skills in "human engineering," your personality and ability to communicate, negotiate, and lead. Shockingly, only 15 percent is due to technical knowledge.[31]

Good speaking skills is also very important to have a good life without much chronic pain. A January 19, 2017, article in the *New York Times* pointed to a study done by Canadian researchers on how communication helps reduce pain.[32] The study found that a sham treatment that included a good conversation between a caregiver and a patient decreased pain. When a good conversation was coupled with a real treatment, the decrease in pain was even greater. Now there is research that supports the importance of communication not only for success in life and work, but even in health, too.

The Day Marissa Mayer Made It to the Big Leagues

For Marissa Mayer, former CEO of Yahoo!, making it to the top in the corporate world was no accident. It took time, effort, and talent. I think it all started the day she made the move from the minor league (not being visible to the outside world) to the major league (being visible to the outside world). When you get to the major league in business, you get noticed. You are sought after to join corporate boards; you are in demand for plum speaking engagements; you are on track to join the exclusive CEO club of a billion-dollar company.

Mayer was always smart, hardworking, and focused. At Google, she handled user interface meetings, product review meetings, and the launch calendar to review Google's products. The latter brought in key decision makers from marketing, legal, PR, engineering, support, and so on. The launch calendar gave Mayer insights into Google's new products, and it gave her a lot of visibility inside Google—but little to no visibility outside Google.

Mayer's limited visibility to the outside world changed when Walt Mossberg, then from the *Wall Street Journal*, was coming to

Google's headquarters to get an update on Google's products. Cindy McCaffrey, then the head of marketing, asked Mayer to update Mossberg.

Initially, Mayer refused, saying that she was going to be busy with meetings. The real reason, according to Nicholas Carlson, author of *Marissa Mayer and the Fight to Save Yahoo!*, was that Mayer was shy.[33] She had not done this kind of a media update before. It's been reported that it was only after McCaffrey added a little incentive of a gift certificate to a spa that Mayer finally agreed.

When Mossberg came to Googleplex, Mayer showed her mettle by publicly demonstrating three things that catapulted her to the majors:

- **Knowledge.** Since Mayer handled the user interface (UI) meetings, she showed that Google didn't make UI decisions on intuition; rather, they based decisions on hard data and solid statistics. She had the opportunity to take a deep dive into the UI decisions Google was making and gain valuable knowledge.

- **Preparation.** Ever since she was young, Mayer was always thoroughly prepared. When she joined Google, she was always well prepared for interviews, presentations, and meetings.

- **Passion.** Mayer was passionate about the work Google was doing, and that passion helped demonstrate to others that she was on top of her game.

McCaffrey was very impressed with Mayer's performance, and she was delighted with Mossberg's resulting article, praising Google as "everything a search engine should be: thorough, smart, speedy, and honest." McCaffrey put Mayer on a list of executives she could trust doing a great job with the media. Mayer was already an outstanding worker, but now she was going to get a chance to showcase her talent to the outside world with her communication skills. She got a break, and she was ready to take a leap from the minors to the majors. If you follow her approach and develop your communication skills, including your public speaking skills, not only will you advance within your company, but you will have an open opportunity to go all the way to the top. If you are excellent with only technical skills, however, your path to the top will be difficult. Marissa Mayer and Sheryl Sandberg (COO of Facebook) are great examples of rising to the top by possessing both technical skills and excellent communication skills.

CHAPTER 2

Five Key Success Factors to Winning the High-Stakes Speaking Game

It does not matter what you know about anything if you cannot communicate to your people. In that event, you are not even a failure. You're just not there.

— Saul Alinsky, community organizer and author

High-stakes public speaking would be so much easier if we didn't have to worry about the audience! I joke about this to people whom I am teaching, mentoring, and coaching, so they don't forget why they are giving a speech in the first place: **It's the Audience, Stupid.** Nothing else matters. If there is no audience, there is no speech.

Before you get in front of an audience, there are a few things you need to understand. We need to first address why so many people find this skill so difficult to master. By that I mean they are less successful in engaging, connecting, informing, influencing, and persuading. They are not winning as often as they should.

Many people find public speaking hard, time consuming, and frustrating; hence, they develop fear speaking in front of an audience. You are not immune to fear and anxiety, even if you are a good-to-great high-stakes public speaker. I discussed fear in some detail in the Introduction, but you need to understand here that the best way to manage fear and deliver a good-to-great high-stakes speech is through **caring, time, method, knowledge, and manipulation**—the five key success factors.

Caring

Never believe that a few caring people can't change the world. For, indeed, that's all who ever have.

— Margaret Mead

Caring trumps everything else in a speech. You may be scared to death. You may not have had much time to prepare, you may not have a good method, or you may not possess a vast knowledge. But there is one thing that is a multiplier of whatever you do have: if you show you care about your audience, your topic, and your reputation.

You show you care about your audience by ensuring that they get some value for the time they have invested in listening to you. You show you care about what you are saying by believing in your message and being certain of your purpose. Lastly, you show you care about your reputation by demonstrating that you know that even if you lose everything, you can quickly make yourself whole again with your good reputation.

Without showing that you care for your audience, your topic, and your reputation in a genuine way, you are going to be viewed by some in the audience as a phony and a fraud, and they will quickly tune you out. Do not get on a stage unless you care about those who are investing their time in listening to you. Time may be money, but caring is like putting your money in a bank account that compounds over time. People don't easily forget those who care about them. Sometimes we don't even know how we are touching people by the care we show toward them.

I understood this better when one evening I was watching Megyn Kelly on Fox News thanking television talk show host Dr. Phil (whose real name is Phil McGraw) for how he had changed her thinking. She publicly recalled how something he had said that had changed her life philosophy; it "hit me like a lightning bolt," she said. Here is what Dr. Phil had said: "**The only difference between you and someone you envy is that you settle for less.**"[1]

Soon she quit her job as a lawyer, got divorced, found a new job in the media, married again, had three children, became a successful journalist and host of her own highly rated show on Fox News, and is now a daytime anchor at NBC News. Kelly titled her autobiography *Settle for More*.[2] The point of this story is that just as Dr. Phil had no idea how much influence he was having on Megyn Kelly, you never know how you can influence someone if you show them that you care about them—whether it is during a one-on-one conversation or in front of a massive TV-viewing audience. You don't have to know them, but you must have something valuable to offer, and you must do it in a genuine way.

Another good example of caring is Rodney King, who was mercilessly beaten by several police officers from the Los Angeles Police Department in 1991, after a high-speed chase for eight miles while he was intoxicated. The beating, captured on video for the world to see, showed that police used excessive force, even when King was showing no resistance. The policemen involved in the beating were charged with using excessive force but were later acquitted by a jury. The "not guilty" verdict precipitated riots that caused death and destruction in some parts of Los Angeles.

During the riots, King, looking scared, appeared before the media and made a passionate plea for hooligans to stop rioting and urged everyone with the now-famous entreaty "Can we all just get along?" King, a troubled man, was not a good speaker, but in his brief speech, he showed he cared about people's lives and property. Instead of showing his anger at the verdict, he wanted people—through his example—to express their anger through peaceful means.

If you care about your audience, your reputation, your content, your message, and your performance, then you are naturally going to have some fear. And that is a good thing. You see many speakers, including those at the leadership position, who simply don't care about their audience, and they seem to get away with it. Why? When you don't give a damn about your audience or don't care if you make a fool out of yourself, you are not going to have much fear giving a speech and could come across looking very confident. But that is not a good way to exude confidence. You should earn it by working hard at developing a speech, practicing and rehearsing as if your reputation depended on it. When you are on stage, your audience will quickly sense that you indeed care about them, and they will decide quickly whether they are going to listen—and, if so, for how long and how attentively. If your audience sees that you care, they are going to listen to learn and not listen to look for faults in your speech.

If you don't care about your audience, your content, and your reputation, you are wasting not only your time but your audience's time. People will stop paying attention to you. Caring is hard and can't be easily taught. As entrepreneur and best-selling author Seth Godin writes, "Anyone who cares and acts on it is performing a work of art."[3] Caring is a big multiplier when you are speaking.

Time

If you don't have time to do it right, when will you have time to do it over?

— John Wooden

The second reason that people find public speaking difficult is that they don't realize how much time it takes to prepare to give a good speech. Not allocating sufficient time results in anxiety, since you may not have internalized the content and therefore become uncomfortable when you are delivering your speech. Most people underestimate the amount of time it takes to prepare for a speech.

According to Seth Godin, famous author Elizabeth Gilbert spent four hours a day for three months to prepare for her TED Talk.[4] That was over three hundred hours of preparation for a fifteen-minute speech. Bryan Kramer, author and CEO of PureMatter, also spent over three hundred hours of preparation, which included plenty of guidance from TED's speaking coaches. And the most important lesson that Kramer learned from those coaches was to **"make the end the beginning."**[5]

We all wish we would have the same level of coaching that TED speakers get, but then, who has that kind of time to prepare for a single speech unless it is specifically for TED, or you are getting paid a tremendous amount for giving a speech? TED is excellent at turning speeches into memorable performances. Through their speech magic, TED has a proven track record of turning just about anyone who has a good story to tell into not only a terrific speaker but also an Internet sensation. Unfortunately, only a handful will ever get that kind of coaching to become a great speaker, for at least one speech. Most of us have to do it on our own, with a good method to reduce the time it takes to craft and deliver a good-to-great speech performance.

People often underestimate how much time it takes to prepare for a speech. When you are speaking to an audience, you are not going to be able to "wing it," no matter how good you think you are.

Method

A methodology is only effective when it is practiced consistently.

— Scott Belsky

Even if you have allocated sufficient time, if you don't have a good method, you are going to end up wasting time and are not likely to deliver a good speech. Method is very important to your public speaking success. Most people don't give good speeches, because they don't know a good proven method, or they opt for a method that does not work. Let's examine five possible methods:

First, you might wing it by putting together a few slides, perhaps practice a little, and then give your speech. You would be hoping that PowerPoint slides will save the day, but, unfortunately, you are adding no value to the speech. If you must use slides, limit yourself to just a few slides—unless you are adept at PowerPoint presentations, like Seth Godin. I don't recommend this method; most PowerPoint presentations end in disaster, since you are using the slides not for enriching an audience's experience but for survival. Avoid PowerPoint slides altogether, or use them only if they are going to enhance your audience's understanding and experience. Try to connect with your audience through your speech performance skills only.

Second, you might get your friends and colleagues to give you some feedback. Now, this is better than winging it, but not much better if your friends and colleagues are not good at evaluating a speech. Either your friends will give feedback that is not useful, or they will sugarcoat it to not hurt your feelings. Avoid getting feedback from people who are close to you. They mean well, but they are not going to help you improve your speech.

Third, you might take a three-day public speaking course to prepare for your speech. Now, this method is better than the first two, but here's the problem: Though you will gain a lot of knowledge in exchange for the time and money you spend, unless the instructor can help you with the high-stakes speech on which you are working, the course is less likely to be helpful in the long term. Not only is this type of training expensive, but it's ineffective. Soon after training, you tend to go back to your old ways of doing things.[6]

Fourth, you might hire a speech coach. This is the best way to learn if you have a high-stakes speech that you have to give soon. Do not get impressed by a coach's reputation, however; he or she has to be right for you. Your coach has to analyze what you are doing, what is working, what is not working, and what you *may* need to do more of in order to be successful. Coaching is about generating results in an incremental and iterative manner. I suggest having a free one-hour session and then pay per hour for three sessions before you make a longer commitment.

Fifth, do what I did: Start now, when you don't have a high-stakes speech to give any time soon. Later, when you do have to give a high-stakes, high-opportunity, high-risk speech, you will be ready, and you will not be gripped with anxiety over your speech performance. Having taught and coached public speaking for some time now, I believe you don't learn this skill unless you are giving high-stakes speeches. You have to take your speech seriously, like actors and actresses do, regarding their figure: They have to have a good physique to be marketable. Similarly, if you want to succeed in both life and business, you'd better keep your speaking skills "fit" to ensure your success.

Knowledge

Knowledge is power.

— Francis Bacon

Knowledge alone will not make your speech succeed. It won't. Providing accurate facts with good logic does not result in a win. Emotions get people to pay attention, and as I stated in the Introduction, an audience is moved by a message that is simple, memorable, and repeatable. For some that is sufficient. But for others, emotions will get them to look at your facts and evidence closely before they make a decision.

However, knowledge is a double-edge sword when it comes to public speaking. It can also prevent you from connecting with your audience. You don't want to use too much of it and risk coming across as a pompous fool who is not relatable to your audience. Often this is a hard choice to make when you are giving a speech. You have to know the audience and try to appeal to a majority among them.

There is a difference between dumbing it down and challenging your audience. If you dumb it down and focus only on entertaining, then people will not take you seriously. You have to include some history, clever anecdotes, current events, and insights. You have to find the happy medium between entertaining and informing. If you are too content-heavy in your speech, then you are going to come across as too smart for the audience. Remember: your purpose is to make the audience feel smart themselves, so you need to limit how much new information you include in your speech. Don't overwhelm.

Author and prize-winning *New York Times* journalist Charles Duhigg cites research done by Brian Uzzi from Northwestern University along with others, revealing that research articles that are considered "creative" have only 10 percent new information. Approximately 90 percent of the information is old information presented in a different way. According to Duhigg, "It was this combination of ideas, rather than the ideas themselves, that typically made a paper so creative and important."[7]

Manipulation

The most amazing thing for me is that every single person who sees a movie, not necessarily one of my movies, brings a whole set of unique experiences. Now, through careful manipulation and good storytelling, you can get everybody to clap at the same time, to hopefully laugh at the same time, and to be afraid at the same time.

— Steven Spielberg

As I was writing this, I thought of the question that businessman, philanthropist, and author Peter Thiel likes to ask candidates interviewing for a job: "What important truth do very few people agree with you on?"[8] I thought about this as it is related to public speaking, but it is applicable to other things too. I came up with manipulation. No book on public speaking ever mentions how powerful manipulation is to get people to pay attention. Some will not like my using the word *manipulation* in this context, but as Thiel writes,

> It's intellectually difficult because the knowledge that everyone is taught in school is by definition agreed upon. And it's psychologically difficult because anyone trying to answer must say something she knows to be unpopular.[9]

According to the Holy Bible, life would have been so much easier if it hadn't been for the serpent who manipulated Eve to eat the apple from the tree of the knowledge of good and evil. When God found what Eve and Adam had done, he made life difficult for mankind. Since then, we have learned all kinds of good and bad things, including how to manipulate people. But manipulation is good if your intention is good and no one gets hurt. Manipulation justifiably gets a bad name when it is used maliciously or to benefit oneself and perhaps a few at the expense of others. *Let me be clear: I don't advocate that kind of manipulation.*

When it comes to public speaking, you can do everything else right, but you are unlikely to win if you don't use manipulation techniques in your speech. I view manipulation as your "secret sauce" in a speech. It is like Coke, which is really just sugar water without their secret formula. Without some manipulation, you are going to have a hard time making people remember your speech, spread your message, or take deliberate and decisive action.

Manipulation sounds like the Machiavellian principle that "the ends justify the means." What Niccolò Machiavelli actually said in his famous book *The Prince* was the following:

> [I]n the actions of all men, and especially of princes, which it is not prudent to challenge, one judges by

the result. For that reason, let a prince have the credit of conquering and holding his state, the means will always be considered honest, and he will be praised by everybody....[10]

As long as your end benefits you and others without harming anyone, then you can use manipulation techniques to get your point across, and no one is going to complain unless they view it as some moral violation. Politicians and business leaders routinely use manipulation techniques to win. But, sadly, they often use it to harm others to get ahead, which is often legal but unethical and potentially destructive.

When you are giving a high-stakes speech, you have a very short time to achieve your overall objective. You can provide information and facts and then hope and pray that the audience can reason and help you achieve your objective. Unfortunately, life doesn't work like that. You have to use manipulation to capture your audience's attention and then keep it, so that later the audience can persuade themselves and come up with their own reasons to agree with what you said.

Now I am going to manipulate you by telling you a story. (You knew that was coming, didn't you?)

I lived in India when I was little. One time, my mother took me to a village, where I saw a bullock cart. I wanted to get a ride on the bullock cart, because I lived in Mumbai, where I did not see any bullock carts. My mother cajoled the driver to give me a short ride, to which the driver agreed. I happily got on the cart and sat next to the driver. The driver made some noise to the bullock and pulled the chain to get the bullock to move. The bullock did not move. He did it again with no success. He then proceeded to whip the bullock's backside, and the bullock slowly started moving. Being a city dweller, I was shocked that the driver had hit the bullock. I asked the driver, "Why are you hitting the bullock?" He said, "Son, bullocks are lazy animals. If I don't hit the bullock, it will not move, and you will not get a ride." I never forgot that story.

Metaphorically, our brain is like a bullock. It is a lazy organ; you can't easily persuade it. Nancy Duarte, author, entrepreneur, and thought leader on public speaking, notes that "moving people is hard."[11] You have to manipulate the brain to get it to think so it can persuade itself. If the brain were easily persuadable, then we would not need advertising, marketing, and sales.

Without manipulation, people would not make a decision. Most of the things we do are done without our giving them a lot of thought. Presidential candidates are judged on the basis of emotion versus logic. The candidate who uses emotions more often wins, since he or she can move people better than the candidate trying to get people to use their logic. Hence, if you want to win, you can't afford to ignore manipulation.

When I think about manipulation, I am reminded of that famous scene from the movie *The Sting*, where Henry "Shaw" Gondorff, a con artist, is playing high-stakes poker on a train with a crime boss, Doyle Lonnegan. They are both cheating, but Gondorff is a better cheater and wins $15,000. When his partner Johnny "Kelly" Hooker comes to collect the money, Lonnegan says to him "Your boss is quite a card player, Mr. Kelly, so how does he do it?" Hooker replies, "He cheats."

We all manipulate, and some are better than others. Again, as long as you achieve your objective and others benefit without anyone getting hurt, then is that a good thing or a bad thing? If you are giving a high-stakes speech, you have to win. Otherwise, you are going to lose. Every speech matters.

If you are a good manipulator like the famous magician Apollo Robbins, you will pick people's pocket but then give everything back to them; however, if you are a bad manipulator, you will pick people's pocket and keep everything. Robbins ends his TED Talk by saying, "Attention is a powerful thing.... If you could control somebody's attention, what would you do with it?"[12]

Tying the Five Factors Together

Now that you know the five reasons why people struggle at public speaking, I am going to throw a little math at you. I realize it is never a good idea to do that, since as theoretical physicist and cosmologist Stephen Hawking related, someone told him that each equation he included in his famous book *A Brief History of Time* would halve the book's sales. However, he did include one equation: $E = mc^2$. He wittingly wrote in his acknowledgments section that he hoped that the equation would not scare off half of his potential readers.[13]

I also don't want to scare off half my readers; nonetheless, like Hawking, I can't resist including just one equation—which, in my case, I have made up (so please don't go looking for the equation's proof). I created this equation to show what it takes to succeed in speaking. The only way you can prove this equation is by doing it.

$$\text{Speaking Success} = \text{Caring} * (\text{Time} + \text{Method} + \text{Knowledge}) + \text{Manipulation} - \text{Fear}$$

You don't have to be a math genius to see that you first have to care. Then put in the requisite time, follow a good method (the method I used to develop this hard skill), and share the right amount of your knowledge. You also need to employ a bit of manipulation, and you need to control your fear. Following this equation, you can succeed in any public speaking situation that you may face.

We are always amazed at great speeches that have been given throughout history by such famous people as Patrick Henry, Abraham Lincoln, Winston Churchill, Martin Luther King Jr., Ronald Reagan, Margaret Thatcher, Barack Obama, and many others. But they did not become great speakers by fluke. They honed their public speaking by working on it for their whole life. Their speeches are an amalgamation of a lifetime of knowledge, experience, insights, and performances. To speak like the great ones, you have to start today and work on improving this skill every day of your life. It is a skill that anyone is capable of mastering, since you control how good you want to become. You have all the physical and mental attributes to be a great speaker. There are no obstacles other than the ones you create for yourself.

CHAPTER 3

What Causes a Speech to Fail?

You can't be afraid to fail. It's the only way you succeed. You're not gonna succeed all the time, and I know that.

— LeBron James

You might be asking, "Why does this book have a chapter on failure?" The reason is that no matter how good your speech is, achieving your objective is still unpredictable. You can do just about everything to understand your audience as well as you can and hope that your speech resonates with them, but remember, you have control only over your content, your message, and your performance; there are, nonetheless, a lot of factors that are completely, or nearly completely, outside your control. Creating a speech performance is a costly endeavor. Before you do it, you need to know what causes speeches to fail.

Before I discuss those causes out of your control, however, I must address a few considerations you should make that are obviously in your control:

Are you likable? One of the main reasons your speech might fail is that you might not be likable. Likability is critical to your success in anything. If you are likable, your audience will pay attention, at least in the beginning.

One of the best ways to gauge who will win the presidential election is by asking a simple question: "Which candidate would you rather have a beer with?"[1] Except for Richard Nixon, the candidate who won this test also won the election. I think likability is a superpower. It can get you out of trouble. Bill Clinton and Donald Trump are very good examples of men who seem to get out of trouble because of their high likability factor, though not with everyone.

When you are giving a speech and if you are likable, you are in luck. However, if you are not likable, then you have some work to do to make yourself likable. You have to take care of this before you get into your content. You don't want to lose people right from the get-go. Likability is critical to your success in just about everything, including your speech.

Best-selling author and international keynote speaker Tim Sanders says it well:

> Your life is really determined by other people's choices.... The more likable you are, the more likely you are to be on the receiving end of a positive choice from which you can profit.[2]

According to Sanders, if you want to be likable, you have to be friendly, relevant, empathetic, and real, which are the next considerations.

- **Are you friendly?** You need to treat the audience as your friends. You need to come across as though you are happy to be giving a speech at a venue. You have to say it and then show that you mean it.[3]

- **Are you relevant?** You may be likable, but if your speech is not relevant, then people are going to lose interest in it.[4]

- **Are you empathetic?** You need to show you understand how the audience feels about a topic on which you are speaking, and then you need to address their needs and wants. You have to make them feel good about themselves.[5]

- **Are you real?** I will use the famous Texas saying "Are you all hat and no cattle?" You may be great at giving a speech, but make sure you are being real. You don't want your audience, on closer examination, to conclude that you are a phony and a fraud.[6]

Now we can discuss factors that are out of (or nearly out of) your control.

The Speech Is Not That Important

"Wha'choo talkin' 'bout, Willis?" as Arnold would say to his brother Willis in the famous television show *Diff'rent Strokes* when he did not understand what Willis was saying.

Let me explain.

Unless you aspire to get to the top, speaking well is not that important in the larger scheme of things. You need not read this book and spend hours, days, weeks, months, and years trying to get good at this skill if you are satisfied with your current situation. You are probably good enough to succeed and go quite far both personally and professionally, although not to the top, where excellent speaking skills are usually a necessity. You can get quite far with hard skills alone and adequate communication skills. Just look at all the doctors, lawyers, accountants, engineers, athletes, and creative people who do well in spite of the fact that they are, at best, adequate public speakers.

A speech's importance is both overrated and underrated. I have never been swayed by a single speech, ever. But a speech is also underrated, especially today, since if it is published in newspapers, as in the old days, or if it is recorded and put on YouTube, it has a way of spreading the message. It becomes a product of persuasion. A speech is good only if it grows over time. But unfortunately, most speeches have a very short half-life, if any. They are simply not that important, or worse, they were made unimportant for the audience by the speaker.

Speeches unfortunately have such a short half-life so that even if your speech bombs, no one will remember your speech, your name, or even what you looked like on stage. You have very little time being in front of an audience, so don't think that anyone cares about your speech. People have other things that will consume them after your speech is finished. You are not that important to your audience.

When Mitch Joel, author, entrepreneur, and marketing expert, appeared on Michael Port's *Steal the Show* podcast (at the fourteen-minute mark), he described a recent TED Talk he saw live that, according to him, was a disaster.[7] Joel did not know who the speaker was or could even remember much about the speaker. All you can do is be prepared, be well rehearsed, and do your best. You do have to take it seriously, but don't be disappointed if your audience doesn't give much importance to your speech.

Since Donald Trump won the presidential election in 2016, you can say that he is without a doubt one of the best speakers in America, since what does a presidential candidate do besides giving a boatload of speeches? But if you think he is an awful speaker, then you have to ask yourself how important is a speech? Do you have to give a great speech to get the job done? You should ask these two questions before you put a lot of time and effort into working on a speech. If you can win by winging it, then you should do that. Winging a speech did not hurt Donald Trump. But if *you* need to win with your speech, then you'd better put in a lot of time to put together a good-to-great speech. There are a lot of factors that determine your overall win and giving a good-to-great speech may occasionally have little to do with it. Often, a speaker is only as good as his or her audience. Unless you can get the right audience for all your speeches, you must put in hard work to win your audience.

Out of all the speeches that have ever been given in the United States, there are three that could be sculpted on the "Mount Rushmore" of American speeches. They include Patrick Henry's "Give Me Liberty or Give Me Death" speech, Abraham Lincoln's Gettysburg Address, and Martin Luther King Jr.'s "I Have a Dream" speech. Would any of these speeches rank as one of the greatest speeches ever given by an American if the outcome had been different? I doubt it. A great speech is great only if the outcome is great. Otherwise, the speech is not that important.

The Speech Is Telling But Not Selling

We don't make money when we sell things. We make money when we help customers make a purchase decision.

— Jeff Bezos, CEO and founder of Amazon

When you are speaking, you are either telling or selling. When you are telling, the only person who cares about your speech is most likely you. But when you are selling, your audience will start caring about your speech, since it resonates with them. Never forget that whenever you are speaking, you are absolutely selling something.

I know you are probably saying that you are not some sleazy used-car salesman and that you hate to sell. I hate to break this to you, but here is the cold, hard fact: **You are always in the mode of closing.** Sleazy salespeople want the prospect to see the world from their frame, whereas non-sleazy salespeople try to see it from the prospect's frame. The non-sleazy approach is much harder and requires patience and calibration on what is realistically possible to close. When you are giving a speech, you have to define your "close"—which may be as simple as getting people to check out your website to get more information and stay in touch with you.

Today, we are all selling ideas, whether our selling is one on one, in a small group, or in front of a large audience. Best-selling business writer Dan Pink says that the definition of sales has changed. Today, he writes, "we are all in sales"; hence, when you are speaking, you are indeed selling something.[8] Otherwise, why give a speech?

What you are selling is the message. Nothing will result from your speech if people don't buy your message. No matter who the audience is, it comes down to these three simple questions:

- Why should I buy your message?

- Why should I buy from you?

- Why should I buy now?

To sell, you have to learn constantly, you have to know your audience, and you have to adapt to the changing environment. As I discussed in the Introduction, today people's attention has become a lot shorter due to constant distractions, so you need to learn how to engage and connect quickly. You need to sell to get the other person to pay attention—and you need to do it fast.

With so much information that is readily available today, the most important person in any sales process is you—the salesperson. The sales product is your speech. Your message may be great, but your audience can get that same message from just about anywhere. However, they can't get that message delivered in the unique way that only you alone can deliver. If your message can be delivered equally well by anyone, then you are not adding value to the sales process. Instead, you are merely occupying space. You have to show your audience that you are different in the way you add value by what you say and how you say it.

For example, have you ever noticed that all motivational speakers say pretty much the same thing? What makes some of them so successful, however, is that they each have a unique style of speaking. The late Zig Ziglar said the same things that Tony Robbins says, but they each sound different. We notice what makes one different from the other, not what makes one better than the other. That is what you have to do when you are giving a speech. If you listen closely, there is not that much originality in the content of what these motivational speakers are saying; what differentiates them is how they say it. In the same way, we can enjoy hearing the same story told by different people, each rendition told in a different way. People notice when you say something in a different way. That is your differentiator.

A better salesperson also coaches people how to buy. Selling a message is not enough. You have to *show* them how to buy your message. You also have to ask. There has to be an "ask" in your speech. As you know, if you don't ask, you don't get. But make sure you ask with a purpose.

You'd better know how to ask, since if you don't, you might get a polite ovation but no buyers. What do you want: ovation or buyers? In the movie *Jerry Maguire*, soon after Jerry gets fired, he gives a moving speech and, as he is leaving the office for the last time to start his new venture, he is successful in getting Dorothy Boyd to join him. He was able to convince Dorothy to leave her safe job for an uncertain future. He would not have gotten her to join if he had not asked this simple question: "Who is coming with me?" But that was not what closed the deal. Dorothy was moved by Jerry's mission statement on the ethical way his sports management company should be doing business.

One thing you have to be very careful of when it comes to selling: As the stakes rise, you can't always charm your way to success. Today people have access to your body of work through the Internet. You are no longer "an ordinary fellow from another town," as Mark Twain is said to have defined an "expert." People can also find out more about what others are saying about you, especially as you are becoming successful. You just can't expect that people are going to believe you; you have to show it, and you have to prove it. Personally, I do not do business with people who have little or no social media presence or a website where I can see their body of work. I want to be close to 70 percent in my decision-making process before I contact someone. And I hope others are doing the same with me, too.

Another thing you have to watch out for when selling is not to get overconfident and start exaggerating things. Some salespeople delude themselves into thinking they can sell ice to Eskimos. The only way that can happen is if the Eskimos are ill informed and don't know how to Google. You need to approach any sales situation by respecting people's intelligence. And no matter how good you think you are at selling, the sale happens when you are not there. People may trust you, but they will take their time to verify whether you are legitimate and whether your ideas are any good. Whether it's products, services, or ideas, you need to sell with integrity.

We are living in a transparent world, and if people can't find a lot about you when they Google you, then you are likely to be ignored. When you are speaking, they can learn about you instantly, and they can tweet things about you and your speech to others. You can't afford to be a phony or a fraud when you are speaking. You need to sell with integrity when you speak. If you don't, you risk damaging your reputation, perhaps permanently.

The Speech Is Unpredictable

Everyone has a plan 'till they get punched in the mouth.

— Mike Tyson, former heavyweight-champion professional boxer

Often you think you might have given a great speech, but you soon discover that many in the audience were not persuaded. Or you might have given a poor speech, according to your high standard, and discover that many in the audience were persuaded anyway. You can't control how well your speech is going to resonate with your audience. All you can do is focus on your speech so that it achieves its objective by being interesting, informative, and entertaining, thereby capturing and retaining the audience's attention, making them feel smarter.

The main thing that makes a speech so unpredictable is that people have a short attention span. No matter how good a speaker you are or will become, you have about eight seconds to succeed when you are giving a speech. In his *New York Times* op-ed, Timothy Egan quoted Satya Nadella, CEO of Microsoft, saying that "the true scarce commodity" of the near future will be "human attention."[9] Indeed, you face a tough challenge whenever you are giving a speech.

Capturing people's attention is a highly valued skill if you want to succeed at anything today. Time is still money, and getting other people's attention today is like striking gold. You need to get the attention of those who have the power to make decisions. Unless you speak the language of those decision makers in a way that resonates with them, you are not going to be successful. According to economist, academic, and author Tyler Cowen, "getting attention will continue to be a critical function in the new world of work and is likely going to require ever-greater effort and sophistication."[10]

On the other hand, even if you are among the top 1 percent of speakers, you face a challenge in that you are hyperspecialized. Unless you can speak well and get your message across clearly and crisply to the people you are trying to influence and persuade, you are not going to resonate with them and spread your message, market your products, or be viewed as a thought leader. Speaking well is important if you intend to rise to the top 1 percent of your field, but to remain there, you also have to constantly hone your speaking skills. Today, you are how well you speak. You simply can't afford to ignore this critical skill for success.

The Speech Is Telling the Truth

Men are liars. We'll lie about lying if we have to. I'm an algebra liar. I figure two good lies make a positive.

— Tim Allen, actor, comedian, author

I know you should not lie, but today you are at a tremendous disadvantage when you are dealing with someone who is a pathological liar. It seems as if everyone is lying shamelessly today and are getting away with it at the highest level. We all know politicians are known to stretch the truth, but today they don't even try to correct it when presented with facts that contradict what they said. Not only do facts and evidence not matter to them, but they double down on their lies.

Today we have both facts and "alternative facts."[11] Addressing those who believe in "alternative facts," you are not going to win this crowd over with objective, provable facts. Your trying to convince people who believe in "alternative facts" will further solidify their opinion of those "facts." Can you persuade an audience when you take an ethical stance and refuse to engage in exploiting "alternative facts"? No.

You need to know what your audience "knows" and how they came to "know" what they believe. Then you can determine if they are open to hear something contrary to what they believe. Remember, you are never going to win all the audience members unless they are already sold on your message. So, don't even try. You want to stick to your game plan when you are speaking.

According to a recent cover story in *The Economist*, we have entered the era of "post-truth politics."[12] And if the people that we are electing face no consequences for lying, then why would others feel restrained from telling lies? The article points out that since we are so overloaded with information today, "feelings trump facts." If lying becomes the new normal, then "the power of truth as a tool for solving society's problems could be lastingly reduced."[13]

A big red flag should go up in your head when someone tells you a story when there is no way to verify it; no matter how compelling the story is, it is often filled with lies. How often have you ever fact-checked anything someone says? Hardly ever, probably. Lies are working today, since we are so overloaded with information that we are either too overburdened or too distracted to verify facts.

Former TV anchorman Brian Williams lost his job on NBC for embellishing his story when he was in Iraq.[14] He took a true story and stretched it to a point that was unnecessary. I am not sure what his motivation was, but evidently he wanted to show how brave he was for taking the incoming fire from the enemy. Now, this is unacceptable, and when you are an anchorman of a major TV news organization, it is a firable offense.

Another reason you might stretch the truth is because you don't remember the details. But this can get you into a big trouble later. When famous people get caught lying, they have probably been doing it for a long time; they just can't get away with it when the stakes are high, however. For one thing, it is much easier to fact-check these days. And let's face it: A lot of people are going to scrutinize everything you say. So, if you are in the bad habit of lying, understand that it is likely to catch up with you sooner or later.

Why do leaders lie so much? According to columnist and internationally acclaimed speaker Jeffrey Pfeffer, leaders frequently lie because "they seldom face serious consequences for doing so."[15] In fact, Pfeffer says that according to his research studying many business leaders, "The most important qualities of a leader is the ability to lie successfully."[16] Those who are good at it tend to have a better career and make more money.

One of the most honest speeches ever given in American politics in the last thirty-five years was by Walter Mondale, vice president under Jimmy Carter and presidential candidate in 1984. At one point in his speech accepting the nomination at the Democratic National Convention, he said, "Mr. Reagan will raise taxes, and so will I. He won't tell you. I just did."[17] Mondale never got to raise taxes to reduce the deficits and debt, because he lost to Ronald Reagan in all the states except his own state of Minnesota (and the District of Columbia). During the election, Reagan ran on cutting taxes; however, after the reelection, he did go on to raise taxes. The point is that if you want to win, you must tell people what they want to hear. A speech that wins is the one that faithfully sticks to that tried and true formula. Mondale didn't stick to the formula; he told the truth, and he lost by a massive landslide.

This lesson applies in our daily lives. A few years ago, a relative informed me that the environment at his new job was very political. But, he said, he was going to focus on doing his job well. I told him that is all well and good, but from my experience of having been laid off several times in my career, I have learned there are only two kinds of employees: those who are political and those who are victims of politics. "Your being sacked from a job," I said, "is a political act—unless you did something ethically or morally wrong or the entire company were being shut down.... If you want to get ahead," I said, "you'd better learn to be political in everything."

To speak well, you need to be political. In other words, you'd better know what your audience wants to hear. You don't give a speech that *you* want to hear; you give a speech your audience wants to hear.

But what should *you* do? When you need sound advice, turn to a quote attributed to that famous wise man Mark Twain: "If you tell the truth, you don't have to remember anything." When you lie, you will have to come up with all kinds of explanations and waste time on something that may hurt your main message. And today when people have a short attention span, you don't want to waste time correcting lies.

The best thing to do when speaking to an audience that believes "alternative facts" is to know what is going on, so you are not clueless. You have to point out to them that speaking truth is caring about your audience. You want to mention it, so they have an opportunity to know that they should trust you. Honest content does matter.

The Speech Is Not Making the Audience Feel Smarter

Be smarter than other people, just don't tell them so.

— H. Jackson Brown Jr., best-selling inspirational author

If you want to be a good-to-great speaker, you need to know how to teach. Many people often take a public speaking course once they have to start teaching something. Teaching is hard, since you need to engage, connect, inform, influence, and persuade. To be a good teacher, you at least need to be a good speaker. But to be a great speaker, you need to be a great teacher. Best-selling business author Sydney Finkelstein quotes Jack Nicholson on what kind of a teacher Roger Corman (movie producer, director, and actor) was: "[W]ith Roger, you learn the basics, good basics and tough basics; you never really forget it."[18] Keep in mind that when you are speaking, you are teaching, and do it in a way that the audience remembers it for a long time. The student's (the audience's) retention is a hallmark of a good teacher.

Teaching is one of the most important skills for success in business today. The reason for this is very simple: For a company to win today, not only must it learn fast as an organization, but it also must have people who can teach well. A company must find ways to be productive, and that means it has to learn faster than its competitors. But to learn well, it needs a lot of good teachers. In fact, it needs a teaching culture. If employees don't cultivate teaching skills, the company will not be able to compete effectively.

We are living in a world where things are getting more complex and changing fast. People are overwhelmed with information overload and don't have time to learn new things. If you can teach, you will succeed, since you are making people smarter much faster. A company values those who can teach well.

Bill Clinton was put in this position of teaching when he was asked to nominate Barack Obama as president at the 2012 Democratic National Convention.[19] Prior to Clinton speaking at the convention, the Republicans had done an excellent job portraying Obama as a failed president, and Mitt Romney was in fact ahead in the polls. But with his speech, Clinton put Obama ahead in the polls, since he was able to explain the rationale for Obama to be reelected. Many political pundits credit Bill Clinton—and this speech in particular—for changing the narrative in the 2012 election.

How did Clinton accomplish this difficult task? By being the "Explainer-in-Chief," he clearly showed people where they were before Obama became president, where they were then with Obama as the president, and where they were going to be with Obama as the president for the next four years. He removed any hesitation of those in the middle of the political spectrum. Similarly, when a 1-percenter is explaining, people are listening. If you want to be in the 1 percent of the communicators, you have to explain in order to win, often in high-stakes situations.

The Speech Is Not Risky Enough

Speeches often are not memorable, because speakers don't take any risks. Most speakers play it safe; hence, what they deliver has no winning speech moment. What made Martin Luther King Jr.'s 1963 speech at the Lincoln Memorial create a winning speech moment was that he had the "I Have a Dream" speech in his repertoire, and he could use it if he felt he needed it. During the speech, he felt he needed it, and he seamlessly included that famous part, thereby creating one of the greatest winning speech moments of all time.

But how do you do this?

I suggest you write a safe speech that will be "boring good," in that it gets the job done. Once you have the safe speech completed, focus on giving a risky speech. You don't have to make the decision until the last possible moment. In fact, you can do as MLK did: Start with the safe speech, and then midway bring in the risky speech.

I did this for my father-in-law's funeral, and it worked. I had worked hard on the safe speech, but on the morning of the funeral, I decided to put together a risky speech, and I used it when my turn came to give a speech.

It is always easier to play it safe, but then you are not going to develop the instinct to be spontaneous. The safe speech will be quickly forgotten, but not the risky speech, provided that you indeed create a winning speech moment.

A week after I gave the funeral speech, two professors I met at an event told me that they remembered my speech and that they liked it. That was one week after I gave the speech. I was caught completely by surprise, since I did not know these two professors, and I hadn't expected that anyone would remember the speech.

To be able to hack a risky speech for any occasion, you have to go through what I teach in this book, so you can hack content, hack a message, and hack a performance, thereby turning a safe speech into a risky speech on short notice so that it is memorable in a good way.

The Speech Is Not Crafted and Delivered to Win at Any Cost

If you are not willing to win at any cost, then you need to accept that you might not win so that you will not be disappointed if you lose. Winning is everything to successful people, and this is especially true the more successful they are. People will lie, cheat, and steal to win. You have to decide how far you are willing to go in order to win. I would be committing malpractice if I did not point this out. I would be setting you up to fail. Books on public speaking rarely ever go into what makes a winning speech. They focus on all kinds of techniques that are going to make your speech good, but they do little to help you achieve your overall objective.

Often it is how low are you willing to go with your audience that will help you win. Hillary Clinton learned this lesson the hard way during her campaign against Donald Trump when she kept repeating Michelle Obama's line "When they go low, we go high."[20] Going high was the right thing to do, but it did not result in a win when the other side had no bottom. Donald Trump did not play the game by going high. Instead, he scared voters over immigrants, over Muslims, and over trade with China and Mexico. His scare tactics worked. Though Trump did not win the popular vote, he did win the Electoral College vote and became the president of the United States. He won, and he gets to set the future of the United States and the world. This just goes to show that you may not like to go low, but you have to also remind yourself of the consequences of losing. If you believe in your cause, you have to do just about anything in your speech to win.

Jeffrey Toobin, lawyer, author, and legal analyst for CNN and the *New Yorker*, writes that when O. J. Simpson was charged with murder, his lawyers knew that he was guilty.[21] But when O. J. refused to plea-bargain, his team of lawyers decided that to have any chance of an acquittal, they needed to play the race card. Their strategy was to make O. J. the victim of the racist Los Angeles Police Department, accusing the LAPD of framing him for the two murders because he was African American. O. J.'s lawyers believed that using the race strategy would work well, since the jury pool consisted of mostly African Americans, who they felt would be sympathetic to that argument, based on their bad experience with the LAPD. It worked. It didn't take the jury much time to return a not guilty verdict.

Civil rights lawyer, jurist, and best-selling author Alan Dershowitz, who was also one of the lawyers on the O. J. defense team, said it best:

> Once I decide to take a case, I have only one agenda: I want to win. I will try, by every fair and legal means, to get my client off—without regard to the consequences.[22]

You have to ask yourself whether you want to win by being a leader or by being a demagogue. Each of them uses the same tool for being a great public speaker. Leaders use their public speaking skills to take people from their negative state and elevate it to a positive state through persuasion. They play to people's hopes and aspirations. Demagogues meanwhile take people's current negative state and amplify it, scaring them to win support. They play to people's fears. Demagogues have it easier, since it is easy to scare people by appealing to emotions than it is to uplift them through reason and logic. When you are giving a speech, you need to decide how you want to win.

The Speech Does Not Create the Right Winning Speech Moment

Who has words at the right moment?

— Charlotte Brontë, English novelist and poet

There is one thing many people do not understand, yet it's something the Greeks figured out early: In order for your speech to resonate, you need *ethos*, *logos*, and *pathos*. I will explain it a little bit differently by providing an equation and then by providing a couple of examples.

Uh oh. Paraphrasing Stephen Hawking near the end of Chapter 2, I said that I hoped my including a single equation would not halve the sales of this book. And now I can't resist including one more equation.

Right Moment = Right Person + Right Time + Right Place + Right Audience + Right Message + Right Speech

From this equation, you can see that each element has to exist simultaneously to create the right winning speech moment that people will remember. The following are two examples of speeches that created the right winning speech moments.

Robert F. Kennedy: One of the Greatest High-Stakes Speeches Ever Given

Often it is hard to look back and determine how high-stakes a particular speech was at the time it was delivered. But one speech was definitely high-stakes when it was delivered, and it has stood the test of time. It was given by Robert F. Kennedy in the poor African American section of Indianapolis immediately after the assassination of Martin Luther King Jr. on April 4, 1968.

The police warned him not to go to this poor black section of Indianapolis, and they withdrew their escort when RFK decided anyway to go and address the black crowd. The crowd did not yet know that King had been assassinated in Memphis, Tennessee. It was Kennedy himself who had to inform them of the tragedy, and he used the opportunity to focus on love and justice, calming the crowd down with his eloquent words and his heartfelt empathy. He knew that people would be angry, but he was able to make the crowd understand that violence was not going to solve anything, and he said that he could relate to how they felt, since his very own brother had been assassinated by a white man.

NPR's forty-year commemorative article pointed out that

> a well-organized black community kept its calm. It's hard to overlook the image of one single man, standing on a flatbed truck, who never looked down at the paper in his hand—only at the faces in the crowd.[23]

Many cities burned across the United States—with the exception of Indianapolis. Indeed, Kennedy delivered one of the most high-stakes speeches ever given, which could be measured by the lack of violence in Indianapolis. His power of oratory prevented death and destruction that night.

Using the equation I presented earlier, let's analyze what made RFK's words create a right winning speech moment:

Right person. Robert Kennedy was well known, and he had credibility, since his brother (JFK) had also been assassinated.

Right time. The tragic death of Martin Luther King Jr.

Right place. The African American neighborhood in Indianapolis.

Right audience. Kennedy was speaking to African Americans in their poor neighborhood who had not yet heard that MLK had been assassinated.

Right message. Love and justice.

Right speech. RFK's speech was filled with empathy and hope; his speech was heartfelt, and he never looked at the notes that he had jotted down.

George W. Bush: The Best Speech He Ever Gave as the President

Presidents have speech writers who craft their speeches, so it is often difficult to know their personal involvement in developing the speeches they give. They get the credit, though, just as actors do for their performance, and no one cares who actually wrote the words. That is not the case when they have to give a speech on their feet, however. George W. Bush was not known for his talent for giving great impromptu speeches; nonetheless, he gave the most memorable speech of his presidency when he visited Ground Zero in Manhattan after the 9/11 attack to pay his respects to those who had died, thank the first responders, and rally the nation to fight terrorism.

As he was speaking, someone in the crowd yelled, "We can't hear you." Bush yelled back,

> I can hear you. The rest of the world hears you. And the people who knocked these buildings down will hear all of us soon.[24]

The crowd started chanting "USA! USA! USA!" A few weeks later, Bush delivered on his promise at Ground Zero by attacking the Taliban in Afghanistan.

How did Bush's words create a right winning speech moment?

Right person. George W. Bush was the president.

Right time. Three days after the 9/11 attack.

Right place. Ground Zero, where the towers stood.

Right audience. First responders who were dealing with the aftermath of the death and destruction.

Right message. "We will get those who attacked us."

Right speech. President Bush's speech was short, crafted ostensibly to thank the first responders, but the impromptu was what made this speech great.

CHAPTER 4:

The Most Important High-Stakes
Speech You Ever Give

Ninety-nine percent of opening bands stink.

— Gene Ween, alternative rock musician

N o matter what self-help book you read, you should walk
away with at least one tip that you can use immediately.
When it comes to public speaking, the most important
high-stakes speech you give is **the introduction speech.** I will
show you in this brief chapter how to get off to a good start
through different ways you can introduce yourself. Do not
underestimate the importance of your introduction speech with
anyone, anytime, anywhere. You just don't know what
possibilities it can lead to if you connect with someone right away.
And you need to do this well, since people make a like/dislike
decision in just a few seconds.

The introduction speech is the shortest speech you give, but
it's in that speech that you need to make a good first impression.
You want to keep it simple, but at the same time, make the speech

87

result in a short conversation. Hence, the main purpose of an introduction speech is to elicit a short conversation. But that conversation depends on what you say after you give your name.

Maybe you don't think of introducing yourself as a speech, but if you don't handle an introduction well, treating it like a speech, you may never get a second chance to make a good first impression. In fact, you may have already lost someone at "Hello." How you introduce yourself makes a huge difference when you speak to anyone for the first time. People are not going to invest much time in you if you don't intrigue them in some way. The burden is on you to make the introduction as high-stakes as possible.

After you say, "Hello, How are you?" it comes down to an informal *introduction speech*, which is a make-or-break moment in any first interaction. What are you going to say?

Here is what I would say to you if you were just meeting me: "I help people give high-stakes speeches." Or I can be a little playful: Depending on whom I am talking to, I might say, "I save lives." Wouldn't you be at least a little bit curious as to what I could possibly be doing? You would likely think I am in the medical profession, right? I would have to follow up with, "I help people not 'die' on stage when they are speaking." At this point, you might either have a story probably about yourself or someone you saw recently "dying" on stage while giving a speech. If I can elicit this type of response, then I have achieved my objective, which could lead to just about anything. I will have connected, and I can then move to see if I can engage with you.

That's it. It's simple, clear, and direct. It's my superpower. It can be your superpower too. As you can see, it's not that hard to extend your introduction into a little speech, but you need to be prepared. Seth Godin writes that without that prepared introduction speech, you are "just another handshake."[1] You are not bragging with your speech, you are just letting the other person know a little more about you and how you can help them. It is the easiest speech you will give, so you must not blow it at "hello." You have a superpower, so lead with your introduction speech the next time you introduce yourself!

After I give the person I'm introducing myself to my name and tell him or her something important about me, such as that I save lives, I would expect the person to ask more about what I said. If my introduction speech does not pique the person's interest, then he or she is not likely to have a conversation I am interested in having. I will know quickly whether I am dealing with a *conversation ender* or a *conversation extender*. You want to talk to someone who enjoys having a conversation with you so you can make that all-important connection. Even if it leads to nothing, having a conversation means that you will have enabled a conversation to happen by the way you introduced yourself. You will have showed that you are a confident speaker, and you gave a person an opening to engage with you.

You will find that many people would like to engage but are reluctant to initiate. So you have to take a risk and initiate a conversation, which often is the hardest part of any connection. As the famous lotto slogan said, "You've gotta to be in it to win it." You can adopt this slogan to communication: "You have to converse to connect."

Without a good introduction, you are more likely to end a conversation quickly. Don't just introduce yourself by telling someone what your job function is without telling how you help people. Next time you introduce yourself, pay close attention to how you do it. You need to practice this opening, since it is a speech you often give, which makes it the most important speech you ever give.

You just introduced yourself, and you have the other person's attention, so what are you going to do next to sustain the conversation and take it to the next level? You had the confidence to introduce yourself, because you were prepared. Now you must do the same for other speeches that are likely to follow. And that is what this book is about. How do you develop the confidence to give an introductory speech, an impromptu speech, an informative speech, a persuasive speech, and other kinds of speeches? By developing competence.

World-renowned personality expert Tomas Chamorro-Premuzic writes that "your self-improvement depends not on feeling more confident, but on being more competent."[2] I will teach you how to develop competence through the steps that I went through (and am still going through) to become a confident speaker.

I use the word *confidence*, whose increase is something you control by incrementally becoming competent in your public speaking skills. As you work on developing your speaking skills, people may judge you to be an average speaker, a good speaker, a great speaker, or even an inspirational speaker. You don't control how others judge your speaking skills. You just need to keep on learning and practicing so you become competent. As you become more competent, and start to exude genuine confidence when speaking before an audience, people will start noticing that you are a good, or even a great, speaker.

But because everything starts with a conversation, you have to treat a conversation as if it is an important speech. Whether you are speaking to one person or to many, you are on a stage, even if that stage is a "virtual stage" rather than a physical stage. You need to be confident and deliver your speech, which you have prepared to achieve an objective. **You don't just prepare for formal speeches; you prepare for *all* the speeches.** If your informal speech is not impressive, you will not engender much trust that your formal speech will be any better—that is, if you even get a chance to give a formal speech. People do start judging you from the time you say "Hello," so you can't afford to blow it at "Hello."

What should you do in an introduction speech? Read on.

Make People Remember Your Name

You should help people to never forget your name. What I do may be a little corny, but it works. I say that it is amazing how many people forget my last name "Oza." I make remembering it easier by telling them to think of "Obama" but to replace the *bam* with a *z*. People might think I am a little bit weird (perhaps they might be right), but they are not going to forget my last name. Of course, I am playing with them, but it also shows that I don't take myself too seriously. In fact, if they have any sense of humor, they may even call me "Ozama" when they bump into me later; it becomes our little inside joke. What I have done is connect, and all I did up to that point was to just introduce myself.

You have to bring something that people can work with. And even if they think you are little weird, look at it on the bright side: You are most likely not going to see them again anyway. You have nothing to lose. You need to take some risk, and you may as well start right from your introduction speech.

Suppose someone is introducing you to a third person. Make sure the introducer knows how you want to be introduced (how you want to be "framed"). And keep the introduction simple. We often forget this and get framed by the person introducing us in a way that is difficult to reframe later. Your introducer can give you instant credibility that will help you connect quickly, or, sadly, he or she can do the opposite. Do not assume that others are good at introducing you. You need to take charge of this simple thing. You have to let your introducer know exactly how you want to be introduced and not leave it to his or her good judgment.

If the person is not good at introducing you, just let him or her say this much: "I want to introduce you to…" You step in with your name, just as if you were James Bond with his "Bond… James Bond." Isn't the first introduction of James Bond one of the highlights of any James Bond movie? What are you going to do?

Instead of Giving Your Job Title, Tell How You Help People

No one cares whether you are a business development manager, a vice president of marketing, a senior director of technology, or whatever. Who cares? No one. Instead of giving your job title, tell the person you are meeting how you help people or how you make a difference. For example, if you are a real estate agent: "I help people get their dream house." In my case: "I help people become confident public speakers" or "I coach people how to win with their speeches."

When you meet people, they want to see how you might be able to help them. Before you tell them what you do, you might want to ask them one or two questions. For example, I might ask the following: "Do you know people who will do anything to get out of giving a speech?" Or, taking a line from the website of Nick Morgan, author of *Power Cues*:[3] "Do you know people who have been known to 'kill' their relatives to get out of giving a speech? Well, I help people keep their relatives alive by helping them overcome their fear of public speaking."

Use this approach if you can make it relevant to the person's hidden needs, since it shows that you know how to solve a problem that people run into. Your little introduction speech might lead to an extended conversation. Also, the person might refer someone to you who has a problem that you can solve. I would suggest using some humor in your speech and rehearse it, so you come across naturally instead of sounding like you are reading a script.

Again, an introduction is where it all starts. A bad introduction is like giving a verbal "dead fish" handshake. You want to avoid both the physical "dead fish" handshake and the verbal "dead fish" introduction, which creates a poor first impression and will likely lead to nothing. You will have blown your chances, since you will not be remembered. On the other hand, your introduction speech done well, following some practice and rehearsal, is likely to lead to your giving an impromptu speech, and perhaps even an informative speech and a persuasive speech in the near future. You have to treat your introduction speech as high-stakes.

Do Your Homework

Suppose you are listening to a speaker whom you'd like to network with in order to advance your objective. When you introduce yourself to the speaker, you have a very short time to make your introduction count. What are you going to do? Networking, especially with important people, is something you need to be good at, since these people are not thinking about what you do; they are too busy with what they do and what energizes them. If you just wing it, then you will have wasted a golden opportunity to connect with a potential influencer who could make a difference in your achieving your objective. Before you approach the speaker, know how you are going to handle this situation: Do your homework, so you know what the speaker does and what energizes him or her.

Sheryl Sandberg, COO of Facebook, writes how Garrett Neiman, cofounder and CEO of CollegeSpring, got her attention after she gave a speech at Stanford.[4] He approached her and said that he had founded a nonprofit company that provides SAT tutoring and college counseling to students coming from low-income households. He wanted to speak to her for a few minutes to see if she could help him with some introductions to increase his company's reach.

According to Sandberg, she gave him time because "he had done his homework and knew that I care deeply about education."[5] What would *not* have worked with Sandberg would be someone asking, "What is Facebook's culture like?" because you can find an answer to that on the Internet.

What can you learn from this example, according to Sandberg?

- **Be prepared.** Before you approach the speaker, make sure you know what would get his or her attention.

- **Be clear and direct.** Don't waste time. Briefly tell the person what you do, how you help people, and what you are looking for. Be clear, direct, and succinct.

- **Be professional.** Sandberg writes that during every meeting she found Garrett to be "crisp, focused and gracious." You want to make life easier for the person who is helping you; keep him or her updated on your relevant activities. Again, do not waste the person's time.

Whenever you are faced with this situation, do take a shot at networking with the speaker, provided that you have prepared and that you are clear, direct, and professional. Networking such as this can pay off for you in a big way. In fact, this is a skill you can learn and practice at the next big event that you will attend. The skill takes work to develop, but it's worth it when you look at the potential upside. I use this method to get guests to appear on my YouTube show *Speech Talk Live*.

When I meet people face to face, my success rate is very high. (It is not that high, however, when I don't know the person at all and I am essentially cold-calling them. I have to work on improving my cold-calling ratio. I use the same approach by e-mail, but the success is not as high as it is when I meet someone face to face. Even with all the technology we have today, nothing beats face-to-face interaction to connect quickly.)

Work on Your Introduction Speech Before You Proceed

I know this is so simple that your natural tendency might be to proceed further without working on your introduction speech. I suggest you spend a few days working on it, however, so you can anticipate how people will react to your introduction. Again, if you don't make a good first impression with your first speech (your introductory speech), you are not going to get a chance to impress people with your second speech (your impromptu speech, discussed in Chapter 9). And just in case you are wondering, the third speeches—your informative speech (Chapter 11) and your persuasive speech (Chapter 12)—are more formal. But your introduction speech is one place where you don't start with the end in mind. You need to start with the beginning in mind, because there is no end if your beginning is bad.

CHAPTER 5

Overview of the Steps to Become a High-Stakes Speaker

Adapt what is useful, reject what is useless, and add what is specifically your own.

— Bruce Lee, martial artist, actor, philosopher, and filmmaker

You are reading this book because you want to learn a public speaking method that is simple, practical, and proven. You can learn to become an effective high-stakes speaker if you are willing to put in the time and follow the method I teach in this book for at least ninety days. If you see the results, then you will have a method that you can use forever. You can easily tweak what I teach as you see fit so it produces results for you.

Since I have been working on this for a while, I have developed this method so you don't have to struggle to figure it out on your own. Think of working on public speaking skills as an infrastructure project: It's always under construction. Everything I am going to teach you in this book will cost you nothing, but one thing that is not free is your time, your effort, and your energy. However, if you aspire to get to the top, then it will be well worth your making the investment now.

When it comes to improving your public speaking skills, there are no shortcuts. The only way you get good at this skill is by putting in the work—a lot of work. Just look at how much work you have already put in since your birth to become an adequate speaker or perhaps even a good speaker. You no doubt have at least a high school degree, and you possibly have one or more college degrees.

Note: The numbers of years of education you have does not predict that you are going to be a good-to-great public speaker. Public speaking is not exclusively a knowledge-based skill, but it is a practice-based skill. Anyone can become a good-to-great public speaker, just like a rock star.

I am not even counting the speaking you may well have done since you entered the workforce. That is a lot of time that you have spent on learning and practicing how to communicate. Even with all that, you may well be, at best, an adequate public speaker. To become a confident speaker and then take it to the next level, you will need to become a student, a teacher, and a coach of public speaking, especially your public speaking.

And, unless you have a boatload of money to hire a public speaking guru to coach you one on one, you will need to do it on your own. This book contains all the steps necessary for you to do it on your own. (Nonetheless, once you become a confident speaker, you may want to find a coach so you can focus on improving specific aspects of your high-stakes public speaking skills.)

The main reason I keep saying that you have to learn this skill on your own is because it is very hard to find someone who can teach and coach you to make a significant improvement. Public speaking is not a "drive-by" skill, which you can learn from taking one-and-done courses. To develop and master this skill, you have to be committed to stay the course for a while. Before you hire a professional coach, you should first become a confident speaker on your own, so you will be able to assess what specific areas you need to improve with targeted coaching. If you are committed, focused, and motivated, then you can easily become not only a good speaker but even a great speaker on your own, as I am currently doing.

In this chapter, I provide the steps you can take to become first a confident speaker and then a high-stakes speaker. I recommend that you not fast-track your way through this book, since you need to learn each hack thoroughly so you know it is working for you.

The Method

The following are the steps you can take—starting today—that will move you from being a confident speaker to becoming a high-stakes speaker.

First Phase: Becoming a confident speaker (Part Two):

Step 1: Record your goals video (Chapter 6).

Step 2: Learn the content hack (Chapter 7).

Step 3: Take the 3/30 Challenge to obtain a baseline of where you are (Chapter 8).

Step 4: Practice by giving impromptu speeches both socially and professionally (Chapter 9).

(Steps 1 through 4 should take no more than thirty days.)

Second Phase: Becoming a good-to-great high-stakes speaker (Part Three):

Step 5: Learn the message hack so you know how to convey your message (Chapter 10).

Step 6: Integrate the message hack into your impromptu speeches (still Chapter 10).

Step 7: Practice the message hack with an informative speech (Chapter 11).

Step 8: Practice the message hack with a persuasive speech (Chapter 12).

Step 9: Learn the performance hack (Chapter 13).

Step 10: Practice the performance hack with all the speeches where the stakes are high (Chapters 14–16).

Step 11: Master all three hacks, and integrate them to create a great experience for your audience (Chapter 17).

(To become and remain a good-to-great high-stakes speaker takes a lot of practice, and the effort varies, based on your motivation and level of interest.)

Again, high-stakes public speaking is always a work in progress. Even though I have a lot of work to do (as you can see from my videos on my YouTube channel), I am working hard on further developing and mastering the advanced public speaking skill; in fact, I consider myself a "speaking athlete" by the way I am learning / training, preparing, performing, evaluating, assessing, and winning.

You will need to approach this craft like a world-class athlete if you want to go from a weekend speaker to a good-to-great professional or an inspirational speaker. The good news is that it is all up to you. You get to control your speaking success. You get to practice when you want. And you must want to become a speaking athlete like Barack Obama or Bill Clinton.

Your Goals

You need both a method (or system) and goals. In this book I teach a flexible method (outlined in the preceding paragraphs) for becoming a high-stakes speaker, a method you need to follow diligently. But you also need goals so you know what you are trying to achieve for the long term and are able to make the necessary changes to correct anything that needs improvement. Goals help you reach your destination faster.

Here is how Scott Adams, creator of the *Dilbert* comic strip, puts it:

> Goal-oriented people exist in a state of continuous pre-success failure at best, and permanent failure at worst if things never work out. Systems people succeed every time they apply their systems, in the sense that they did what they intended to do.[1]

I agree with Adams that you can get disappointed if you don't achieve your goals, disappointed enough to eventually quit. But, according to research, goals do indeed work. *Forbes* blogger Ashley Feinstein cites research performed by Dr. Gail Matthews of Dominican University that found that those who wrote down their goals accomplished significantly more than those who didn't write them down.[2] But writing the goals is not enough. You need to back up your goal writing with an action plan, staying committed and motivated, assessing progress periodically, and finally having someone hold you accountable with specific measurements, such as progress reports.

Since many people are adequate speakers, the first thing you have to do is go from being adequate to being confident, following the first four steps in the method (the first phase, described in Part Two). Next, you can take your speaking even higher by following the remaining steps to become a high-stakes speaker (the second phase, described in Part Three). If you wish, after you become a good-to-great speaker, you can leverage your speaking skills to become a professional speaker. And perhaps you can even go to the pinnacle in public speaking and become an inspirational speaker.

How do you make your goals work for both the short term and the long term? In his book *Smarter Faster Better*, Charles Duhigg cites research that demonstrates the importance of goal setting and describes the traps you can fall into if you are not careful.[3] I have taken many of the ideas from Duhigg's book, ideas that you can use for setting up your goals to become a confident speaker. I am covering this subtopic in some detail, because I believe it is important to be goal-focused when you are developing a skill.

SMART Goals

You need goals that are SMART, which is an acronym that stands for **S**pecific, **M**easurable, **A**chievable, **R**elevant, and **T**ime-bound. It is a good method for short-term goals, enabling you to achieve quick, small wins so you feel confident that you are making progress. This approach does not work well with a long-term goal, which does not meet SMART criteria. For that, you need to come up with stretch goals, which you then break into manageable parts that you can apply the SMART criteria to. (Stretch goals are described in the next section.)

Note: Goals are necessary so you have a map for success, but you also should be ready to take detours if you run into roadblocks. In some cases, if something changes, you may have to abandon your goals altogether and develop new ones without becoming discouraged or paralyzed.

This SMART process is effective, since it gets you to focus on what you want to achieve, how you are going achieve it, when you are going to achieve it, and how to measure if you achieved it. But one question SMART does not address is, should you even try to achieve what you are trying to achieve? What is the point of achieving something that may not be that important in the long term?

The weakness of SMART goals is that they may make you more process-oriented and not make you ask whether a goal is even worth accomplishing. It is a productive method: People who establish goals that are SMART are focused, they persevere to finish them, and therefore they feel good about themselves. But the question that is not often asked is the following: Is it worth being productive in something that is not that ambitious?

As you create short-term goals, answer the following questions to be sure that you are applying the SMART criteria:[4]

- What is specific about the goal?

- Is the goal measurable? (How will you know the goal has been achieved?)

- Is the goal achievable?

- Is the goal relevant to performance expectations or professional development?

- Is the goal time-bound? (How often will this task be done? Or, by when will this goal be accomplished?)

Here is a sample goal that many might have: "I want to become a confident public speaker." Unfortunately, this goal does not meet the SMART criteria, since what does "confident" mean? You would need to make some changes to make this goal SMART.

Consider the following goal:

I want to become a confident public speaker in thirty days by performing the following steps:

1. Record a goals video to start the process (Chapter 6).

2. Learn the content hack (Chapter 7).

3. Take the 3/30 Challenge (Chapter 8), where I will record one three-minute speech every day for the next thirty days.

4. Assess my progress after completing the 3/30 Challenge to see if I indeed feel more confident as a speaker than before, or do I need to do anything more and come up with a new plan.

This goal meets all the SMART attributes:

- **Specific.** It has four steps that I have to take to become a confident speaker.

- **Measurable.** I will know where I am in the course, based on whether I am posting speeches for others to review.

- **Achievable.** Thirty days is aggressive but achievable.

- **Relevant.** If it is relevant to my achieving my goal, then I will remain committed.

- **Time-bound.** I am saying that I will do it for thirty days to become a confident speaker.

Stretch Goals

Stretch goals are a very successful concept used in companies such as General Electric. Now, there are critics of this approach (especially in business), but I don't see a problem with thinking big, as long as you don't view stretch goals as the be-all and end-all goals. You want to pick some goals that you have no way of knowing how you are going to achieve them. You can even call them "dream goals." In fact, that is the whole point of these goals. If you can't dream them, then you are limiting your growth potential.

A stretch goal can be something like "I will speak before an audience of one thousand people" or "I will write a book, go on a speaking tour, and appear on various podcasts" or "I will give a TED Talk." You probably have no way of knowing when you write these stretch goals on how to get them done, but they are something you have identified, and gradually you will put together a plan to achieve them.

If you can't break your long-term goals into manageable parts, then they will remain unrealistic and unachievable. For example, if you say you want to write a book when you have never written one, then you might see it as a stretch goal that will never be realized. However, if you say that you want to write a book in one year, and you plan to write an outline, then do the research, interview people, write one thousand words a day (at a minimum), then slowly, in six months, you will have more than enough material for a book.

After that, you can organize your written material and get the first draft completed, receive feedback, write some more, and go through more drafts. After nine months, you will have a book ready for a professional edit, for getting a cover design, for the book design, and for focusing the last two months on developing a marketing plan for the launch. Now this long-term plan, your stretch goal, can be broken down into multiple SMART goals.

And if it is not going well or if something changes, then you must either make changes or even end it. You always start with the intention to get to your destination, but you always need to be on guard for the changing environment. You can't just follow the goals and not look at the things that are changing around you.

For example, I started working on a book that was about helping people get a job. I wrote the first draft, but then I decided that I had to put the project on hold, since what I was recommending would work only if the reader had good speaking skills. Hence, I pivoted and started writing this book. Along the way, the book had to go through multiple changes, since I was trying to boil the ocean, so I had to tweak some parts and remove other parts. You will be the judge whether I accomplished that or not. But even if I didn't, I will fix it in the next version. Just as there is no one decisive battle that wins a war. Similarly, there is no one book that defines you or your writing skills. You have to fight the battles, even if you lose, and eventually you will either quit or win.

Here is an example of a stretch goal: "*I want to become a professional keynote speaker.*" Now, this is a good aspirational goal, but it needs to be broken into manageable parts and combined with the SMART method of goal setting.

Here are high-level SMART goals that break down that stretch goal (and each SMART goal would need to be broken down further):

- Take the Coursera courses on public speaking.

- Take the 3/30 Challenge, but do it twice a week.

- Practice splitting your speech into various time durations, such as five minutes, twenty minutes, and forty minutes.

- Start a YouTube show.

- Get as many speaking gigs as possible to speak in front of people.

- Get paid for speeches.

- Deliver a keynote speech before a large audience.

This stretch goal may take some time to achieve, but if keynoter is what I aspire to become, then I have to come up with many SMART goals that will ultimately result in my becoming a keynoter.

If all these steps don't sound like much fun, I have to cite what Yale Law School professor Amy Chua writes in her best-selling book *Battle Hymn of the Tiger Mother*, which I believe applies not only to raising children to help them realize their potential but also to developing lifelong skills for success such as in public speaking.[5] You are trying to realize your potential as a public speaker, so you have to be your own tiger mom who will kick yourself in the butt when needed. She writes, "What Chinese parents understand is that nothing is fun until you're good at it.... Tenacious practice, practice, practice is crucial for excellence." **Your getting good at a skill** (by gaining competence and thereby building confidence) **"makes the once not-fun activity fun."**

Got it. It is not going to be fun in the beginning. But if you stay the course and keep at it, you will get better and start having fun giving speeches and whatever might result from that.

Hierarchy of Goals

Another way to look at goals is what Angela Duckworth writes about in her book *Grit: The Power of Passion and Perseverance*. She discusses the hierarchy of goals, where you have one long-term (top-level) goal, a few mid-term (mid-level) goals, and several short-term (low-level) goals.[6] Your short-term goals can be viewed as "means to an end," and the long-term goal is the "end."

So, my top-level, long-term goal is to help people, by teaching, mentoring, and coaching them on public speaking, so that they can deliver winning high-stakes speeches whether the speeches are one on one, in a small group setting, or in front of a large audience. This top-level goal of mine will remain fixed for a long time, if not forever—unless I get sick of public speaking, which is highly unlikely.

Based on my top-level goal, I may have a few mid-level goals, such as giving a few keynote speeches to thousands of people, giving speeches to students (for free) and companies (for pay), coaching CEOs of top companies, and teaching an online course on public speaking. Ideally, you should limit yourself to three mid-level goals, using the 60/30/10 rule (based on their importance to your success).

Here's what *I* mean by the "60/30/10 rule": I have taken the 80/20 rule (also known as the Pareto Principle) and modified it, considering how the ancient Greek poet Archilochus (680 BCE – 645 BCE) contrasted how a fox and a hedgehog each approach a problem: πόλλ' οἶδ' ἀλώπηξ, ἀλλ' ἐχῖνος ἓν μέγα ("a fox knows many things, but a hedgehog one important thing"), an idea elaborated by the Russian-British philosopher Sir Isaiah Berlin.[7] Simply, the ways you prioritize items vary: the first one is most important and gets a 60-percent priority, the second one gets 30 percent, and the third one gets 10 percent. Items after the third are not that important.

Again, you do have to prioritize; otherwise, you are less likely to achieve your mid-level goals. Does the first mid-level goal get you 60 percent of the way toward achieving the top-level goal? Does the second mid-level goal add 30 percent more toward that top-level goal to 90 percent? Finally, does the third mid-level goal add the final 10 percent, the "frosting on the cake," to take you all the way to 100 percent?

Now, if I want to achieve my mid-level goal of giving a keynote speech, I would need to achieve a lot of low-level goals, such as writing a book, speaking before a small crowd, appearing on different podcasts to spread the word, writing blogs, recording a lot of videos, creating an online course, getting a speaking coach to improve my speaking for paid events, and so on. Low-level goals are generally short-term, so you can assess in a relatively short time whether they are helping you achieve your mid-level goals.

You need to review your low-level goals often and change them as needed. It is much easier to change low-level goals than it is to change mid-level goals. But the one goal that is not likely to change for the long term is your top-level goal. The top-level goal is something that defines you. For example, I plan to be helping people with their speaking skills. What can change is my mid-level goals, perhaps every year, if I want to do something different related to my top-level goal.

In the next chapter, you will take the most important step in developing your goals to become a good-to-great speaker. I am helping you become a good-to-great speaker in the next two parts of this book by breaking the process down into steps so you can achieve your stretch goal—say of becoming a good-to-great speaker—into eleven steps. These are the steps I am following. You can tweak the steps so they help you improve.

But first things first. You must record your goals video in the next chapter.

PART TWO:

Becoming a Confident Speaker

CHAPTER 6:

Get Your Goals on Video!

People who won't take step number one never take step number two.

— Zig Ziglar, author, salesman, and motivational speaker

"Begin with the end in mind," writes Stephen Covey in his excellent book *The 7 Habits of Highly Effective People* as one of the habits to follow to be successful in both business and life. He adds that

> to begin with the end in mind means to start with a clear understanding of your destination. It means to know where you're going so that you better understand where you are now and so that the steps you take are always in the right direction.[1]

You began life with a quick breath and a loud yell, announcing your arrival into this world. Amazingly, you immediately captured people's attention without uttering a single word. But, as you get older, it gets much harder to capture and maintain people's attention. Since there is so much speaking you do in your lifetime, your success depends on how often and how well you can engage, connect, inform, influence, persuade, and win with the speech you give to anyone, anytime, anywhere.

My purpose is not to just teach you a forever skill, so you know it, but to motivate you to develop a mindset through deliberate practice, so you can do it naturally and become successful in anything you pursue where you have to use your speech to win. With the hacks, I teach you that giving a winning speech will no longer be a one-time event; it will be an everyday occurrence. If you are ready to become a high-stakes speaker so you can speak with anyone, anytime, anywhere, then you will learn three hacks, which will help you achieve that.

But before you go any further, I would like you to record your goals on video. As I pointed out in Chapter 5, this is step 1 in my eleven-step method for becoming first a confident speaker and then a good-to-great high-stakes speaker. Even if you don't do anything besides this step, you will at least know what you look and sound like to yourself.

Note: If you need a refresher on setting the goals you are going to record, please reread the section "Your Goals," which is the second half of Chapter 5.

After recording your goals, ask yourself the following question: "Do I like the way I look and sound when I'm speaking?" If not, then you need to fix that now by recording why you want to develop a skill, the lack of which is probably keeping you from being successful both personally and professionally.

Many people who give speeches have no idea what they look like and sound like when they are at the podium; hence, they have no idea what they are doing well and what they need to improve. I wish I had done this right after I graduated college. I had a VHS video camera, but I never used it to improve my speaking skills. Today, video cameras and camera phones are everywhere, so there are no excuses for not recording a video of yourself giving a speech.

For this exercise, you are recording your personal video, so you do not need to share it with anyone. I do recommend that you do share it with at least one person you trust, however; that person will keep you accountable to your goal of becoming a confident speaker. When you feel you have become a good-to-great speaker, then you can use the video to motivate others, helping them start their journey to becoming a good-to-great speaker like you.

Since this is your first video, do no more than three takes. There are *no* rules for this video. Whatever fear you might be feeling, you want to get it out of your head. Many people have a lot of potential but are paralyzed by their fear of public speaking; thus, they hurt themselves from succeeding in both life and work. You want to talk about this in this video, so you can go back to it and view it in case you fall off the wagon or somehow lose motivation.

Don't worry if you ramble on in this video; don't worry if it is long; don't worry if you get stuck; don't worry if it is not good. You are not recording this for the world to see. I always joke with people who are hesitant to come on my show *Speech Talk Live*, which I record and post on YouTube. I tell them that they should have no fear, since, as I like to say, there are only two chickens and a pig somewhere in Idaho who ever watch my video channel. You are fortunate that you will have at least one person whom you trust who will watch your goals video.

By making this video, you will take a huge first step—probably the most difficult one—in getting your high-stakes speaking journey started. You will look back and be amazed at this video you are about to record.

I did something similar when I started my blogging, with a post I appropriately titled "My First Blog Post: It Starts Today."[2] I had to do a lot of work to get that first blog post up, such as securing a domain, finding a good host site, developing courage, having a point of view, and so on. I have been blogging for several years since I put up that first post on my blog. And I still think that first post was my toughest post. I enjoy blogging so much that I don't have much time anymore to watch TV shows or even sports. And I don't miss them at all. I suddenly found a new hobby, which later turned into my way of sharing ideas on speaking, jobs, and sales. And because of my blogging, I mustered sufficient courage to write this book.

So you just never know what will result from your starting anything. Never forget that you control the start, the middle, and the end of anything you do. Do not let others try to take this away from you. If people don't like what you are doing, screw them. (I am telling you this, because I had to deal with this crap.)

I want you to record your goals video answering the following simple questions. (You need to limit the number of questions to only a few, so they are simple and straightforward, yet impactful.)

- **Why do you want to improve your high-stakes speaking skills?** You need to be clear on why you would want to spend time, money, and energy to develop these skills.

- **How do you plan to improve your high-stakes speaking skills?** You need to be specific on what you plan to do and when, and how much time you are planning to spend in order to improve these skills.

- **What do you see yourself accomplishing once you become a high-stakes speaker?** What is your end goal?

- **What will you not achieve if you quit?** Same as the preceding question, but with this one, you will realize that you control what you achieve.

- **Who will hold you accountable to your high-stakes speaking goals?** This person should assess your progress on a quarterly basis. You need to keep the person updated on your progress. Ideally, this is someone who is either your mentor or someone who is learning to develop and master these skills along with you. Do not choose a friend, family member, or other relative for this responsibility; they should be used for providing emotional support, however.

- **How often will you assess your progress?** I recommend you do this on a quarterly basis.

- **Whom do you plan to serve when you become a high-stakes speaker?** Once you achieve your goal of becoming a good-to-great high-stakes speaker, whom are you going to help to do the same?

After you have answered the foregoing questions and before you move on, you need to state in your video something like "I will be a great speaker." You need to come up with something aspirational, some meaningful mantra that you can keep repeating when things get difficult or when you start losing your motivation. You may think this is hokey, but take the chance anyway: It is your mantra, and it could make a difference in your staying the course.

Why should you say this?

You want to talk yourself up, so you record this positive aspiration into your subconscious. If you secure that mantra into your subconscious, then when you are under stress, you will *not* be saying to yourself or to anyone else, "I suck as a speaker" or "I will never be a confident or high-stakes speaker." You need to realize how easily these thoughts have a way of coming back when you are under stressful situations. If you can't say "I will be a confident speaker" or "I am going to be a high-stakes speaker," then why should anyone believe you?

Say your mantra till you achieve your goal and beyond. If you think this is misguided advice, understand that there is some science that supports giving yourself this kind of self-talk. In a study published in the journal *Frontiers in Psychology*, several interventions were used to increase performance, such as imagery, self-talk, and an innovative "if-then-plan."[3] The researchers found that self-talk yielded the best improvement, so keep on saying, "I am going to be a great high-stakes speaker."

You are going to gain confidence by following the steps described in this part. As you follow them, you are going to become competent, since you will also be producing a body of work. Gradually, a sense of security from your growing competence will enter your subconscious mind, and you will be able to give your speech confidently. By this I mean that you will have fewer things to worry about when you are giving a speech in any situation, since you are going to be more competent even if your confidence is low. By following these steps, you will increase your competence so it slowly builds your confidence.

You also need to stay motivated. You need to focus on the eleven-step process in Part Two and Part Three and trust that it will work. You did the right thing by starting your speaker's journey, but you may occasionally get disappointed in your progress. How do you motivate yourself? You have to stay the course even when you are not seeing much progress and when it is getting hard either going through the course or recording your 3/30 Challenge videos (Chapter 8). To keep going, you need something that motivates you. You can even try a catchy song and adapt it to what you are doing.

Do you remember Helen Reddy's song, "Keep on singing, don't stop on singing, you are gonna be a star someday"? Probably not. I didn't either, but today you can't plead ignorance when you have Google and YouTube, which today act as our auxiliary brain. Here's how you can adapt Reddy's song to your speaking: "Keep on speaking, don't stop speaking, you are gonna be a great speaker someday." If you need motivation, just sing it.

Do you know who used this technique to become very successful? Sara Blakely, founder of Spanx. On the James Altucher podcast, she said that after number of failures, she identified that she was good at sales and wrote down what she wanted to do that would give her purpose. She wrote the following: "I want to invent a product that I can sell to millions of people that will make them feel good."[4] She has become a billionaire, so apparently she achieved what she wrote down. You should do the same with one sentence regarding your speaking goals.

Public speaking, like many other skills, is like some highways you travel on that are always under maintenance. The day you stop maintaining your speaking skills is when you stop engaging, connecting, informing, influencing, persuading, selling, and leading. Speaking is always going to be "under maintenance," no matter how good you become. The reason for this is that public speaking is a "people" skill, and people are different and unpredictable. Never forget that; if you do, you are more likely to make a speaking mistake, especially as you become more successful and get overconfident.

Before you move to the hacks in the next several chapters, I want to clarify one thing to ensure that you set proper expectations for yourself. I present the three hacks using the 60/30/10 rule. By this I mean that the first hack, the content hack (Chapter 7), will get you to 60 percent of the way toward giving a good-to-great speech. The message hack (Chapter 10) will get you another 30 percent of the way—that is, as far as a 90 percent total toward giving a good-to-great speech. Finally, the performance hack (Chapters 12–16) will add the final 10 percent, getting you all the way to 100 percent. The hacks are presented in order of difficulty. Maybe all you need is just a content hack to get the speech done. And that's fine. You do not have to use all three hacks for all speeches.

Often you have limited time, so all you can do is the content hack to craft a speech together quickly. Though I have written this book to give you a good idea of what a good-to-great speech looks like that creates a winning speech moment, it may not always be possible to do this, due to time constraints you might face.

I need to be clear on this, since public speaking is hard, time consuming, and unpredictable. The only thing you control is how well you craft and deliver a memorable experience that is likely to result in a win. When I am giving a speech, I have a very high expectation of my preparation to craft and deliver a good-to-great speech, but I have little to no expectations on how the audience will react to it, since I don't have any control over that. I raise the expectations during preparation, and I lower it as low as I can before I speak so I am not gripped with any performance anxiety. If you are not enjoying the experience of giving a speech, then the audience will sense it and not enjoy the experience of listening to your speech.

You now have enough to get started and to keep a single-minded focus on developing this skill. Congratulations on making your first video! You have taken the most important step—the first step—to becoming a confident speaker. Now you must keep going. As I've mentioned before, you have to become competent before you become confident. You can say you are going to be a great speaker as long as you are willing to put in the work and engage in deliberate and dutiful practice to achieve your goals.

CHAPTER 7:

The Content Hack

If I am to speak ten minutes, I need a week for preparation; if fifteen minutes, three days; if half an hour, two days; if an hour, I am ready now.

— President Woodrow Wilson

If you want to win a job interview, a sales deal, support for your idea, or whatever, you need good content for your speech. But if you don't have a lot of time to put one together, what are you going to do?

I suggest you hack a speech iteratively and incrementally so that it is good enough. Then you can test it to make it better, though not perfect. Remember, there is no point spending a lot of time in trying to develop a "perfect" speech. A speech is a means to an end, and the end is to achieve your overall objective.

Many people give up at this stage when they have to give a speech, or worse, they do a haphazard job by just winging it. Winging a speech wastes time, since you are not likely to achieve your objective. But if you use the content hack method, you will be able to put together a speech quickly that will do its job.

The content hack will help you improve your speaking skills quickly—without your needing to give a lot of speeches in front of a live audience. I will dispel one oft-propagated myth right now, the myth that you need plenty of stage time to become good at this skill. You don't. However, you do need to practice a lot and make the most of whatever you have of speaking opportunities in front of an audience, whether small or large. If you become comfortable speaking in front of a camera, then you will find speaking in front of an audience a little easier—especially since you can then get some valuable feedback.

I use the content hack to produce a boatload of content. I have hundreds of videos that I have recorded and made public. (There are a lot of ideas that I have made public.) Here is the process I use:

1. When I listen to a podcast or an audiobook while I go for a walk, I come up with ideas.

2. I record many of my ideas on my audio recorder.

3. I select one or two ideas and record a video.

4. I make the video public on YouTube to get feedback (and I ignore the feedback comments that are not constructive).

I can stop at this point, since I have generated content and made it available for anyone to see and comment on. But since I have the content, I can go further:

5. I refine the video and convert it into a blog post.

6. I can repurpose my blog posts into a book, a speech, an online course, a workshop, or a seminar.

As you can see, it all starts with the content hack. Once you start the content hack and get good at it, many possibilities open up to you—including your giving a speech. Even more important:

You will start thinking better; you will come up with ideas and turn them into content that you can share with others. You can even monetize those ideas. You can write a book, as I have. Now you know the process I use. You can use what I do, or you can come up with your own content creation process that works for you.

Use the content hack and become a "content machine."

The Minimum Viable Speech (MVS)

Before I describe the content hack in detail, I need to tell you that you first need to create a *minimum viable speech (MVS)*, terminology you will appreciate in the section "A Hack Helps You Get Your Speech Started," which follows. Then test your MVS by getting feedback so you can improve the speech. Since you are often going to be severely time constrained, I recommend that you go through no more than two iterations of your MVS. I know this works, since I use it all the time for any speech that I am working on or when I record a video of the speech that I post on YouTube. By using this hack, you are going to improve and will need no more than two iterations.

But before you follow the simple steps I teach in this chapter, I want you to do something even simpler: Without thinking too hard,

1. Come up with a topic,

2. Start the video recording, and

3. Talk about that topic.

That's right. Many can't do these simple three steps, since they are perfectionistic. I want you to do these steps and get it done rather than trying to create a "perfect" video recording. Talk till you run out of ideas.

Again, repeating from Chapter 6 about recording your goals video:

- Don't stop.

- Don't worry if you are rambling.

- Don't worry if it is lousy.

- Don't worry if it makes little sense.

This MVS (your "version 0") is something for you to work with. You have gotten started (and you have not wasted time thinking about getting started). If you keep doing this whenever you have to prepare content for a speech, you are going to be way ahead.

Remember, version 0 is your version that you are not going to be showing to anybody. You are going to show others only your version 1 and version 2. Now it is time for you to make version 0 better with version 1, version 2, and (if necessary) version 3.

This is how I develop my content for any speech I give. The procedure is fast, content-rich, and effective.

A Hack Helps You Get Your Speech Started

Artists often use the word *hack* in a negative way, since, according to them, a hack is created primarily for the mass market rather than for themselves out of their own aesthetic integrity and sensibilities. Prolific author Steven Pressfield, for example, calls a writer a hack who, "writes what he imagines will play well in the eyes of others.... [He] asks, What's hot, what can I make a deal for?"[1]

But I am using the word *hack* in a positive way, the way it is commonly used in writing software and in the startup world. In software development, a hack is code that is written fast in order to test a feature so that it can be validated quickly by customers who are willing to pay for it. In the same way, when you are hacking a speech, you are developing a speech for an audience to achieve your overall objective. You don't give a speech that you like; rather, you give a speech that the audience will like, so that they will spread the message and/or take action.

The idea of hacking comes from the *lean startup method*, which was adapted from the proven lean concept that had been pioneered by Toyota with their Toyota Production System (TPS). Implementing this concept helped Toyota build quality products quickly based on what its customers wanted, thereby eliminating a lot of waste and enabling Toyota to become a leading global automobile manufacturer. Now many software companies use the lean startup method to develop something quickly, something they commonly refer to as the *minimum viable product (MVP)*, which can be validated by a few customers before the startup launches the final product.[2] In the past few years, the lean method has become very popular with the startup community to build software products faster, better, smarter, and cheaper.

I have adopted the same lean concept for building speeches. I view a speech as a product; hence, my definition of waste as it applies to public speaking is simple: Waste is giving a speech that does not achieve your objective.

A Hack Mitigates Speech Failures

The dirty secret of public speaking is that most speeches fail—often miserably. By this I mean they do not achieve their overall objective. Assuming such a speech is serious, all it typically accomplishes is making a bit of noise and wasting people's time. Can you remember anything you heard from the last speech you attended? Or the one before that? You get the picture. Delivering a memorable speech that results in a win is hard. Almost every speech you ever listen to is forgotten shortly after it is given—hence, it is a loss.

Your speech is your opportunity to communicate your idea to an audience. Instead, what you often have is that famous line from the movie *Cool Hand Luke*: "What we got here is failure to communicate." You need to talk to your audience as though you were having a conversation, so that they pay attention to what you are saying. Otherwise, they will tune you out in a second with their smartphones. It is getting harder and harder for a speaker to capture and keep the audience's attention. You cannot afford to be an average speaker today, especially when you are competing against all kinds of distractions.

According to Microsoft's conservative estimate, businesses waste close to $252 million a day on bad PowerPoint presentations.[3] Giving a speech is an expensive endeavor for both the speaker and the audience. If you are going to invest time, effort, and money for a speech, you'd better make sure you have a good chance to achieve your overall objective.

When I explain how expensive speech giving is, one of the questions that I am often asked is, "How do I get started working on a speech that resonates with an audience?" Many struggle with how to organize their thoughts in a way that makes it easier for their audience to understand. They are quickly overwhelmed; hence, they often wing it, or in some cases, they get frustrated and give up. Not only will the consequence of their giving up prevent them from getting better at speaking, but, worse, they will become even more fearful of giving a speech in the future, whether it is one on one, to a small group, or in front of a large audience.

With a content hack, however, you can reduce the chances that your speech will fail to communicate.

A Hack Simplifies Speech Development

Public speaking is frustrating for many, because it is hard, time consuming, and sparse. By *sparse* I mean that you often don't get many opportunities to give speeches in front of an audience unless you are a professional. And when you do get an opportunity to speak in front of an audience, you often don't have time to do the research, prepare, and rehearse. Unless you can wing it on short notice, you are going to be nervous and not feel confident. You will likely fail to achieve your overall objective.

After recording each version of your speech, you should put it on YouTube. You want to make it "unlisted" but solicit feedback. If you think you can make it better, work on one or two versions and make the one you like "public" on YouTube. At this point, your content is set, but it might change a little as you develop your message and create a memorable performance.

Develop a habit of turning on your video camera. I know you think you know the content well and are going to do a good job, but it never hurts to see it with your eyes before you get on the stage. Turn on the camera and prove it to yourself so you don't regret not using this simple tool that could have made a huge difference. Again, habits are hard to develop and harder to break. Using your video camera to record your speech is one habit you want to develop and master. It will pay off big time.

To overcome the lack of confidence, you need simple rules that work. Unless you are giving a TED Talk or someone is paying you a lot of money to speak, you are not going to spend the hundreds of hours necessary to put on a great speech performance. You need some simple rules that can work for any situation that you are likely to encounter.

MIT Professor Donald Sull and Stanford Professor Kathleen Eisenhardt wrote about simple "how-to rules,"[4] which can help you accomplish a task when you do not have a lot of time. When it comes to speaking, even though you often do not have a lot of time, you still have to perform like a pro in order to win. Without simple rules, it is impossible to perform well on a consistent basis. One of the examples Sull and Eisenhardt wrote about is the task of announcing sports events in a way that makes watching the event both informative and entertaining. The person who developed the simple rules for this task was a BBC sports announcer named Seymour Joly de Lotbiniere. The following simple rules he recommended for commentators changed the way sports announcing is done everywhere:[5]

- Set the scene.

- Describe the action.

- Give the score or results, regularly and succinctly.

- Explain, without interrupting, the stadium's reaction to the game's event.

- Share "homework," such as historical facts and figures or personal information.

- Assess the significance of the occasion and key moments.

When it comes to crafting content for a speech, I use these simple rules:

1. Select a topic.

2. Brainstorm to come up with ideas.

3. Prune the ideas, using three to five of them.

4. Create an outline with one to three of the ideas, according to the idea's importance.

5. Review. Keep the speech simple and conversational.

6. Record the speech.

7. Iterate and improve. (Since you already have recorded version 0, it should not take much time to go through these steps and record version 1.)

The content hack, like every hack, can be viewed as an iterative and incremental method for crafting and delivering your speech:

1. **Practice.** You have to keep practicing until your speech is good enough.

2. **Test.** Once your speech is good enough, you have to test it so you get some feedback.

3. **Refine.** Based on the feedback, you may have to make some changes to your speech, if necessary.

4. **Deploy.** You are now ready to ship (use your speech) and not worry about it being "perfect."

Keep going through this iterative and incremental process until you are satisfied, but don't record more than three versions. Again, the purpose of this hack is to create a good-enough speech and not focus on creating a "perfect" speech.

I like this hack a lot, since it's easier to improve your speech once you have recorded it on audio or video, even though often the first version may not be good enough to be delivered. But the main thing you get out of this exercise is that you get this "ugly" version completed. Now, if you are not happy with this first version, you can make it better. It is a lot easier to improve a speech once you have finished it, rather than keep thinking for a long time about how to make it perfect at the outset.

This mode of acting by recording an audio or video and then thinking about how to make it better draws from the "Outsight Principle," which Herminia Ibarra, an economist and professor at the leading international business school INSEAD, verified in her research: A good leader acts first and thinks later, instead of the other way around.[6] Since you have to speak to lead, I think this principle applies to public speaking, too. Ibarra writes,

> We try something new and then observe the results—how it feels to us, how others around us react—and only later reflect on and perhaps internalize what our experience taught us.

This idea is also similar to what best-selling novelist Jodi Picoult said about writing: "You can always edit a bad page. You can't edit a blank page."[7] Similarly, you can't improve a speech that you have not recorded on audio or video.

The content hack has a bias toward action, not perfection. You are unlikely to get your speech right the first time, but that's fine. By doing your speech again, you can make it better. You can think of hacking like learning to ride a bike: by falling a few times and eventually figuring it out instead of reading a textbook on Newtonian mechanics. Hacking is simple, fast, effective, and fun, so you are motivated to work on your speech instead of working hard to come up with excuses to avoid it.

Common Presentation Structures

Vitruvius, a first-century BCE Roman architect-engineer, said that in order for an architecture to be considered great, it has to have an excellent form, function, and structure. Form refers to the beauty of an architecture, function refers to how practical it is, and structure refers to what keeps the architecture stable under different load conditions. I think this analogy applies to a great speech, too: It must be beautiful to watch, provide practical content, and be memorable so it is long-lasting. This section focuses on the structure, so that the speech can stand on its own.

I am an engineer and am thus biased, so I believe that unless your speech has a solid structure, its form and function will not be easy for the audience to follow in a speech.

Before you use the content hack method, you first need to determine what kind of presentation structure you want to use for your speech. You have several options to choose from, depending on what works for your speech. According to organizational behavior lecturer and coach Matt Abrahams, several structures are commonly used:[8]

- **Past-Present-Future.** Use this structure when you want to show what the situation was, what it is right now, and what it will be.

- **Comparison-Contrast.** Use this structure when you want to show why what you are proposing is better than other alternatives.

- **Cause-Effect.** Use this structure when you need to provide some logical explanation for something.

- **Problem-Solution-Benefit.** Use this structure when you are trying to persuade someone why to choose the solution you are proposing.

- **What? So What? Now What?** Use this structure when you are wanting the audience to take some action concerning what you are proposing.

- **Challenge/Approach/Outcome.** Use this structure when you are selling your consulting or coaching services. (I have added this structure to the ones Abrahams recommended.)

- **Current State, Future State, Path to Get There.** Use this structure when you are interviewing, securing funding, or getting approval of a project. (I have also added this one.)

Here is one more structure that I recommend for a content hack:

- **Tell them what you are going to tell them, tell them, and tell them what you told them.** Though this presentation structure, attributed to Aristotle, is simple, it works when you have to deliver a speech that it is good enough. It is the structure that I opt for when I don't have a lot of time. (See the section "The Aristotelian Structure" for more about this structure.)

Once you determine the presentation structure you are comfortable with—and I especially recommend the last one in the foregoing list—then it is time to hack a speech together with the content hack.

Content Hack Steps

The idea of the content hack comes from Mark Levy's book *Accidental Genius*, where he uses a similar approach to get people to write down their ideas.[9] I have taken some of what he covers in his book and adapted it to public speaking. Let me summarize the content hack method I use for all the speeches I work on:

Idea Selecting

Pick a topic. The topic should be very narrow, so you can deliver it in three minutes. Even if your intention is to give a longer speech, break it into approximately three-minute subtopics.

Free Thinking

You need to come up with lots of ideas, including questions on the topic you chose. You can call this "free thinking." Write your ideas on a board (whiteboard or blackboard). In this step, try not to guard yourself; let your ideas flow. You can categorize them into good, bad, and ugly later. In this step, all ideas are good. Your free thinking should take, say, ten to twenty minutes.

Pruning

Now you need to prune your ideas down to no more than three. Reducing your ideas to three is the first major decision you need to make for your speech.

Outlining

Now create an outline from the ideas you generated using the presentation structure with which you feel comfortable (and I highly recommend the structure attributed to Aristotle). You want this outline to be simple; do not get bogged down by turning this into a mini-project. Remember, you are trying to get this done fast. You can write a thin outline if you are time constrained, or a fat outline if you have time and want to put more meat on the bones, as described in an excellent blog by Josh Bernoff.[10]

Reviewing

Now you need to go over the outline and prioritize the points for free speaking. By *free speaking*, which I elaborate on in the next section, I mean to speak without stopping, no matter whether you make any mistakes. During this reviewing stage, though, I often go with one main idea, to keep it simple for the audience. Leading with one idea is similar to the "Ivy Lee Method" for productivity, which helped improve Charles M. Schwab's executives' productivity.[11] You can use the other two ideas for backup, if needed.

Free Speaking

Now you need to record your free speaking on video. Remember, you have to let yourself go here, since no one is ever going to see this crappy first version. You are doing this to present the material you have thought about in an organized way. Actually, you may do your best speech when free speaking, since you don't have any expectations—and that often makes it the best version. Instead of going at 110 percent with your expectations, try 90 percent instead, and it will make a huge difference in the outcome.

Note: if you view a speech as a product, as I do, this speech is the one you are not going to like in its first version. It is a "quick and dirty" speech, so you need to temper your expectations. Reid Hoffman, founder of LinkedIn and author, is quoted as saying that "if you are not embarrassed by the first version of your product, you've launched too late."[12] The entrepreneurial community has followed the philosophy that Ben Parr, journalist and former coeditor of Mashable, writes about when they are developing a product.[13] By their doing this, the product is the one the user wants instead of what the entrepreneur thinks the user will pay for. You can use the same philosophy when you are trying to hack a speech to find out how well it resonates with people.

Free speaking is a big confidence builder, since you will have already gone through your speech once, without using any notes or PowerPoint slides—except your outline. You may not see the importance of free speaking when you are starting out, but when you start speaking in front of an audience and you feel a little nervous, you can draw upon this exercise to get back on track.

Simplifying

When you record, pretend that you are trying to explain your idea to a six-year-old, or to your grandmother. Remove all the jargon, and make it simple and direct. Keeping it simple is not easy, since you know so much about the topic that you are speaking on, but the imaginary six-year-old or grandmother in front of you does not know anything about your topic. You will see how hard this can be. It is better to test this out, so you don't lose the people when it counts.

Refining

Keep tweaking your speech, record it again, and ask, "So what?" Ask, "Who cares?" These are the questions your audience will be asking when you start speaking.

Iterating

On the first take, you should not speak under any time constraint. On the second take, you should try to come a little over the time allotted. On the third take, try to come a little under the time allotted. At this point, you are done; do no more than three takes, since you are not trying to turn this into a TED Talk. But if you are going to deliver this speech, your recording it three times means that you have practiced it well.

Now, out of the three takes, select the take you like.

Of course, if you really want to do one more take, go ahead. But before you work on improving your speech further, you need to stop to get some feedback. Otherwise, you are going to go crazy trying to make your speech "perfect."

Remember, you don't have to memorize anything other than just the opening, the transitions, and the closing.

Note: It is not a good idea to memorize this speech, since you don't want to look scripted, an indication that you cannot connect with people.

The Aristotelian Structure

I will defer to Aristotle, since he gave a lot of thought on public speaking, and he developed the structure that has worked since his time for giving a speech.

- Tell them what you are going to tell them.
- Tell them.
- Tell them what you just told them.

I included this structure as the final one in the list of common presentation structures I provided earlier.

Speaking in front of people is hard, so try your best to make the delivery simple, since your objective is to get your point across so that others can remember it. If you get that point across three times, as Aristotle suggested, the result may not be pretty, but your audience will remember what you said.

If you use this Aristotelian presentation structure, you will be able to give your speech confidently. In the beginning, you can put a speech together in one hour. But as you become more competent, you will be able to put a good speech together in less than thirty minutes. (Often, I can do it in on the first take if I don't have time to go through multiple iterations.)

Here is another thing a student whom I mentored told me that he liked about this presentation structure: He has attention deficit disorder (ADD), and this structure of developing a speech by breaking into parts really eases his anxiety. Today we all seem to have some type of attention deficit problem, so I think this structure should work for just about everyone.

The 3x-2x-1x Method to Hack a Speech

You have learned about how to hack a speech, so how do you use it for an actual speech that you have to deliver? Suppose you have to give a speech that is approximately fifteen minutes long, so how do you use the content hack to craft a speech as fast as you can? In this section, I show you how I would do it, by making five video recordings as part of my speech development.

Note: This information is just for the content hack. I am not focusing here on the message hack or the performance hack, which I cover in subsequent chapters.

- **Knowledge take.** For this take, you want to use three times the amount of time, which in this case would be approximately forty-five minutes. You can start with several points that you want to convey about a topic. Focus on having a conversation with the video camera for the next forty-five minutes. And don't stop the recording. You want forty-five minutes of video that you can review later. You will see what you have to say and how you sound and look saying it. After recording, do a self-feedback. Listen to just the audio, since you are not going to use this take to post on the web to get others to provide some feedback. Now you have your raw content.

- **Structure take.** With your raw content from your knowledge take, you now structure it so it is easier to present and so it will make sense to your audience. You can use the simplest of the presentation structures, the Aristotelian structure, where you tell the audience what you are going to tell them, you tell them, and then you tell them what you told them. I like this structure, and it works when you have limited time.

- **Time take one.** After you have set the presentation structure, you are ready to record three takes, in each take reducing the speech's overall time from forty-five minutes down to fifteen minutes. Then you can select the take you like, which you will actually deliver (or post on the web for additional feedback). Your challenge here is to trim the speech, preferably to slightly under fifteen minutes. The reason for coming under the time allotted is that when you give the speech live, it will inevitably go longer than planned. And you don't want to go over, if you can avoid it with a little practice.

    At this point, you are ready for solid self-feedback. The first time you view it, mute the sound, so you see what you look like when you are presenting. On the second view, only listen, so you know what you sound like. On the third view, you can see it as you recorded it. After viewing it three times, make whatever changes are needed and repeat this process one or two more times.

- **Time take two.** You want to do this second take only if necessary.

- **Time take three.** Again, you want to do this third take only if necessary.

At this point, you are finished. You have put in quite a bit of work. You now know what your content is and what you look and sound like delivering that content. After the small amount of time you had to put this speech together, you should be confident giving this speech.

Use your best judgment on how to deploy this method, based on the time you have to prepare. What I showed you here would take me from half a day to a full day to do a good job. As you use this method often, you will learn roughly how much time you need and what steps you can eliminate. If I know my topic well, I often record my videos using one take and post them on my YouTube channel if I think they are good enough.

Note: Don't try to make your videos on YouTube "perfect," and understand that you are going to make mistakes when you are delivering a speech live in front of an audience.

The "One Shot" Practice to Raise the Stakes

When you are speaking in front of an audience, you get only one shot to deliver a good speech. You can't stop in the middle and start all over again. So, how do you practice that "one shot" when you are hacking a speech?

After I have come up with an outline, I use my audio recorder to record my speech, and then I tweak it as needed till it is good enough. Once I am satisfied with my speech preparation, I try to record it in a single take in front of a camera, pretending that I am in front of an audience. Doing the speech in one take, I put some pressure on myself, as though I were giving it in front of an audience and I had to do it in a single take. I do this for most of my video recordings, and I have found that if I think I am going to do a good job in one take, I always do. Conversely, when I think I am likely to screw it up, I always tend to do that.

Unless my speech is incoherent or I lose my thought in the middle, which is rarely the case, I will go with my first recording. After years of practice, I rarely ever have to do an additional take when I am recording. That happens principally because I take care of all the changes when I am practicing my speech using the audio recorder. When you are starting out, you will find this difficult, but after doing some deliberate practice for a while, you will not need more than one take when you are doing your video recording.

The content hack is so simple that you can get started right away. But to turn the hack into a habit, you need to do it for the next thirty days, a process I cover in the next chapter. If you stop here, however, you have the basics to craft and give a speech for most situations. Now get one done before you move on to the next chapter!

CHAPTER 8

The 3/30 Challenge

Sometimes it takes a while to discover the best approach to whatever you're doing, and only by doing it over and over again do you get it right.

— Grant Cardone, best-selling author, motivational speaker, and sales trainer

You now know how to use the content hack to build and deliver a speech quickly, so you can use this hack for any speech you have to give. To continue to improve your speaking skills, you need to keep the foot on the pedal. Before you spend a boatload of money, time, and energy, take the 3/30 Challenge. All you have to do is record a three-minute video every day starting from today for the next thirty days and post each video on YouTube.

By going through this exercise for thirty days, you will turn crafting and recording a speech into a habit. By undertaking this speech blitz, you will gradually become more confident giving speeches. I don't know any method that is more effective at improving your public speaking skills than taking the 3/30 Challenge. It works.

Why a Three-Minute Speech, and Why Thirty Days?

Most of the time we give short speeches, rarely long ones. Short speeches are flexible, in that you can give them to anyone, anytime, anywhere. If you see people being interviewed on television, unless the interview is on C-SPAN, interviewees have to give short answers, often less than ninety seconds. You will rarely find someone talking for more than three minutes to answer a question. The interviewees are prepared by producers before they go on live, since TV shows have to sell commercials to exist. If you want to become a confident speaker, you need to master the ability to make your point in less than three minutes.

Another reason I like the 3/30 Challenge is that it even helps you in making long speeches. Why is that? If ever you have to give a long speech, say more than fifteen minutes, you can't practice it easily with people. It is difficult to find people who will want to listen to your fifteen- or thirty-minute dry run. But people will usually give you at least three minutes to listen to your speech before they stop you or tune you out. What a short speech enables you to do is test different arguments of your speech with others, without boring them by going on too long. Now, if you can give a good short speech, then all you have to do is stitch a few of them together to craft a longer speech.

If you don't think a speech you recorded is good enough, then just rerecord it. But remember, you are not trying to make a "perfect" three-minute video. When you think it is good enough, post it on Facebook, YouTube, or your website (if you have one), and make it public. Let others know. Just do this for the next thirty days.

Note: If you don't want a search engine to find your YouTube speeches, then mark them as unlisted or private. But put them somewhere so you can see, after thirty days, how you have been improving.

Where Did the 3/30 Challenge Come From?

I adopted the 3/30 Challenge idea from entrepreneur and author Jia Jiang, who wanted to get over his fear of rejection. He set out to deliberately get rejected for one hundred days. He overcame this fear and learned a lot of interesting things, which he shared in his book *Rejection Proof*.[1] Jiang came up with this idea after being rejected from getting funding for his startup company. He took it hard. But instead of giving up, he wanted to understand rejection better, especially how to overcome the fear of rejection. This is a very good book, since what can keep you from succeeding in anything is the fear of rejection. Soon you will not even think about rejection, you will quickly strengthen your rejection muscle, and others will approach you in a more accepting manner. An analogy: Golf is a game of misses; similarly, life is a game of rejection. Enjoy and have fun playing the game of life. And if you do get rejected (which you will often, no matter how good you are at this game), don't stop playing; instead, focus on your next shot.

In golf, you control how well you play and score. If you have the lowest round, you win. No matter how good you are as a golfer, you are going to miss shots. And if you are like me, a lot of shots. But golf does test you in how you comport yourself during play and after you are finished with your round of play. When you are done, you should look the same no matter how well or poorly you played. Speech performance is no different. If you want to win, you must get on the stage to speak. No matter what the outcome is, you should look no different from how you would look if you were a professional. If you can do this, then you are on your way to becoming a good-to-great speaker.

On his journey to get rejected for one hundred days, Jiang videotaped his encounters. He then put his videos on YouTube, and he began to acquire a huge following. Through something that was supposed to help him understand and overcome fear, he discovered that his postings were helping other people, too. Soon he was being interviewed by the media and was a guest on talk shows. To help others who are paralyzed from being rejected, he even gave a TED Talk, and later he wrote his book *Rejection Proof*.

Jiang learned the following lessons about rejection:

- **Rejection is constant.** You get rejected no matter who you are.

- **Rejection is an opinion.** You should not take rejection personally, since it is just someone's opinion, and there is nothing you can do about it.

- **Rejection has a number.** Each time you get rejected, you can learn and improve your odds for the next time.

- **Rejection is learning.** You have an opportunity to see how you can up your game in order to reduce your chances of rejection.

- **Rejection is not final.** You (not someone else) get to decide when you are rejected.

Similarly, by making a three-minute video every day for the next thirty days, by documenting your journey of becoming a confident speaker, you can do the same as Jiang. And once you overcome your fear and become a confident speaker, you can then help others do the same.

Why Take the 3/30 Challenge?

Most people have no idea of how they come across when they are speaking. You first need to establish some baseline measurements before you can make improvements. If you are committed, disciplined, and focused on making a tangible improvement in your speaking skills, you need close to thirty videos, so you have a decent sample size to see what you are doing well and what you need to work on. You simply can't get lucky thirty times in a row, so you will have some good ones and some bad ones to assess. After assessing where you stand after recording thirty videos, you will be able to target specific areas that you need to work on to continue to make improvements.

Another reason for doing the 3/30 Challenge is to turn crafting and giving speeches into a habit. You are not likely going to be invited to give a speech that often unless you are involved in some activities where you are giving a lot of speeches. If you are like me and don't speak that often in front of a lot of people, you still have to develop this skill and turn it into a habit. Many people feel that after they complete the Coursera course, they are good speakers. The course does provide you the knowledge, and it helps you create, record, and receive feedback on the four speeches the course has you work on. But the real work begins after you complete the course.

So rather than waiting weeks or months before you get to prepare a speech, you need to keep your speaking skills current by doing the 3/30 Challenge, and you need to keep working on this skill. You want to have an athlete's mindset by "staying fit" and keeping your skills sharp. Speaking skills, like other skills, can atrophy quickly if you are not working on keeping them sharp. You have to if you want to be a speaking athlete. That's why you need to take the 3/30 Challenge.

What Will Result from the 3/30 Challenge?

What will result from your taking the 3/30 Challenge? First, you will at least have a good thirty videos. Second, you will have done something that you can talk to others about. Third, hopefully, at least one third of the videos you will have recorded (about ten of them) are going to be excellent, one third of them are going to be good, and one third of them are going to be average. That is how it works. No matter how good you think the videos are, it is hard to predict what people will like. I have always been surprised by what resonates with people, so the only thing you can do is experiment a lot with all kinds of videos.

And remember, you are doing this for *yourself*. If others like it, great! It will give you some idea of how well you are resonating. If others don't like it, just accept it and move on. If you have ten videos that you think are excellent, then that is a great accomplishment.

Once you have made an improvement, let others know, so you can help others overcome their fear of speaking. The more you do it, the less likely you are to get disappointed if one video is not good. But you learn from all the videos you record, whether you like them or not or whether others like them or not.

You need to make a commitment to make public speaking your core competency. By this I mean public speaking is one thing you do better than anything else. If someone ever asks you, "What is that one thing you do well?" without hesitation, your answer should be public speaking. Unless that is your answer, you are not going to focus on developing, testing, and mastering this skill.

How to Record a 3/30 Challenge Speech

You need to go through the following ten steps (adapted somewhat from the procedure in Chapter 7):

1. Select a topic.

2. Brainstorm using bullet points, and limit yourself to five to seven bullet points.

3. Create a rough outline with one to three points.

4. Record the speech using Aristotle's technique: Tell them what you are going to tell them, tell them, and tell them what you just told them. The technique is simple, and it works.

5. Review the video, tweak the video, and record again (if necessary).

6. Review the video again, tweak the video again, and record again (if necessary).

7. Stop at this point, since you should not do more than three takes.

8. Select the take you like, and evaluate it yourself before you ask one or two people you trust to evaluate it.

9. Post the speech on YouTube as "public" if you want others to see it, or keep it "unlisted" if you don't want anyone to be able to find it. If you don't want anyone to see the speech at all, make it "private." ***Note:*** I have never made any of my videos private.

10. Move on to your next speech.

The first few speeches will take maybe an hour, but after doing a few of them, you will be able to record a three-minute video in less than thirty minutes.

What Kind of Videos Should You Record?

After you do an introductory video, you can record a speech on any topic, but you need to challenge yourself and make your speeches interesting. You need to make all kinds of videos, such as giving an opinion, providing information, trying to persuade, telling a story, and even practicing humor. One thing you have to remember is that anytime you are talking, even to yourself, you are trying to achieve some objective. You have to be "on" all the time.

Example of My First Video Script

> Hi, My name is Jay Oza, and I have decided to take the 3/30 Challenge.
>
> My goal is very simple. It is to become a confident speaker and then become a good-to-great high-stakes speaker.
>
> I plan to record videos in a wide range of topics and post them on YouTube. I am putting myself out there, which is outside my comfort zone. But unless I do this, I will not improve. I am making a commitment to improving my speaking skills by taking this 3/30 Challenge.
>
> The first video is my "hello world" video, and I am glad I've done it. I plan to do twenty-nine more speeches in the next thirty days.
>
> I hope you take this challenge with me, and I wish you good luck.

You can come up with your script for the first video and record it.

Crafting a Three-Minute Video Script

The Outline

In drafting a three-minute speech on why it is important to send children with musical talent to rock band camp, I started with the following rough outline:

    I.   Opening statement

    II.   How do I know about this?

    III.   Why is this skill important for kids' future?

    IV.   Provide some research info for support

    V.   Concluding statement

This is a very rough outline, which I would now use to write down the speech. Note that I would not be writing this speech to be read aloud word for word to an audience. I would write this speech and record it only to practice delivering it so I can later give a three-minute speech with just my outline. (If this were a blog post, then I would need to convert it into a speech.) After you practice writing down your speech like this for a while, you can dispense with this writing exercise; all you will need then is just the outline. Most of the speeches I record, I do it from an outline like the foregoing.

The Written-Down Rock Band Camp Speech

> If you have a child with musical skill, then you have to look into sending him or her to a rock band camp.
>
> Why?
>
> Besides doing what he or she enjoys, your child will get a head start in

147

developing an important skill of the future: Teaming.

How do I know this?

My son attended rock band camp for four years and now plays with a professional band during the summer as part of a children's concert series. I can see a big difference in him wanting to work with others, which I think will continue as he gets older and enters the workforce. I preferred a music camp, since he got to interact with both boys and girls with different skills, backgrounds, and experiences.

The future success of children does not depend just on what they know or on how fast they learn, but also on how well they get along with people who are different. If your child starts early learning how to get along with different kids at a rock band camp working on a musical piece, then he or she will know how to do it well later in life, when the project is going to be much tougher and more complex.

Companies that are successful know how to team well. And they look for people who have teaming skills. Today, anyone can do this. You can do this as a *solopreneur*. For example, my sister is a solopreneur who teams up with people from different states and countries to get her work done.

Rock band is a good head start for kids to begin learning how to do this on a smaller scale, working with both boys and girls of different musical skills, backgrounds, and experiences to create a musical performance in one week. When I see their performance at the end of the week, I am very impressed with what they have accomplished so quickly through teaming.

Amy Edmondson, professor at Harvard Business School, has done a lot of research in this area. She defines teaming as "teamwork on the fly," which is assembling diverse people over a short time to complete a task or project and then disband. To thrive in the future, you have to become an expert at working on one-off projects. Individuals who are good at teaming will have a competitive advantage and will be highly marketable and well compensated.

So sending your child to a rock band camp is not likely to make him or her the next Bruno Mars or Katy Perry, but it will help him or her develop critical skills of the future to have a good career.

Rehearsing and Recording

Now with this speech written, I would practice it by recording on video no more than three times. I would now be ready to deliver it without the written version. Since I am not reading the speech, it may not sound exactly as I have written it. I would probably improvise based on the flow of the speech. When you rehearse it often, you will be able to easily improvise. You can and should improvise, so you are having a conversation with the audience.

Note: This is the minimum I would do to ensure I am prepared to give a speech to anyone, anytime, anywhere.

You can pick any topic you want, but the main point is to do it.

Benefits of the 3/30 Challenge

The following are some of the benefits of taking the 3/30 Challenge:

- **Test your commitment.** Unless you are committed, you are not going to improve your speaking skills. You have to try hard to get a three-minute recording done every day.

- **Turn speaking into a habit.** By completing the 3/30 Challenge, you will turn the content hack into a habit, so you will not need the massive amount of willpower that you needed when you first started.

- **Organize your thoughts quickly, clearly, crisply, and compellingly.** One of the things you will like about the 3/30 Challenge is how good you become at organizing your thoughts on any topic quickly and at presenting those thoughts clearly, crisply, and compellingly.

- **Identify areas for improvement.** After you finish the 3/30 Challenge, you will be in a good position to know what you are doing well and what areas you need to improve. You will not be wasting time on areas that you are strong in, and you can focus on specific areas that need work.

- **Enjoy speaking.** In the beginning, it will be hard to get started, but once you get past fifteen speeches, you are going to start enjoying giving a speech. You will not be paralyzed with fear of speaking into a camera.

- **Develop confidence.** The only way you are going to become confident is by doing something over and over for a period, so you are not thinking about it. When you have recorded thirty speeches, you will have produced a good body of work to draw on.

- **Manage your fear of speaking.** You never overcome your fear of public speaking, but after recording thirty speeches, you will know how to manage the fear better. If you can get through thirty speeches, then you know that you have given your speeches in front of a camera. Now, you may be anxious if you have to give a speech in front of an audience, but your experience of taking the 3/30 Challenge will help you manage your anxiety better.

- **Learn to finish.** One of the best things about the 3/30 Challenge is that you have to finish. If your take is not good, you can forget it and focus on the next one. For this 3/30 Challenge, you should not do more than three takes since you have to learn to improve quickly and get it done. In the beginning, doing a speech in three takes will be difficult. As you record more speeches, however, you will become more comfortable.

- **Establish a baseline of your speaking skills.** After taking the 3/30 Challenge, you will be able to baseline your speaking skills and focus on areas of improvement. You can document this when you do your assessment. Then you will be able to see what you are doing better and what you need to improve.

- **Improve your thinking.** In the beginning, recording a speech is going to be hard, but as you make progress, you will begin to enjoy doing it, and you will be amazed at how good you are at thinking. You will quickly become an idea machine. The problem you are going to face is deciding on which of your many ideas to select, outline, and record.

After you complete the 3/30 Challenge, you should be much better at public speaking than you were before. I would say, conservatively speaking, you are at least a good speaker. However, you will find that people who you think are very good at speaking are not learning and training as you are. They may be "winging it," so don't get lulled into a sense of comfort and stop here. You have to keep going to remain good. Public speaking is a skill that does not allow for complacency.

So now you are good, perhaps very good. But you can get even better! To become a better speaker, you can't stop here. You have to keep going. You have the knowledge, you have the habit, and you have the motivation. All you have to do now is keep doing it and make it work for you in both social and business settings.

CHAPTER 9

The Magic of Impromptu Speaking

It usually takes me more than three weeks to prepare a good impromptu speech.

— Mark Twain

The next most important speech you ever give after the introductory speech is the impromptu speech. It is a speech that you are expected to give with little or no preparation. But don't be fooled when you hear people say, "She is good at thinking on her feet." The impromptu speech is the most dangerous speech you can give. If you are not well prepared, you are likely to put your foot in your mouth.

You can deliver a speech on your feet, but you can't do a good job unless you have already given a lot of thought to what you are going to say and how you are going to say it. For example, if you ask me about the Higgs boson, I would not say anything, since I don't know anything about it. But if I were attending some event where there were going to be physicists present, I would be prepared, instead of winging it, because I would have anticipated that the subject would likely come up. I would do some research and prepare an impromptu that I could give if it came up, or perhaps I could even broach the subject in a casual meeting.

Let me repeat. No one is good at thinking on his or her feet all the time. This is nonsense that people perpetuate all the time. And after a while, you may even start believing it and admire people who seem to be good at giving impromptu speeches. To ace your impromptu speeches when they come up in a debate, a meeting, or an interview, you need to be prepared. I agree with public speaker, marketing consultant, and author Michael Port that "improvisation without preparation is just winging it."[1] Many speakers simply don't prepare, and they wing it. And often, when the stakes are high, especially when the speaker is famous or important, winging it can be a disaster from which it is hard to recover.

A good example of putting one's foot in the mouth was what José dos Santos, CEO of Cell C, South Africa's third-largest telecom company, did during a TV interview, speaking about women in the workplace and how they work with one another: "Women do have a bitch-switch and, boy, if you see two women fighting, it's worse than two men having an argument."[2] Later he apologized for what he said, but the damage had been done, and he looked like an idiot. Why? Though he is the CEO of a company, he could not think on his feet like he thought he could.

One of the most egregious examples of a CEO completely botching an impromptu that he should have been well prepared for was Chip Wilson, founder and chairman of Lululemon. When women were complaining of the sheerness of the Lululemon yoga pants, Wilson appeared on Bloomberg TV *Street Smart* program to address the issue. When asked to explain the "see through" complaints from customers, he said that

> quite frankly, some women's bodies just actually
> don't work [for the yoga pants].... It's really about

the rubbing through the thighs, how much pressure is there over a period of time and how much they use it.[3]

Not only was Wilson ill prepared for the interview, but he made matters worse when he recorded an apology that was directed to his employees rather than to his customers. With the outcry from customers and the stock falling, Wilson had to resign as chairman a month after the comments. The stakes are very high for people at the top, and to remain there, you have to be prepared and ready to deliver when it's speech time.

When former Veteran Affairs Secretary Bob McDonald was asked about the wait time for veterans to get medical care, he compared it to waiting in line at Disneyland to go on a ride. Here's how he answered a reporter's question about the wait time:

> When you go to Disney, do they measure the number of hours you wait in line? Or what's important? What's important is what's your satisfaction with the experience?[4]

It was an unfortunate comparison, but my point in showing you this is to point out that most gaffes occur when people have to think on their feet. The only antidote for this mistake is to spend time preparing for this speech instead of leaving it to your own prowess to think on your feet. If presented with an opportunity to speak spontaneously, you should resist the temptation. It is too risky, especially if you are in an important or visible position. What you probably should do is say as little as possible and leave it at that. You may take heat from some for saying little, but it is a lot better than to say something inappropriate that you may regret later.

Example of a Well-Prepared Impromptu Speech

Do you know we elect our president (probably the most important job in the world) on how good the candidates for that position are at giving impromptu speeches, particularly in a debate? How many people are going to see a presidential candidate give a prepared policy speech, stump speech, or convention speech? So, if a presidential candidate wins by being adept at giving good impromptu speeches, you, too, need to learn to win by being good at giving impromptu speeches wherever they are needed. And it can be just about anywhere. You have to be prepared to hit it out of the park, since you need to assume that you may not get to bat again.

Why prepare? A textbook "real-world" example of how to give an impromptu speech is how Justin Trudeau, prime minister of Canada, explained the difference between normal computing and quantum computing. Trudeau, who appeared at a press briefing in Waterloo, Ontario, was prepared to speak, primarily, about quantum computing—and he had made it clear that this was the topic he wanted to talk about. Here's what he said:

> When we get to the media questions later, I'm hoping people ask me how quantum computing works because I was excited to deepen my knowledge of that this morning.[5]

Later, when a journalist started by saying that he was going to ask a question on quantum computing but instead asked a question about ISIL (the Islamic State [ISIS], or Daesh), Trudeau ignored the question about ISIL and launched into an impromptu speech explaining the difference between normal computing versus quantum computing. Since Trudeau was well prepared, he stayed with the message about quantum computing. Moreover, he showed that he cared about the research subject, and he gave exposure to quantum computing, since the mainstream media was there to cover his presence. Trudeau enhanced his image as a politician who likes science, and he gave exposure to a research field that many simply don't know much about. Impromptus work when you are well prepared, especially since often you have no more than ninety seconds to make your point. Trudeau's impromptu is a textbook example of how to give an effective impromptu for any occasion in which you find yourself.

Restrict Yourself to One Point

People often have a hard time remembering even one main thing, one point you are claiming. Do not ever forget this. So don't add more points, since **when it comes to speaking, less is more**.

I recommend that you structure the one-point impromptu as shown below:

I.   Main point

II.   Evidence 1

III.   Evidence 2 (if needed; often only one piece of evidence is all you need, but you can be the judge whether you need a second piece)

IV.   Evidence 3 (only if another piece of evidence is needed; try to avoid including it, since it may confuse the audience)

You might think from this outline that you are not doing much—and you would be right. Getting your single point across crisply and efficiently, in say ninety seconds, is not that easy. You will find that out when you do it. Resist any tendency to ramble on or repeat things. Also resist doing your speech in ninety seconds but without much clarity or power. For the impromptu to be effective, you want to keep it simple, straightforward, and clear.

For example, let's take a closer look at the 2016 presidential debates. Candidates got between seventy-five and ninety seconds to answer some of the most important questions, such as "What is your strategy to defeat ISIS?" or "How do you plan to create good high-paying jobs?" or maybe "What is your plan to lower the health-care costs?" Though entire books can be written to answer many of these weighty questions, a political candidate gets no more than ninety seconds to answer each of them.

If you want to become a pro at giving impromptu speeches, I strongly urge you to watch the political debates. In my opinion, they are the gold standard of how to give an impromptu speech, since there is so much at stake with how each candidate answers a question. And many voters make decisions on whom to vote for based on the candidates' debate performance. You can immediately tell who has prepared well for this kind of format, and the candidate who handles the format well is deemed a winner by the media, and as a result, that candidate's poll numbers increase.

You need to restrict yourself to only one point in your speech, because you shouldn't try to make your audience think too hard. If you address a single point, your audience is likely to understand that point and the evidence you are presenting to support it. But if you give the audience two points, you make it difficult for them to process the information, and they are likely to stick to their original thinking. Psychologists attribute this phenomenon to cognitive bias, where adding one more point makes people think that much harder. Your audience consists of cognitive misers, in that they don't like to think too hard. Ideally, you should give one claim or point and one or two supporting facts. But you should stop at two supporting facts unless you are asked for more.

You need to think of an impromptu speech not as a speech but as a conversation, due to the limited time you have to answer a question and still keep the audience's attention. Even in a presidential debate, the moderator will interrupt the candidate, asking him or her to be more specific. I would prefer to start with being general and get specific upon request. When people ask you to be more specific, it indicates that they are interested in what you have to say. You can't get that kind of feedback by being specific if there are no follow-up questions.

Though you may be tempted to provide more evidence to support your argument, you should resist doing so. Instead, lead with your strongest piece of evidence and stop. Often one piece of evidence is sufficient for someone to decide. If you provide two, you may think you have made your case stronger, but you risk confusing the audience, since they now have to make sense of two claims. And when people are confused, they don't make a decision. They stick with their default position.

Next time you are giving an interview, prepare to deliver your message quickly.

And also, remember: The more words you use, the more people you lose. Or worse, if you are not careful, you can easily shoot yourself in the foot.

PART THREE:

Becoming a Good-to-Great High-Stakes Speaker

CHAPTER 10:

The Message Hack

My life is my message.

— Mahatma Gandhi

I was at my aunt and uncle's wedding anniversary celebration, and since I am the oldest nephew, I was asked to say a few words. Since I had very little time, I focused on just one word that I could use to help me build a quick speech. I came up with the word "passion."

I focused on the following aspect of passion in my speech:

- My aunt and uncle have a passion for dancing. They have been doing ballroom dancing for over fifteen years.

- My aunt and uncle have a passion for pets. They have a shih tzu named Haley.

- My aunt and uncle have a passion for fitness. They like to work out and stay healthy and in excellent shape.

- My aunt and uncle have a passion for travel. They purchased an RV so they can see the United States by road—with their dog.

- All this adds up to one thing: They have passion for life.

My aunt and uncle were pleased with my speech.

If you have mastered how to hack the content of a speech, you should be feeling comfortable and even confident in giving a speech to anyone, anytime, anywhere. But you are still less likely to achieve your objective if you don't have a clear message that resonates with your audience. In this chapter, you will learn how to craft a message incrementally, so you can deliver a three-minute speech that is impactful and more likely to achieve your overall objective in any situation.

Note: How you convey your message during your performance (which is covered in Chapters 13–16) will help you create a winning speech moment.

Before we proceed, you may be asking, shouldn't the message hack precede the content hack? No, because often you don't have the time to develop a compelling message. Developing a good message is time consuming and has to be tested to see how effective it is. If the speech has to be delivered soon, you may not have much time to test the message, and if the message is not right, your speech is going to fail. One of the main reasons speeches fail is that they have no clear message. A speech without a message is just words—or, worse, noise.

One of the concepts I use when developing a message is one called the *red thread*, which Tamsen Webster applies to public speaking to ensure that a message runs throughout the speech.[1] Webster adopted this concept from Greek mythology, where Theseus killed a monster called the Minotaur. Every seven years, seven unwed young men and seven unwed young women had to be sacrificed to satisfy the monster. When the third sacrifice approached, Theseus volunteered to slay the monster. Before entering the cave, Princess Ariadne, who had fallen in love with Theseus, gave him a red thread that he could unwind as he entered the labyrinthine cave and then wind it back to find his way out of the cave. Theseus killed the Minotaur and used the red thread to find his way back to make Princess Ariadne happy.

If you want your audience to resonate with your speech, you also need to have a red thread: good content, memorable performance, and a solid message that runs throughout the speech. If you do that, not only will you get your speech done, but you will achieve your objective.

The main idea of the message hack is to use five simple steps to ensure that your message remains consistent as you go from a word to a speech that includes the following steps: One word, a tagline (a sound bite), a logline (one sentence), a thirty-second pitch, and a three-minute speech. When it comes to creating a message, here are the simple steps:

1. Come up with **one single word** to describe your speech topic.

2. Create a **tagline**, or sound bite, which will be a memorable slogan that defines your speech.

3. Develop a **logline**, or simple one-sentence concept, that captures the main idea or your speech.

4. Develop a **thirty-second pitch** to describe the big idea at a high level, without much detail.

5. Develop a **three-minute speech** to describe the big idea with sufficient detail for your audience to make a go/no-go decision.

Just as with the content hack, you can view the message hack as an iterative and incremental method for crafting and delivering your speech:

1. **Practice.** You have to keep practicing until your speech is good enough.

2. **Test.** Once your speech is good enough, you have to test it so you get some feedback.

3. **Refine.** Based on the feedback, you may have to make some changes to your speech, if necessary.

4. **Deploy.** You are now ready to ship (use your speech) and not worry about it being "perfect."

In a nutshell, this is how the process of hacking a speech with a message works. As you can see, it is not that complicated.

Note: This speech is never really finished. It can be changed based on the situation, but you should formalize it, so you do not have to start from scratch every time. You need to make it better as you go along, based on the feedback you receive.

You can use this method for just about any situation and build a speech quickly that has a clear message. You don't have to wait for people to invite you to speak. You can use this approach and develop a speech to deliver to one person, to a few people, or to many people. With the message hack, you have the flexibility to develop many speeches quickly, so you can engage in meaningful conversations with anyone, connect with different people, pitch an idea, and promote yourself as a thought leader.

You can use this method to hack a speech for any occasion, but it is especially suitable for job interviews, debates, Q&A sessions, business meetings, and social events. Remember: You may get only one opportunity to make a good first impression, so you should never miss an opportunity to be a fabulous speaker or a good conversationalist.

Short speeches are so important in the political debates, since, according to debating rules, the candidates often have little more than a minute to answer questions on such weighty topics as the economy, immigration, foreign policy, environment, and healthcare. If the political candidates can tackle some of the most complicated issues in about one minute, then what's your excuse for needing more than three minutes to convey a message in a social or business setting?

Once you learn the method I teach, you will be able to repurpose your message within a span of time of between thirty seconds to three minutes. But to master what you want to say within three minutes, you need to be so well prepared that you deliver your short speech like a natural speaker. Unfortunately, during high-stakes situations, if you are thinking on your feet, you are likely to make mistakes. It is difficult to come up with a crisp, clear, and concise answer within such a short time unless you have put a lot of time into crafting short speeches.

You must learn to develop a salable message from a single word to a compelling three-minute speech. Do not waste time building a fifteen-to-twenty-minute speech until you know that your speech is resonating with people. That is, do not craft a longer speech until you have given your three-minute speech and find that people are genuinely interested in knowing more. If you can't discern any interest in your speech, then you have to fix it. The lean (MVS) method enables you to validate your speech with different people based on their constructive feedback. The beauty of the message hack is that it is incremental and iterative, so you are always testing it to see how it works with different people. The message has to be refined further based on its measured success.

By measured success, I mean how well it is resonating with people and helping you achieve your objective.

Keep in mind what political consultant, pollster, and author Frank Luntz has for the subtitle of his book *Words That Work*: **It's not what you say, it's what people hear.**[2] I will also add, **it's what they process.**

The First Step: Your One Word That's Hard to Beat

You often don't need more than a single word to get your message across. In the movie *Man on the Moon*, which is about the life of the famous 1970s comedian Andy Kaufman, played by Jim Carrey, Kaufman attends a session to listen to a spiritual guru. Hesitantly, he asks the guru a simple question, "Is there a secret to being funny?" The guru looks at him and confidently replies, "Yes. Silence."

Kaufman takes that one word of wisdom, creates his famous "Mighty Mouse" act, and performs it on *Saturday Night Live*. Watch the video on YouTube, and you will see that he says nothing; he merely creates tension, plays a record of the Mighty Mouse song, and simply mimes a part of the lyrics, "Here I come to save the day!" He never utters a single word, proving that the guru was right, that he could be funny with silence. If Kaufman can make people laugh using no words, then I am sure you can get your message across by emphasizing one word.

The guru was able to communicate with using just one word, *silence*. Kaufman turned that one word into an idea of crafting a performance where he would not use any words at all, a performance that became a classic comedy act. If you can't do something with a single word, then more words are not going to help you much, which is a tip I always give to the people I coach.

One word can get you out of any stressful speaking moment. You can do this in any high-stakes situation.

One word is very important in business. If you can get people to name a company based on its one-word brand (assuming it is positive), then it is highly likely that company is going to dominate both the mindshare and the market share.

Maurice Saatchi, cofounder of the advertising agencies Saatchi and Saatchi and M&C Saatchi, writes about the importance of "one-word equity" today.[3] Why? "Because nowadays only brutally simple ideas get through. They travel lighter, they travel faster."

For example, if I say "search," what company comes to your mind? Google.

What about "innovation"? Apple.

What about "books"? Amazon.

What about "sneakers"? Nike.

Though the one-word branding is an advertising concept, it can also be applied to a speech, since every word matters, and it is your job to capture the audience's attention.

What is the one word that best describes the main idea of your speech?

Is it "investment"?

"Data"?

"Confidence"?

"Cybersecurity"?

"Automation"?

"Teaching"?

As you saw in the beginning of this chapter, I started with one word, "passion," to build a short speech. I suggest you always get the one word right. It will make the rest of the speech clearer.

When Donald Trump accepted the resignation from his national security adviser, Michael Flynn, his White House press secretary, Sean Spicer, used one word to explain Trump's decision: "trust." Spicer said at a press conference on February 14, 2017, that "the issue, pure and simple, came down to a matter of trust."[4] Spicer's message worked, since that is how the media reported the resignation. If you can't get the one word right, you are losing control of your message right from the start. It is like not taking the golf club back correctly a few inches from the address position. The errors compound during the rest of the swing, so when you hit the ball, you are going to miss the fairway and land in the rough or, worse, in an unplayable lie, resulting in a penalty.

In the James Altucher interview with Sara Blakely, on his podcast at the thirty-eight-minute mark, she talks about how she learned the importance of one word when she was doing stand-up comedy when she was young.[5] She realized that one word in her stand-up act would make a difference between laughter and crickets. Though she did not become a stand-up comic, she did learn the importance of a single word. It took her a long time to come up with the name of her company, Spanx. She uses Mark Twain's famous quote on the importance of one word: "The difference between the almost right word and the right word is really a large matter—it's the difference between the lightning bug and the lightning." When Spanx was not well known, she would joke that "you have to spell it right or you will get a treat."

If you think that coming up with a single word is merely some marketing gimmick, you should try it and see if it works for you. I know it works. It has been used to change history. A good example of this is the construction of the Panama Canal. Philippe-Jean Bunau-Varilla, a Frenchman, was a lobbyist who helped sell the U.S. Senate on approving the canal in Panama rather than in Nicaragua, the preferred location at that time. How did he do it? He successfully used a single word that scared the senators enough that a majority of them changed their minds. The word was "volcanoes."[6] Nicaragua had been struck by a volcano a long time before. Though there was little danger of more volcanoes, the majority of the senators did not want to take any chances, so they voted for the Panama Canal. So don't disregard the story you can tell with just a single word. In fact, if you don't have that one word to create a story, you are less likely to win.

To build your one-word pitch, you need to test it on people to gauge their interest. You have to keep tweaking the word till it starts resonating with people. The word you come up with is the branding for your speech. People may not remember much, but at the minimum, they should be able to tell others using one word what your speech was about. Lao-Tzu, a philosopher and poet of ancient China, once said that "the journey of a thousand miles begins with one step." Similarly, building a three-minute speech begins with one word.

The Second Step: Your Tagline (Sound Bite, or Slogan)

We are living in an attention-deficit world; you need a catchy sound bite, or slogan, since that is what many people will remember. And you need something catchy, so they will be able to tell others. If you don't give people a sound bite, you are making your audience work too hard. You don't want them to think hard when you are explaining your message. If you make your message simple and catchy, it will impel people to repeat it and tell others. You want people to spread your message, not to forget it. Even with all the technology we have in our hands, a good sound bite is still one of the fastest and most effective ways to transmit a message.

Though many decry sound bites, they are nothing new. When America was founded, it had two very popular sound bites: "Join, or die" and "Don't tread on me." And they haven't changed much; consider Barack Obama's "Yes We Can!" in 2008 and Donald Trump's campaign slogan, "Make America Great Again," in 2016. People may not remember you or your speech, but they will remember your catchy slogan.

The same slogan can be used effectively both by those who support someone and also by those who oppose that same person. A good example is the slogan "Muslim ban." Donald Trump used this slogan to win votes from those who feared terrorism from Muslim radicals. However, after the election, when Trump issued an executive order to prevent people from seven Muslim countries to come to the United States, those who opposed the executive order because they said it was religious discrimination used the same slogan to mobilize people and corporations. Slogans are very powerful. Trump hopefully learned a hard lesson on sloganeering: **You can win and lose through a slogan.**

In politics and business, you live and die by sound bites. If you don't have a good sound bite or a catchy slogan, you are not going to succeed. Do not diminish the importance of a sound bite. It can be the difference between winning and losing, since if it is easier to remember, then it is also easier to spread. It enables your brain to travel "lightly" when you talk to people.

Right after Steve Jobs rejoined Apple in 1997, one of the first thing he did was to promote a sound bite that spoke about what Apple enabled people to do. He was wowed by the sound bite

"Think Different." It spoke to Jobs on what Apple was all about and what it enabled others to do. Having a campaign around this sound bite started Apple's renaissance and made it one of the most innovative tech companies since the late 1990s.

The "Think Different" message was conveyed in a famous sixty-second commercial. The voiceover in the commercial is done by the actor Richard Dreyfuss. After all these years, it is hard not to shed a tear when you watch this great commercial. It speaks to all of us who are trying to create a speech or anything creative. That is the genius of a well-thought-out sound bite. It speaks to you viscerally.

Here is what Steve Jobs said when Lee Clow first brought the "Think Different" idea to him:

> It choked me up, and it still makes me cry to think about it, both the fact that Lee cared so much and also how brilliant his "Think Different" idea was. Every once in a while, I find myself in the presence of purity—purity of spirit and love—and I always cry. It always just reaches in and grabs me.[7]

This is a very important step in the message hack, since the slogan, or sound bite, you come up with becomes your signature, which you can use when you are performing to create a signature moment and a winning speech moment.

The Third Step: Your Logline, or One-Sentence Message to Inspire Curiosity

If you've bought yourself some time, don't start celebrating yet, since people have a very short attention span, something like eight seconds. You don't have much time to get your message across quickly, crisply, and persuasively.

Roger Ailes, former president of Fox News and a media consultant for Republican presidents Richard Nixon, Ronald Reagan, and George H. W. Bush, wrote in his book *You Are the Message* that

> it takes only seven seconds for you to make an impression on other people.... The seven seconds is crucial in the making and breaking of impressions, relationships, sales, and decisions that affect the direction of our lives.[8]

If you can't make someone curious about what you have to say, then you will not get any more time. You have lost them for good.

A good example to understand the power of the first few seconds comes from music. Do you know how the Beethoven's Fifth Symphony begins? For those who may not know, it sounds something like this: "*Da da da daah... da da da daah.*" It takes Beethoven less than five seconds to hook you onto what's to follow. The musical sound bite (the technical term is *motif*) gets repeated throughout the first movement. At the end of the concert, you may not know anything else you heard, but you are certainly going to leave the concert humming, "*Da da da daah... da da da daah.*" Though this music was composed more than two hundred years ago, people still today are familiar with its opening. Though Ludwig van Beethoven was a musician, not an orator, he knew the importance of the first five seconds to hook an audience. No one has ever done it better than he.

Winston Churchill often compared a well-crafted speech to Beethoven's Fifth Symphony. Churchill is quoted as saying that

> a speech is like symphony. It can have three movements, but it must have one dominant melody: da, da, da... daah.[9]

Your speech does not have to reach the heights of Beethoven's Fifth Symphony, but you too can easily come up with a sound bite—through tweaking and testing—that people will remember after your speech is finished.

Hollywood agents, managers, producers, and film executives are very busy and have very little time to go through the thousands of scripts they receive. They base their decision to read the script on its *logline*, a one-sentence summary of a script (but it could also be a TV show or a book) that, according to Wikipedia,

> states the central conflict of the story, often providing both a synopsis of the story's plot, and an emotional "hook" to stimulate interest.[10]

The decision to read the script or not is made in ten seconds. In that time, the script had better answer the following questions:

- Is it understandable?

- Is it different?

- Can it be marketed with a good tagline?

- Can it be sold in theaters and on TV with a thirty-second trailer?

What makes a concept work? A "pitchable" concept has to be brief, clear, original, and salable.

- **Brief.** To pass the ten-second test, you need to answer this question: What are you talking about?

- **Clear.** There is no way the concept can be misunderstood.

- **Original.** The concept is simple, different, and fresh.

- **Salable.** The concept should be such that people want to see it.

Also, the concept should answer the following questions:

- Whom is the story about?

- What goal is the character trying to achieve?

- How does he or she overcome obstacles in pursuit of the goal?

As I pointed out earlier, the other important thing in getting a script read is whether it can be marketed with a thirty-second trailer. If it can't be marketed, it can't make money. Making movies may be a lot of fun, but it is business first. Hence, before a single dollar is spent, the success of a pitch comes down to ten seconds. If you want a script approved, before you start writing a single sentence, you need to work on a pitchable concept that can be explained in ten seconds and marketed with a thirty-second trailer. Similarly, you can use this same approach when you are building your speech that can be understood quickly and be marketable, meaning that a person hearing it can easily spread your message to others.

Many people struggle when they are trying to describe what they do. They try to squeeze too much into that description. A long, detailed description may work for you, but it is too much for another person to process if it is more than one sentence. For example, if I want to tell someone what I do, I might say the following:

> I coach people to win by helping them create a great experience for their audience when they are giving high-stakes speeches.

This one-sentence introduction is too long, and the person's eyes are probably glazed over by the time I am finished. Besides being long, it makes me sound too pompous. I would be better off with something simple and direct, in no more than eight words, such as the following:

I coach people to win with their speeches.

You can use a logline like this when giving your introduction speech. The purpose of such a speech is to start an engagement. You are giving the person you are talking to three paths you brought up in that little eight-word sentence to pursue if he or she is curious: coaching, winning, and speaking. If the person does not engage, then either he or she is a conversation ender or is simply not looking to engage with you. In that case, you move on. What you are trying to do with your logline is to move onto the next part, the fourth step of the message hack, which is to give a pitch in about thirty seconds.

The purpose of your seven-to-ten-second logline is to evoke the following curious response: "I want to know more." That response enables you to go into your topic a little more, but not much more, with a simple pitch.

The Fourth Step: Your Thirty-Second Pitch— from Curiosity to Attention

If you were successful in piquing people's curiosity, then you have to capture their attention with a few more details, but not too many. Again, you don't want to waste time, money, and energy on something that is not going to resonate. The thirty-second pitch will let you know whether the message is still resonating or whether you have to make further tweaks and test it some more. With some people, you are not going to get more than thirty seconds. For example, if you are on TV, you have to be quick, crisp, and impactful. If not, then you are not going to be invited again. But in the attention-deficit world we live in, this TV restriction happens to you even when you are communicating with relatives, friends, colleagues, or strangers.

You want to give them just enough to see how they react. Is it still interesting to them?

In the movie *Django Unchained*, Calvin Candie (played by Leonardo DiCaprio) says to Dr. King Schultz (played by Christoph Waltz) and Django Freeman (played by Jamie Foxx), after Schultz makes a business proposition, "Gentleman, you had my curiosity. Now you have my attention." With a thirty-second pitch, you are moving from curiosity to attention.

You shouldn't think that you will automatically get a shot at a three-minute speech. The odds are that you will not. No one knows this better than Hollywood producers. Most Hollywood films need to make most of the money in the first week of the release. If the film does not do well the first week, it will be considered a flop. And if it was high-budget film, a big flop.

The way a film is sold is with a thirty-second trailer. If a thirty-second trailer can't get people to go to the movies, the film will not make money, so before a single dollar is invested, the most important question is the following: Can the film be sold with a thirty-second trailer? Similarly, you are selling your three-minute speech with a thirty-second pitch. If your pitch is not good, then you are not going to get a chance to give a three-minute speech.

The thirty-second timeframe is your make-it-or-break-it pitch, because you want others to talk about it and spread it to others. Movie studio executives know that if they can't explain the movie in thirty seconds, it will not do well at the box office, since they can't create a good thirty-second trailer. Finding investors is hard. Use the same approach when you are having a conversation where you are looking for potential "investors," so you need to be able to pitch your concept in thirty seconds.

Your objective with your thirty-second pitch is to buy two to three minutes of a person's time. Remember, the purpose of the pitch is to answer the following two fundamental questions: (1) So what? (2) Who cares?

The Fifth Step: Your Three-Minute Speech— from Attention to Interest

Now that you have captured people's attention, you have at most three minutes to close the deal. If you get past this, you will have generated interest to stay in the game. If not, you are "one and done." Ricardo R. Bellino stayed in the game when he pitched a golf club and resort near São Paulo, Brazil, and got to stay for close to thirty minutes to win Donald Trump's endorsement of the plan he had put together. Bellino describes how he was able to take his idea, pitch it to Trump, and get accepted in his book *You Have Three Minutes! Learn the Secret of the Pitch from Trump's Original Apprentice.*[11] The three principles Bellino describes in pitching are the following:

- Capture the attention of the key decision maker in two to three minutes.

- Find out what will make the decision maker say yes, which Bellino calls the vulnerable point.

- Find something in common, even though you may have some disagreements.

When Bellino arrived at Trump's office, Trump said to him, "Look, you have three minutes to sell me your idea."[12] He got close to thirty minutes and got Trump interested in the plan. Here is how Trump describes how the meeting went:

> [The] decisive factor for me to buy into the idea
> was that it really was good. Bellino had analyzed the

179

project in depth, and I noticed it had every reason to work.[13]

When you are working on this part of the message hack, make sure that you can deliver your message in less than three minutes, so you get invited to give a formal speech in more detail later. Anyone can use the message hack to develop an excellent speech. It is hard work, since there is a lot of tweaking and testing, but if a speech does not move anyone toward an action that you are seeking, then it is a waste of effort. The purpose of the message hack is to eliminate waste early, so that if you get a chance to give a formal speech, it will hit its mark.

The purpose of the three-minute pitch is to either, using Trumpspeak, "get hired" or "get fired." If you are hired, you get to give a formal speech to provide more details to see if you can pass the due-diligence test.

Longer Speeches: Spreading the Message and Invoking Action

Now that you understand how to develop a three-minute speech, you can easily take several three-minute speeches and stitch them together. For example, after testing them, you can stitch three to five short speeches together to comprise a TED-like fifteen-minute speech. Think like an entrepreneur, and use the hack, deploy, and scale approach to craft your speech; you have hacked each three-minute speech and deployed them, and now you are scaling a larger speech by stitching several short speeches together. So as you can see, creating a longer speech is both incremental and iterative.

You may often be asked to speak for more than three minutes, but remember that three minutes is all you really need to explain anything, even to reframe the nation the way Abraham Lincoln did with his Gettysburg Address.

Except for a few historical speeches such as Lincoln's, there are no "perfect" speeches. The purpose of a speech is to sell your message by making the audience feel smarter so they spread the message or take action. Do not let your speech just be a "spray and pray" endeavor. If you do that, you will be wasting your time and the audience's time.

You need to approach your speech as aiming to achieve your objective; do not worry about the outcome, since that is out of your control. Often you can give the best speech you can possibly give, but it may fail to achieve your objective. Or you can give a lousy speech and nonetheless achieve your objective. Never forget that a speech is about generating results, not about going through the motion. If you follow the steps I have outlined in this chapter, you are more likely to advance to the further due-diligence step.

Developing a Message Incrementally So It Sticks

So far this chapter has shown you how you can craft a message using the message hack method. It has shown you how to incrementally develop your message step by step into a three-minute speech. The chapter does not show you the iterative part, however, since that is something *you* have to keep tweaking. In a sense, all of the speeches you are going to develop are living speeches, in that you can always tweak them to make them better.

To get an idea of how you can do this, suppose you are trying to convince a person why it is hard for someone laid off to get a job. You want to go into this incrementally instead of giving them information that the person may not be interested in. You can do it using the message hack method.

Now that you have learned to incrementally build your message from one word to a three-minute speech with the message hack method, you can use the same approach in an impromptu speech (Chapter 9), an informative speech (Chapter 11), and a persuasive speech (Chapter 12). It is difficult to succeed in any situation if you don't have a message that is simple, relevant, and memorable. Though creating a message takes some time, it is essential when the stakes are high. Again, what was Donald Trump's slogan as a presidential candidate? Was it simple? Was it relevant? Was it memorable? It worked.

Best-selling authors Chip Heath and Dan Heath use the acronym SUCCES to describe what makes an idea stick.[14] SUCCES stands for the following attributes:

S - Simplicity

U - Unexpectedness

C - Concreteness

C - Credibility

E - Emotions

S - Story

Their book begins with the urban legend about a guy meeting a beautiful woman in a bar who buys him a drink; then he remembers nothing till he wakes up in his bathtub and is missing one of his kidneys. That kidney heist story sticks. Why? It is *s*imple. What guy can't relate to having a beautiful woman purchasing him a drink? (That has never happened to me yet.) The story is *u*nexpected, since who would expect that encounter to result in a kidney heist? It is *c*oncrete and *c*redible in its details of the man waking up in the bathtub and calling 9-1-1 to find out what has happened. It has *e*motion in that you will be afraid to even set foot in a bar, let alone having a beautiful woman buy you a drink. Finally, it is a *s*tory that you can't forget.

A classic example of SUCCES is what John F. Kennedy said regarding the mission to go to the moon. He said that we are going to "put a man on the moon and return him safely by the end of the decade."[15]

Simple? Yes. Kennedy captured it in a single sentence.

Unexpected? Yes, since the notion of putting a man on the moon and returning him safely was still considered science fiction at that time. One thing that is amazing: When you visit the Kennedy Space Center at Cape Canaveral, you feel like the notion was indeed science fiction, since we have not sent people to the moon since 1972. When you see the equipment, you feel like it is from a 1960s sci-fi movie.

Concrete? Yes. Kennedy spoke of a round trip to the moon that was going to take place within a decade.

Credible? Yes. Though the idea was futuristic, the president of the United States had credibility.

Emotional? Yes. Who could not get excited about going to the moon?

Story? Yes. Kennedy clearly painted the picture of what that would look like.

Overall, Kennedy's promise was a gold standard on how a single sentence meets the SUCCES test. It is something that you should aim for when you are trying to come up with a message that sticks. People don't remember much, so the burden is on you to be creative in developing that message. Using SUCCES and the steps in this chapter, you can incrementally develop, test, and deliver a message that sticks.

Crafting and Integrating a Message into a Speech

In this section I provide an example of how I would go about incrementally creating a message and then integrating it into a three-minute speech. You can do the same when you are crafting your message. It takes a lot of iteration and testing to get the message right. Once you have your message, then you need to distill it to a single word and then integrate it into a slogan (tagline, or sound bite), a single sentence (logline), a thirty-second pitch, and a three-minute speech. If you can do this, you are on your way to becoming a good-to-great speaker. The only thing after this is to turn your speech into a performance, which is covered in Chapters 13–16.

For example, suppose I want to create a message and a short speech on success.

One word:

> Thrive

Now I want to create a slogan (sound bite, or tagline) that will capture the message.

Slogan:

> Three to Thrive

Once I have the slogan, I want to capture that in one sentence, the logline. Here I am using a famous NFL team as an example that businesses can use. Why use a football team such as the New England Patriots? They are well known to many people, and their success is transparent.

One sentence:

> For your company to thrive, follow the example of the New England Patriots of the National Football League by

putting three talented people at three critical positions—the chairman of the board (or the board itself), the CEO, and the head of HR.

Once I have that one sentence, I expand it into a thirty-second pitch. Often, you may not have more than thirty seconds to convey your message.

Thirty-second pitch:

One of the most successful NFL football franchises for the past fifteen years has been the New England Patriots of the National Football League. Their success can be attributed to three talented people at three key positions: the owner (Bob Kraft), the coach (Bill Belichick), and the quarterback (Tom Brady). Similarly, for your company to succeed, you also need outstanding talent at three key positions, and they include the chairman of the board (or the board itself), the CEO, and the head of HR. Google is a good example of this: It has had a great board, an outstanding CEO, and a visionary head of HR. How well has this worked out? Google's market cap at the beginning of 2017 was over $500 billion.

Once I have the thirty-second pitch crafted, all I have to do is provide more details so I can deliver the message with short examples in three minutes.

Three-minute speech:

> People like to use the National
> Football League (NFL) for all kinds of
> business metaphors, such as strategy,
> tactics, competition, motivation,
> hiring, and winning. Business, like
> football, is all about winning. As Herm
> Edwards, former head coach of the
> New York Jets, once famously said in
> a press conference, "you play to win
> the game!"[16]

> In the NFL, teams that win on a
> consistent basis have three positions
> that are critical to the team's success:
> The owner, the coach, and the
> quarterback.

> Let's take a look at the New England
> Patriots as an example. They have
> been winning consistently since three
> things happened. First, Robert Kraft
> became the owner; second, Bill
> Belichick was hired as the head coach;
> third, Belichick drafted and developed
> a franchise quarterback named Tom
> Brady.

> The other pieces keep changing, but
> these three have remained fixed for
> more than fifteen years. And it has
> resulted in a tremendous success. The
> Patriots won their fifth Super Bowl in
> 2017 in a thrilling fashion in overtime.

And guess who was the most valuable player again?

The Patriots are a great example of how you win or achieve excellence when you have three key positions that are good individually but great as a team when they are working well with each other for a long time.

The interesting thing is that the New England Patriots team has no advantage in the NFL except their system. They have to create it through ingenuity, teamwork, and grit. The only thing they have that other teams don't is Kraft, Belichick, and Brady.

Businesses both large and small can succeed the same way if they have three key positions filled with outstanding, talented individuals. In companies, they include the chairman of the board (or the board itself), the CEO, and the head of human resources.

A good example to look at is Google. They have had an excellent board for many years, outstanding CEOs, and till recently, a visionary head of HR in Laszlo Bock.

To thrive, you need three key positions filled with outstanding talent. What has worked for the New England Patriots

for more than a decade can also work
for a business or any organization,
whether large or small.

Remember: This method of creating a message is incremental and iterative. At this point, what I would do is to record the speech on video no more than three times, test it on few safe people, and then use it in a high-stakes situation.

What I showed you is how I craft a message and integrate it with a three-minute speech. It is simple. Anyone can do it. The hard part is to test it, so you know that it resonates with others.

A Pocketful of Speeches

Before you move on to the rest of the book, realize that you now have everything you need to take care of 100 percent of your speaking. Most of us do only two kinds of speaking: introduction and impromptu. With these two forms, you can speak with anyone, anytime, and anywhere. Many people rarely ever get on the stage, yet they have to give high-stakes speeches in meetings and interviews. You now have all the tools to do that, so start creating a drawer full of speeches that you can open, and put a few of them in your pocket when you need them.

You can use the content hack and the message hack to create that pocketful of speeches in your inventory. You can have a speech for anything, including movies, TV shows, sports, books, current events, whatever. The idea of a pocketful of speeches is adapted from what author and public speaking and sales training consultant Terri Sjodin calls "'plus-ing' your elevator speech."[17] She writes that Ronald Reagan used this idea so he could talk about various topics whenever he was giving a speech before becoming president. He would have a three-minute speech on index cards that he carried in his pocket, which he would select based on the time and the topics he wanted to cover. If you want to speak like Reagan, you can start putting two-to-three-minute speeches on index cards, Evernote, or any other tool, and go over your notes before a meeting, an event, or when networking.

Keep a few of your speeches in your pocket when you may want to use one of them or even test it. I developed this from an embarrassing incident I had, when I wished I'd had an index card available. Though the incident was not high-stakes, it taught me an important lesson: You need to be prepared to engage and connect with anyone, anytime.

I struck up a conversation with a young Asian American woman who had accompanied her father, who is my client. After I had found out she works in New York City in the financial industry, I shifted the conversation to the new Goldman Sachs policy of not letting their interns sleep over. The Goldman thread didn't go anywhere.

The conversation then shifted toward hedge funds. I mentioned that I have a relative who works for a hedge fund company. She was interested in knowing more, so I gave her my card and told her I would broker an introduction with my relative. Then this thread also went nowhere.

I shifted the conversation to something interesting I had read in a book by Amy Chua and Jed Rubenfeld, *The Triple Package*, about why Asian Americans are so successful in the United States.[18] This thread aroused her curiosity, and she wanted to know more. I tried explaining to her that it had to do with the following:

- Inferiority complex

- Superiority complex

- *... What was the third one? I couldn't recall. I told her I would get back to her later. Oops!*

This lapse was embarrassing, since I had brought up the topic but could not remember the third item in the "triple package." I said to myself that I wouldn't let this happen again, since I realized that it had prevented me from making a connection. I had blown it.

That embarrassment of not making a connection got me thinking. Connections don't happen by accident; connections happen through careful planning. I should have prepared in advance, as though it were a habit. What I needed was a "pocketful of speeches" that I could use with confidence.

You need a minimum of three speeches in your pocket when you are meeting people. After you make contact, you will lose attention if you don't have anything interesting to say. Without a pocketful of speeches at your disposal, you will engage in an empty conversation that will go nowhere, and the person will not remember much. Sometimes the other party may not even remember your name. You will have lost an excellent opportunity to make a connection.

The burden is on you when you approach someone or have someone broker an introduction. You'd better be interesting and bring up something that will increase your chance for a connection.

Do you remember that famous scene from the movie *Wall Street* where Bud Fox, a junior stockbroker played by Charlie Sheen, finally arranged a meeting with Gordon Gekko, a legendary Wall Street player played by Michael Douglas? After trying for fifty-nine days, he took a risk and decided to visit Gekko by bringing a box of his favorite Cuban cigars on his birthday. Fox was in, but now the question was, could he stay in, or would it be "one and done"?

Here is a brief description of this famous scene: Fox has to show he has something of value to offer Gekko. Otherwise, he probably will never get another shot with the corporate raider. Fox is smart, gutsy, and desperate. He brought three stock tips to discuss. The first stock he brings up is rejected by Gekko. The second stock he brings up is also rejected. Fox has one last shot. If he blows it, he is done. He comes up with a stock (based on inside info from his father) that immediately draws the raider's attention, and Gekko gives Fox some business to trade stocks. Fox connected and got Gekko as a client.

Now, this example from this famous movie is about financial investing. Similarly, when you are talking to people, they are also looking to "invest" in you, But that can happen only if you can connect. If you can connect, it could lead to friendship, relationship, or business. The question is, do you know how to connect effectively with people?

Like Bud Fox, you have to quickly find something that the person you are talking with is interested in. If the first two topics go nowhere, you'd better have at least one more in your pocket to save the day. If you are not prepared, you may not get another chance. You have to make it count when you meet people. People rarely give you a second chance.

If I'd had my speech prepared and rehearsed, it would have gone as follows:

According to Amy Chua and Jed Rubenfeld, the triple package—which applies not only to Asians but also to Jews, Cubans, Nigerians, Mormons, and others—consists of three attributes that help each of those groups to succeed:

- **Superiority complex.** The groups have some characteristic that makes them feel they are special.

- **Insecurity.** The groups feel that they are not good enough and could lose it all anytime.

- **Impulse control.** The groups defer gratification and stick to something till they succeed. Parents foster this behavior in their children, teaching them that if they don't sacrifice now, they will not succeed.

These groups exhibit an entrepreneurial spirit and believe that only paranoids survive.

After this brief speech, I could have asked her if she had observed this phenomenon with her family, relatives, or friends. The question could then have led to a lengthy conversation, since she could relate to this. I am certain that once I could have got her talking and sharing some information, I would have made a connection. The connection could happen, though, only because I had a short speech in my pocket that was researched, well organized, and rehearsed. The speech could have led to a relationship, friendship, or business. But that result would all start with my first making contact and then a connection.

You need to make the connection happen through making sure you have a pocketful of speeches somewhere to draw upon, like Ronald Reagan did. Once you have them, you can easily deploy them in a way that makes sense based on how the conversation is going. If you have something that can make the other person feel smart, then you will increase your chances of making the connection. Again, you have to be prepared to engage and connect. If you are not prepared, then you will have blown your chances. People do remember those who connect with them, and today face-to-face contact is becoming high-stakes.

A Winning Message

Though I supported Hillary Clinton over Donald Trump in the 2016 presidential election, mainly because of her vast political experience, I couldn't tell you what her message was the way I can even today tell what Donald Trump's message was. The message is extremely important when it comes to winning. Trump had no political experience, but he made up for it with a great message that ultimately resonated with people and helped win him the presidency.

Trump's one-word message: Trump

Trump's main message was unapologetic Trump: "I am Donald J. Trump, and I can make America great again. Would I be busting my butt and take abuse from the media, the Democrats, and the establishment Republicans if I didn't believe I alone could do it? Of course, with your support." Trump was the message.

Trump's slogan: Make America Great Again

The slogan gave people something they could explain to themselves for supporting Trump. Who doesn't want America to be great? Trump the message and the slogan were sufficient to win many supporters.

However, for those sitting on the fence or who needed some reinforcement, he provided high-level solutions in an entertaining way: solving the immigration problem, improving the economy, and securing the country. When the media criticized his plans for lack of specificity or viability, Trump's supporters simply ignored the criticism. Salena Zito, a newspaper and magazine writer based in Pittsburgh, said it best: "The press takes him literally, but not seriously; his supporters take him seriously, but not literally."[19] What does this mean? For example, while Trump was campaigning during the Republican primary, he said that he saw thousands of Muslims celebrating in New Jersey on 9/11.[20] The media took him literally and could not verify the claim. However, Trump supporters didn't care about the accuracy of the claim; they were more focused on the overall threat posed by Islamic radicalism. They took him seriously.

Trump did provide enough details that made his supporters feel like he had plans for how to solve the immigration problem, improving the economy, and providing security.

- **Immigration.** Build the wall along the Mexican border to stop illegal immigration.

- **Economy.** Negotiate better trade deals with China, Mexico, and other countries; cut taxes and reform the tax laws; improve the infrastructure; repeal the Affordable Care Act (ACA).

- **Security.** Increase defense spending and enforce a temporary travel ban to prevent terrorism.

Overall expected outcome: Start winning again.

You may say it's simplistic, but it worked. People thought Trump the brand could get the job done and that he alone could fix the mess in this country.

People already knew Trump from TV and could easily remember his message and spread it, and they acted on November 8, 2016, to give Trump an Electoral College win to become the forty-fifth president of the United States. It didn't matter how inexperienced he was, what controversial things he had said, or how many bankruptcies he had filed as a businessman. What Trump showed is that If you are not the message with a catchy slogan, you are losing before the battle is even fought.

Again, you don't have to like Trump, but at the same time, you can't ignore how he succeeded to capture the most important job in the world.

Your turn.

CHAPTER 11

The Informative Speech

There are three things to aim at in public speaking: first, to get into your subject, then to get your subject into yourself, and lastly, to get your subject into the heart of your audience.

— Alexander Gregg, an Episcopal clergyman

Now that you know how to hack content and how to hack a message, you should be able to craft an effective informative speech quickly with a solid message. You do have to spend some time thinking about the message you want to convey when giving an informative speech, however. If there is no clear message, the audience may like your speech, but it will have no lasting impact afterward, since the audience will not spread the message or take action.

An informative speech can be viewed as a longer version of an impromptu speech (covered in Chapter 9); that is, it is an impromptu speech with a main idea and two to three supporting points. You can make your speech interesting by including anecdotes, stories, and humor. With an informative speech, you have more time than you do with an impromptu speech. The best way to use the time is to elaborate your points rather than stuffing too much information that people can't process or remember. You need to make your audience feel smarter with the content and the message you are conveying. Remember, when giving an informative speech, follow the motto "less is more." You don't have to tell them everything; just tell them enough so they get interested to find out more from your website.

While preparing, you should ask these four simple questions:

- Is my speech informative? Yes or no?

- What are two to three main things I am informing my audience about?

- What is the main message of my informative speech that I want my audience to take away?

- Where do I point people to get more information?

Your audience will focus on whether you are answering these questions in your speech. Every choice you make should be to help you better inform your topic to your audience. You can easily craft an informative speech by stitching two to three impromptu speeches together and tweaking a little.

So, you may be asking, what is the difference between an informative speech and a persuasive speech, which I cover in the next chapter? Many people are confused about what they should do with these two speeches. Both speeches are selling content. An informative speech is selling content with logic in an interesting way, whereas a persuasive speech is selling content with stylistic techniques. In the end, both type of speeches should get an audience to pay attention so they spread the message and take action.

With an informative speech, you want people to trust you, because you have credibility, content, command, and control. The informative speech is heavy on content and light on entertainment. If you have established your credibility and presented the content in a logical manner, then the audience will be susceptible to persuasion, even though it lacks the stylistic elements of a persuasive speech per se, the way I present it in Chapter 12. In fact, even with an informative speech, you must persuade; otherwise, you are committing "speech malpractice."

When you are persuading with your informative speech, pretend that you are an op-ed columnist, such as Thomas Friedman of the *New York Times*, who offers the following purpose of your informative speech:

> [Your] purpose is to influence or provoke a reaction and not just to inform—to argue for a certain perspective so compellingly that you persuade your readers to think or feel differently or more strongly or afresh about an issue.[1]

He adds that you are in both a heating business and a lighting business—lighting in the sense that you are making your audience think differently, heating in the sense that you are making your audience feel or act differently. If you are not doing one or both of these businesses, then you are not likely to change your audience.

Meanwhile, a persuasive speech's purpose, as explained in Chapter 12, is to persuade people to take action using stylistic techniques. In order to do that, the speech often tends to be heavy on entertainment and style and somewhat light on content. If you go too heavy on entertainment and style with your informative speech, you may lose credibility and trust, with the audience possibly doubting your expertise. You need to know what you are trying to do with your speech: inform or persuade? Then, you need to calibrate how you want to balance content, entertainment, and persuasion. With practice and through understanding your audience better, you will know how to make the speech resonate with them.

One mistake you must avoid is to tailor the speech as if *you* were the targeted audience. Rather, you must tailor it to *the audience* you are going to be speaking to. Many speakers look great because they are speaking to the audience that are already sold. For example, Donald Trump would not be effective speaking to those who don't support him.

One thing you also need to understand with the informative speech is that you are not just informing, you are *selling*. Again, you do need to persuade, even with an informative speech. Many speakers forget this and just dump information on the audience. You have to ask, why should the audience care what you are informing them about? The burden is on you to show them why they should care. If you don't, they won't care. But if they like you and trust you, then they are likely to even believe you. Information is cold. By selling it well, though, you are making it hot, and people tend to remember hot stuff.

Remember, your goal is to make the audience feel smarter. You need to figure out whether you are informing in an interesting way that makes it easier for the audience to understand, which will also enable them to spread your message to others.

Preparation

How well you prepare your speech will determine how well it will be received by the audience. You will know you are ready to give the speech when you look like you are in full command of your voice, gestures, body language, message, and the audience's expectations.

The speakers who delivered all the great informative speeches didn't just inform with what they were saying, they were also telling the audience why it was important to know that information. Hence, for an informative speech to be effective, it has to *sell* the information to the audience.

A great speaker who did this very effectively was Steve Jobs. If there is one example that shows what a great informative speech looks like, it is the 2007 iPhone launch presentation that Jobs gave.[2] He did so many things well that anyone could copy it. Just look at how well he used elaboration to clarify each salient part of the iPhone. Also, look at the way he was having a conversation with the audience by asking questions during the presentation. You can tell that Jobs was just a natural, but that's because he was well prepared. He knew this was high-stakes. Though he was presenting the launch of a new product, the *real* product he was launching was his speech. If the speech were not good, then it would have reflected poorly on the product. Jobs understood that a great product deserved a great launch with a great speech performance. When everyone was watching and stakes so high for him and Apple, he was not going to get a second chance. Similarly, you have to view your speech as your most important product, even more important than the information you are communicating.

Though Steve Jobs was talking to a large audience, he made it look like he was talking to each person individually with his conversational style. The secret here is that Jobs was informing, explaining, and selling. He was making the audience smarter so that they could explain the product to others the way he was explaining it to them. Jobs did this with the words and phrases he used throughout the speech, such as "baby software," "amazing," "awesome security," "crippled stuff," "five years ahead," "just wonderful," and, "it's gorgeous."

He would make a point, and then he would sell what he had just stated, and finally he would conclude with something such as "Isn't it wonderful?" to make you appreciate how he was feeling about the product. Soon, you also started thinking and feeling like him, and you would want to stand in line to get your iPhone.

Here are the three things he did effectively:

- He slowed his speech down.
- He used questions that were probably already in the audience's head.
- He used catchy words that made the speech memorable.

He anchored in his audience's mind precisely how he saw the product. Though he was giving a speech, he was also negotiating with the audience and the media. He was helping them write a review of the product. No matter how unbiased someone said he was, it is hard to get the anchored words he used out of your head. All this contributed to Jobs being such an effective speaker and a great marketer.

The good news is that you can do this (and should be doing it) when you are giving an informative speech. It is not that difficult, but it does require a lot of preparation and practice. You, too, can sound like Jobs if you are asked to give a presentation during a product launch.

Putting an Informative Speech Together

At this point you know how to hack a speech and how to hack a message. So, how do you integrate the two into an informative speech?

1. Determine the main message you want to convey, so you can include that message in the opening.

2. Hack three short speeches containing three points, using the main message.

3. Combine the three short speeches into a single speech.

4. Come up with a compelling close, with the main message as the key takeaway. (You are not done yet!)

5. Determine how to seamlessly transition from the opening to point 1, from point 1 to point 2, from point 2 to point 3, and from point 3 to the closing.

Here is an example of how Martin Luther King Jr. stitched two short speeches together with a call to action in his "I Have a Dream" speech. As Nancy Duarte explained in her TED Talk,[3] King made a transition from identifying what is to identifying what could be:

Opening:

> So we have come to cash this check—a check that will give us upon demand the riches of freedom and the security of justice. We have also come to this hallowed spot to remind America of the fierce urgency of now.

King then went on to explain the reason for the urgency of the moment.

"I have a dream" transition:

> I say to you today, my friends, so even though we face the difficulties of today and tomorrow, *I still*

have a dream. It is a dream deeply rooted in the American dream.

Call to action:

Let freedom ring!

Now, this is a classic speech, probably one of the greatest speeches ever given since Lincoln's Gettysburg Address. But you can see how King had a solid opening, a big transition, and an uplifting closing.

Two Important Tips
to Improve Your Informative Speech

I include two tips that I love from Brian Tracy, motivational speaker and author, since they are simple and actionable.[4] At the 28:17-minute mark, you can hear Tracy giving two excellent speaking tips that he attributed for making a profound difference in his speaking career.

In his early days as a speaker, he would cram a lot of information in his one-hour speeches. Then one day, best-selling inspirational self-help author Og Mandino happened to be speaking at a same event as Tracy. After listening to Tracy's speech, Mandino told Tracy that he liked his speech, since it contained a lot of good actionable information, but he left him with the following advice: "You've got to romance your points a little bit.… Give fewer points but give more stories [and] give more examples."

The other important tip that Tracy received came from his speaking coach Ron Arden, who told him that when you are giving a speech, remember one thing: "They [the audience] never know what you leave out."

Two simple tips that anyone can follow:

- **Romance your points a little bit.**

- **The audience won't know what you leave out.** You don't have to overwhelm the audience with every point.

If you follow these two simple tips, you are going to be a much better informative speaker.

CHAPTER 12

The Persuasive Speech
Using Stylistic Techniques

Presidential power is the power to persuade.

— Richard Neustadt, advisor to John F. Kennedy and Lyndon B. Johnson

No doubt you want to be a great persuasive speaker. The persuasive speech is the one that has the highest payoff. You may dread this speech, since the stakes are high, and you know you are going to either succeed or fail. You are giving this speech because you want to influence or persuade. It is a speech you give primarily to win.

To give an excellent persuasive speech, you need to add one more element to the content hack and the message hack: stylistic techniques, which give your persuasive speech its real power. You use the stylistic techniques to hammer the message into people's heads so that they not only remember the main message but are inclined to remember and take action.

Again, what is the difference between an informative speech and a persuasive speech? In an informative speech, you want to inform people so they understand something faster and better and so they remember it. In a persuasive speech, however, your purpose is to get the audience to act; if your speech is not getting the audience to act, it is not persuasive. In order to do that, your persuasive speech, unlike an informative speech, tends to be heavy on entertainment and style and light on content. If it is too heavy on content, you are likely to lose the attention of a lot of people in your audience, and you will not achieve your objective.

You need to have a clear objective on what is it that you want to get. If you don't have a solid "get" (referred elsewhere in this book as your "ask"), then you might be informing, but you are not going to be persuading. The persuasive speech is not an informative speech with a call to action merely tacked onto it. Though you may think you are persuading, such a speech is not likely to persuade your audience. *The persuasive speech is a stylistic speech with a clear logic, presented using simple language.*

The decision you make regarding invention, arrangement, delivery, and style is all about achieving one thing: *winning*. For example, if you have three arguments, you may need to decide to eliminate the weaker two and just focus on the one that will sway the audience. You need to make a decision like this to achieve your objective. Sometimes you may not need additional points to persuade. You need to be impactful but economical with the words you use. Often, less is more. As I like to say, **the more words you use, the more people you lose.**

What makes the persuasive speech so difficult is not that you need to know what the audience knows; you need to know how they *feel* about your topic. If you have a tough audience (meaning that they are mildly unpersuadable), then the specific words you choose to use and the style you employ to use those words will make a difference between your success and your failure. You have to be crisp but repetitive and emotional with your message.

You are not going to win all of the audience all the time, but your job is to get those who are persuadable to at least think about what you are saying. You don't know the number of people in the audience you are likely to sway. It's like polling. Politicians like to say that the only poll that counts is the one on Election Day. With your high-stakes persuasive speech, you need to give it your best shot and not to assume anything. All you need to focus on is delivering a great speech performance. Essentially, the technique that will make you win with your speech is your style. People don't like change. Before they are moved, your audience wants to see you "bleed," so you must deliver an excellent performance.

With your persuasive speech, the only question that matters is the following: *Is your speech persuasive? Yes or no?*

The persuasive speech is the *big* speech you give. At a minimum, your purpose is to get your audience to spread your message, to take some action, or both. You need to use techniques to make the speech memorable, techniques that has been tried and tested over the years. Take a look at some of the great speeches; they use many of the stylistic techniques described in this chapter, techniques that work.

In developing your persuasive speech, follow the stock issues taught by Dr. Matt McGarrity in his course on persuasive public speaking[1] to make a forceful case, which includes identifying ills, blames, cures, consequences, and a call to action.

- **Ills.** What is the problem? How bad are the ills?

- **Blames.** What is preventing us from solving the ills?

- **Cures.** What is the solution to the problem?

- **Consequences.** What are the good, bad, and ugly sides of employing the cures?

- **Call to action.** What action do you want the audience to take?

The way you argue will depend on your audience. If they agree with you, then you don't need to provide any counterarguments; however, if they don't agree with you, then you will have to provide counterarguments (arguments opposed to the audience's position). You are now trying to change their minds, and you will have to work hard not only to argue your position but also to provide solid counterarguments to get them to move closer to your position.

You have to let your audience know what your purpose is for being there. Remember, when you are giving a persuasive speech, you want to get something from the audience. You have to "ask" either in the beginning, at the end, or both. If you don't ask, then you are not going to get.

Not only does the persuasive speech involve the arrangement of ills, blames, cures, consequences, and a call to action, but it also involves the stylistic techniques that you need to use to present your argument. In his course, Dr. McGarrity covers several stylistic techniques, but you don't need to use all of them. I think you need no more than a handful to give a powerful speech. The four that I am comfortable with are anaphora, epistrophe, symploce, and maxim.

- **Anaphora.** According to Wikipedia, anaphora is a rhetorical device that consists of repeating a sequence of words at the beginning of neighboring clauses, thereby lending them emphasis.

  Example: "**We have the** people; **we have the** cause; **we have the** resolve."

- **Epistrophe.** According to Wikipedia, epistrophe is repetition of the same word or words at the end of successive phrases, clauses, or sentences.

  Example: **"Where now? Who now? When now?"** (from *The Unnamable* by Samuel Beckett[2]).

- **Symploce.** According to Wikipedia, symploce is a figure of speech in which a word or phrase is used successively at the beginning of two or more clauses or sentences and another word or phrase with a similar wording is used successively at the end of them. Symploce is the combination of anaphora and epistrophe.

  Example: **"When there is talk of hatred, let us stand up and talk against it. When there is talk of violence, let us stand up and talk against it."** (Bill Clinton[3]).

- **Maxim.** This is a short, pithy statement that is simple, clear, and direct, to motivate people to take some action. It captures the core idea, telling what the speech is about. I love this technique and like to repeat it throughout a speech. People should at least remember this line.

  Example: **"Speak little, do much"** (Benjamin Franklin[4]).

The persuasive speech is difficult for many people, not so much because they don't understand how to develop the stock issues (ills, blames, cures, consequences, and call to action) but because of the stylistic aspect of this speech. Most people who attempt to deliver a persuasive speech do a good job with the stock issues, but although their speech is persuasive functionally and structurally, it fails to persuade because it is not persuasive emotionally. They have failed to use any of the powerful stylistic techniques. When that happens, the speech may be persuasive to the speaker but not emotionally persuasive to the audience who is listening to it live.

Based on my experience mentoring students and reviewing plenty of persuasive speeches, I suggest you start with the stylistic elements first. Focusing on the stylistic elements gives you the emotional part of your speech that will resonate with the audience. You can pick the two that I often use: maxim and anaphora. Once you have them down, then you can move to developing your stock issues.

We all are familiar with Ronald Reagan's famous "Tear Down This Wall" speech, delivered in front of the Berlin Wall.[5] Why? He used the maxim stylistic technique. "Mr. Gorbachev, tear down this wall!" Do people know anything else he said in that speech? I highly doubt it. Most people understand that the speech was about freedom from tyranny.

We are also all familiar with Martin Luther King Jr.'s famous "I Have a Dream" speech, which he gave in front of the Lincoln Memorial.[6] Why? Because King effectively used the anaphora technique of repeating the line "I have a dream." Do people know what he said before that to lay out his argument? Probably not, but they know that he was trying to reframe America so that everyone would be equal.

But you don't need to be Reagan or King to use these stylistic techniques. Even I used it when I had to make a case against a school-related issue that I felt was unfair. It had to do with the school's not awarding a varsity letter to eighth-graders who were participating in a marching band, which is considered a high school varsity sport in my township. I came up with a maxim "School teaches fairness" and then proceeded to use anaphora to explain what was so unfair about the decision the administration was considering. And it worked. I got the administration to reconsider their decision of not awarding varsity letters to eighth-graders.

When you are trying to persuade, start with stylistic techniques, since that is what the audience will remember, not the details of the stock issues you are developing. You have to integrate the stylistic techniques carefully into your stock issues so that people are persuaded emotionally.

Note: It is not sufficient to just include stylistic elements in a persuasive speech. To be effective, you need to perform them, which I cover in the next four chapters. If you don't perform well, the audience will not feel what you want them to feel, know, and do; hence, you are unlikely to achieve your objective.

CHAPTER 13

The Performance Hack: Overview

Here I stand, and here I'll stay. Let the storm rage on.

— From the song "Let It Go" from the Disney movie *Frozen*

You have learned how to hack content and hack a message, and in this chapter and in Chapters 14–16, you will learn how to hack a performance resulting in creating winning speech moments. Performance is the most important part of a speech, since without a good performance, you can at best do only an average job of delivering great speech content with a great message. Your audience processes the performance first, the message second, and the content third. You need to win your speech with your performance.

Though your audience perceives a great speech by its performance, you may find this is difficult, since it is very time consuming; also you need to know your audience well, so that your performance resonates with them. Your performance has to make your speech come alive in the same way that a good actor makes a script come alive.

You are performing in order to guide people toward a direction you want them to go. You have the power when you are on stage, so you have to use all the tools of a performance to be successful in achieving your objective. Performance has three moments that you have to craft and rehearse: the **presentation moment(s)** (Chapter 14), the **memorable moment(s)** (Chapter 15), and the **signature moment** (Chapter 16).

Many speeches are often dull and a total waste of time for both the speaker and the audience. They accomplish very little, if anything. You want to avoid this predicament, but at the same time, unlike a typical TED speaker, you don't have three hundred to four hundred hours to prepare for a great performance. Unfortunately, you probably don't have the time, resources, or access to an outstanding TED speech coach. You are on our own. What you need is something that will help you hack a performance together, which will enable you in a short time to give a good-to-great performance that will get the job done. After reading these four chapters, you will have a better idea on how great speakers do it, and through practice, you will be able to do it, too.

Speaking Is Both Acting and Performing

William Shakespeare said it well: "All the world's a stage."[1] We are all acting, some better than others. You need to act the part that your audience wants you to play. If your audience expects to be entertained, then you'd better entertain them. If they are looking to be informed, then you'd better inform them. Otherwise, you are going to lose them.

So how do you make your speech interesting so that your audience will remember it? Suppose you have to give an informative speech; then you'd better be informative first and entertaining second. You have to make choices during the preparation phase between being informative and being entertaining. Anything that you do that is not informative breaks the pattern, forcing your audience to pay attention. In short, you have to play the part your audience expects of you, and as long as you are meeting their expectations of conveying information in your informative speech, they are likely to let you step out of the part and be a little entertaining. They will give you some latitude and not tune you out.

Though this may sound easy, the only way you can master this, the only way you can learn these kinds of subtleties, is by being in front of an audience. You may have to first test your performance at safer venues, however. Comedians do this all the time: They perform at smaller venues to test their material before they take it on tour or bring it onto a TV show such as *Saturday Night Live (SNL)*. For example, Aziz Ansari tested his comedy routine at the Comedy Cellar in New York's Greenwich Village before he appeared on *SNL*.[2] In fact, he had tested his opening monologue on 111 occasions.[3] Ultimately, his performance on *SNL* was well received, for it humorously addressed the election of Donald Trump with hope for the future. If your speech is high-stakes, then you should pick different venues to test your speech, so you have some idea as to how the audience will react to it. The more you test, the better prepared you will be and the better able to manage the anxiety of high-stakes. You don't want the main event to be the first time you give your speech; it is likely to not go well.

You may be confused by the word *performance* as regards speech giving. When you think of performance, you may be thinking that you have to act on a stage like an actor or an actress. And since you may have little or no acting background, you may be worried that you do not have sufficient skills for success. But let the following fact encourage you: Except for Ronald Reagan, most great speakers (both past and present) have had no professional acting background. Performing a speech is not the same as performing from a script. Though there is some overlap, they are totally different animals, especially when it comes to audience expectations.

I believe that giving a great performance when delivering a speech is actually harder than acting. If an actor bombs, he or she is just a bad actor. If you bomb as a speaker, you are a bad speaker. A bad actor can change his or her profession, but a bad speaker can't. Being a bad speaker hurts your chances of getting a good date, forming a strong relationship, acing a job interview, or winning a business deal.

The stakes are also just as high, if not higher, when you are speaking in front of an audience. An actor is a professional and will do a great job, since he or she has to focus only on his or her acting performance and nothing else. But that is not the case when it comes to giving a speech performance. You have to craft a speech, develop a message, and create a performance that moves the audience—*all on your own*. Now I hope you see why becoming a good-to-great high-stakes speaker takes a lot of practice.

Author and entrepreneur Michael Port says it well in his book *Steal the Show*. When you are speaking, you are putting on a performance that

> delights, impresses, wows, connects, or moves people to think, feel, or do something different.... When you express yourself in meetings, pitch a client, or walk into a job interview, you're performing.[4]

When you are writing, no one sees your first shi**y draft except you, as Anne Lamott refers to it in her book *Bird by Bird*.[5]

214

What your readers see is a well-edited version. Similarly, when you are speaking, your performance is a "well-edited" version of what you want to communicate. You want the audience to understand, appreciate, and feel the content as you do. If you can make the audience feel smarter, then you are likely to win. To make the audience feel smarter with your "well-edited" speech, you need to bring in elements other than just the content and message, elements that will help you communicate your content and message in a forceful manner. These elements include voice, gestures, facial expressions, pacing, controlled emotion, and authenticity—elements that are addressed in the coming chapters. If you can work in most or all of these elements, you will deliver a good-to-great performance.

Your audience will quickly comprehend when you come on the stage whether they are going to see a great performance or not. The question is, Can *you* see it when you are practicing and rehearsing? You are not a movie or TV actor, so when you are in front of an audience, you don't get multiple takes to get it right. You must have something important to say, and you have to say it in a compelling manner with controlled emotion and authenticity. Though an actor's voice or presence would be helpful, however, you don't need them to make your speech great. Purpose, credibility, integrity, and authenticity are your superpowers to change people's minds. With them you are capable of giving a great performance when you are speaking. But to perform well consistently, you require the following: both general and content-specific knowledge, writing, marketing and sales skills, acting skills, knowledge of your audience, and deliberate practice.

When performing, an actor tries to create a portrayal of a character that is memorable. When performing as a speaker, you need to convey a message that is memorable. To be a great actor requires years of training and performing. To be a great speaker, you first have to be the message yourself before you can convey

215

the content of the message in a way that resonates with your audience. You have to live and breathe the message in order to convince the audience through your performance.

In the acting world, there are two terms that are pertinent for this discussion: *surface acting*, pretending to create an emotion of a character the actor is playing, and *deep acting*, embodying the character to make it authentic. Delivering a speech is like deep acting in that you *are* the message. Why could Martin Luther King Jr. improvise during his famous "I Have a Dream" speech? He knew that after he presented his case, he could talk about a better future for everyone moving forward. He didn't need to read that from a script, because he lived it, breathed it, and preached it every day. He *was* the message. Now ask yourself the following questions as you are preparing your speech performance: Why are you delivering the message? How have you been affected by the message? Why is the message important for others? What do you want people to do after listening to your message? What is the message you want people to take away?

What Is Acting?

To answer this question, I will turn to how actor, director, and theater practitioner Lee Strasberg, the "father of method acting in America," who has influenced many famous actors including Dustin Hoffman and Al Pacino, defines acting. During a private class he taught, Strasberg invited two actresses on the first day of class to come to the front of the stage and start acting. The actresses protested that they had not done any preparation. Strasberg then asked them a simple question:

> What is the reality of your present situation? Of course you have not prepared anything for us. I

didn't ask you to prepare anything and would not have wanted you to do so in the first place.[6]

The two actresses started by asking each other's names, and they soon engaged in a conversation with each other. After a while, they weren't paying attention to the class or to Strasberg. The class became engrossed in the conversation the two actresses were having. After fifteen minutes, Strasberg interrupted and pointed out to the class that what they had just seen was a definition of acting. He added:

> What you have just seen… is an example of truthful, believable acting. You have two human beings on a stage behaving exactly as they would in their own living room on being introduced, slightly reticent at first, then gradually warming to each other through their obviously real conversation. Therefore it is safe to assume that a good practical definition of acting would be this: *The ability to create complete reality while on a stage.*[7]

Now, if this is the definition of acting by the great Lee Strasberg, then I believe you can act. Like the two actresses in Strasberg's class, you have to have a conversation with your audience. That is what the audience wants to see, so they feel as though they were part of the performance; it is similar to what Tony Robbins does at his "Date with Destiny" events as shown in the Netflix documentary *I Am Not Your Guru.*[8]

Why Improve Your Speech Performance?

You have heard of the saying that if you want to succeed, you have to fake it till you make it. Amy Cuddy, in her famous TED Talk,[9] modified this to "fake it till you become it." I will modify it even further and state that when it comes to speaking, you have to fake it to make others believe it. Why? People don't care about what you believe; they care only about what *they* believe. Your job is to make them believe strongly what they already believe. Reinforcing someone's belief is a shortcut to success in business, politics, and life. You can't change people; only they can change themselves. If you do this effectively when you are giving a speech, you will not only succeed but thrive.

To make people believe, you must develop your performance skill. You have to put on an act—a good-to-great act. You have to be so credible that people believe that **you are the message.** Actors can pull this off, since they are trained professionals who can deceive people to believe what is fake. Isn't this why we often find actors who play doctors, lawyers, or policemen more credible than the real-world people who perform these jobs? If you look the part, speak the part, act the part, people will naturally think you *are* the part.

According to Robin Dunbar, professor of evolutionary psychology at Oxford University, our brain size became larger because of our need to be social for survival.[10] You use up a lot of brain power for your social skills. Every interaction you have with people is unique; hence, you have to learn to improvise and make quick decisions to connect with people so that you are not perceived as being awkward and therefore shunned. Machines can't improvise like you, and it is doubtful if they ever will be able to improvise the way you can to connect with people. According to the authors of the book *Yes, And,* "Our work and our lives are so much better when we act like improvisers."[11]

I have no doubt that machines will be able to give basic speeches in the future, but I highly doubt if machines will—in the foreseeable future, if ever—be able to improvise like us when we are speaking to one or many. Your ability to make quick changes based on how you read people will help you succeed and can make people believe, pay attention, spread your message, and take action. When you develop and master this skill, you are performing at a high level. People notice performance; hence, you must develop your speech performance skills if you want to succeed. You don't perform just to entertain, you perform to persuade, sell, and win.

First-Party Actor, First-Party Performer: You Are the Message

A first-party actor, first-party performer is the hallmark of a good-to-great performer. But this is hard for most of us, since we lose perspective of how we appear to others, and we may have a fear of revealing too much of ourselves. This is risky, and that's why many speakers hold themselves back. As a result, this prevents them from becoming good-to-great speakers. If you want to be a good-to-great speaker, you need to strive to be a first-party actor, first-party performer.

First-Party Actor, Third-Party Performer: You Are Not the Message

A first-party actor, third party-performer is what you often see when you are in the audience watching some speakers. These speakers do not resonate, since they are not relatable. They have created a distance between themselves and their topic, and they can't make them come together. Watching speeches such as these is a waste of your time, since you are not going to remember much, and you will not be spreading the speakers' message or taking action. I call this kind of speech "one and done" in that it was a waste of an opportunity.

Third-Party Actor, First-Party Performer: You Have to Embody the Message of the Character

An actor who creates this type of performance is a good-to-great actor, since he or she is creating a reality that you can experience. This is why you go to movies to escape and even be transported by the performance. The actor makes you feel the character he or she is depicting, and you will not soon forget that character, who may even change you. That's why movies are so important in how they influence us. I have certainly been influenced by movies, as you can tell by all the movie references in this book.

For example, Ronald Reagan used the phrase "Win just one for the Gipper" often in his career as a politician.[12] In the movie *Knute Rockne, All American*, Reagan, as an actor, played a legendary Notre Dame football player named George Gipp, who contracted pneumonia when he was giving punting lessons after a game. In the movie, while on his deathbed, Gipp, in a moving scene, utters that famous phrase to his coach, Knute Rockne. Later in his career, Reagan used the phrase to rally his supporters. Though Reagan may not have been an A-list big studio actor, he was very successful in turning that acting performance into a third-party actor delivering a first-party performance as a speaker. Reagan metaphorically transferred himself as Knute Rockne to win an important political battle, and it worked for him, since many American people, especially Republicans, understood the metaphor.

Third-Party Actor, Third-Party Performer: You Have No Message

A third-party actor, third-party performer is an actor who does not get many good roles. The actor can't put on a first-party performance to make him or herself believable to an audience.

Unless that actor learns the tools and techniques of a good-to-great actor, he or she will not be making a good living as an actor.

Performance Is Reaching into Yourself

You may be disappointed when you see actors in real life, because they have to be themselves. They suddenly become first-party performers—which is not how you saw them on the Big Screen.

When you are performing as a speaker, you are not performing the way an actor does. You are playing yourself. Actors meanwhile have to perform from start to finish in presenting a reality, portraying a character, that they have crafted, but they do not live in that creation after they are done with their performance. Each actor is a third-party actor doing a first-party performance. Actors can pull this off, since they are highly trained professionals and artists.

Meryl Streep was more persuasive playing Margaret Thatcher than she was trying to persuade you to vote for Hillary Clinton at the 2016 Democratic National Convention. Meanwhile, Khizr Khan, a Gold Star father, was more persuasive in convincing you why you should not vote for Donald Trump. Very few people were talking about Meryl Streep's speech like they were about Khan's speech. More people probably remember Meryl Streep from her great acting performance portraying Margaret Thatcher in *The Iron Lady* or Miranda Priestly in *The Devil Wears Prada*.

On the other hand, Meryl Streep was very convincing when she played herself and criticized Donald Trump at the 2017 Golden Globes Award ceremony for making fun of a disabled *New York Times* journalist during a rally when he was campaigning for the Republican presidential nomination. For a week, just about everyone was talking about Streep's real-life performance.

When you are giving a speech, your audience expects you to make them feel smarter. When you change from speech mode to performance mode, you do something unexpected, and the change is noticed by your audience. You need to keep changing things during your speech from start to finish, and each change is a *presentation moment*. You need to calibrate how many changes you want to make, since you shouldn't exhaust the audience with too many changes (including PowerPoint slides if you are using them). Again, to see how effective your presentation moments are, you need to practice them before a live audience.

When you are giving a speech, you are in a sense reaching into yourself and bringing out who you are, sharing the experiences you have had and the feelings you now have, and you are communicating those experiences and feelings in a way that results in a good-to-great performance. If you incorporate no element of performance, then a speech that may be content-rich is going to be viewed as boring by your audience, and you are not likely to move them to think or to effect a change. However, if you can move your audience with your performance, then you will have achieved your objective, because they are going to pay attention and then possibly take your message and spread it, thereby creating a buzz and attracting more following to your message.

The Zone of Speech Success

One of the traps that singles often fall into when they are dating is the dreaded "friend zone." They want romance, not friendship. And they know that once they are placed in the friend zone, it is hard to get into the romance zone.

Your audience tends to do something similar to you when you are speaking. They quickly put you into either the interesting zone or the boring zone. You do not want to be placed into the boring zone, since it is extremely difficult to get out of it no matter how good your content is. If you are in the boring zone, your audience most likely will have tuned you out. However, if they put you in an interesting zone, then they are going to stick around to listen to you further to see if you can keep your speech interesting. You need to develop a sense of gauging this while you are speaking and make adjustments, perhaps even transitioning to a Plan B speech if you have prepared and rehearsed it.

No matter what, the first rule of speaking is to get into the interesting zone from the beginning and to stay there until the end. When you have finished and no one sticks around to talk to you, then you will know you have unfortunately ended up in the boring zone. You will have to assess whether the problem was you, the audience, or both.

If you want to succeed in speaking with anyone, anytime, anywhere, you need to get into the interesting zone; otherwise you should "cut bait" if you can. Even though the person or persons you are speaking to may be faking interest, you are wasting time; you have lost. Avoid falling into the boring zone at all costs!

How do you know you are in the interesting zone? You can ask a question to see how engaged your audience is. Are they feeling it like you? Are they paying attention? Also, if the crowd is a manageable size, you may even break the pattern by taking one or two questions. If the questions are specific, then you know that your audience is paying attention. You can determine the level of audience interest directly by asking if you are making sense, and you can gauge that interest indirectly from your audience's body language.

To make the audience stay interested in your speech, that speech—no matter what speech it is—must be entertaining. We are living in a world today where entertainment trumps just about everything. You can inform and persuade much more easily if you are entertaining.

The one mistake you simply can't afford to make today, with any speech you give, is to deliver a speech that is not entertaining. We are living in a world where entertainment trumps experience and even competence. The United States elected a president in 2016 who was highly entertaining but lacked government experience. Did people care? No. It didn't matter. Since he was so good at entertaining, people assumed that he probably knew what he was doing. Donald Trump is not alone. Today, we put a high premium on those who can entertain first and inform or persuade second. What this means for you is that when you are giving a speech, you have to make it entertaining first and then figure out how to make it informative or persuasive. Hence, don't give a speech you find entertaining; give a speech your audience finds entertaining. Trump knew this better than anyone else who ran for the president in 2016, and he won.

No matter how entertaining you try to make your speech, however, you are going to lose some members in the audience. If you are losing your audience, what should you do? You need to understand the differences between a tactical performance, an adaptive performance, and a maladaptive performance.

Tactical, Adaptive, and Maladaptive Performances

Don't be intimidated by the fancy words *tactical performance*, *adaptive performance*, and *maladaptive performance*, which I have borrowed from the book *Primed to Perform* by Neel Doshi and Lindsay McGregor, and I have applied them to speech performance.[13]

When you plan to speak before an audience, you need to craft solid content, develop a compelling message, and create a memorable performance that will resonate with your audience and help you achieve your objective. You prepare and rehearse before the speech so you can give a good-to-great *tactical performance*.

But what if the speech you prepared is not resonating? You have a choice to make: Either stick to the plan and muddle through, or change some things in your speech so that it does resonate with your audience. Your changing things on the fly is called *adaptive performance*. Now, to successfully engage in adaptive performance, you still have to be prepared; it is a Plan B adaptation. Your adaptive performance is taking a calculated risk rather than a blind risk.

If your adaptive performance does not work, however, and the speech you give to the audience turns out to be much worse than if you had stuck to your original game plan, then you are giving a *maladaptive performance*.

Let's take a look at two examples.

When Martin Luther King Jr. gave his "I Have a Dream" speech, he was not planning to include the "I Have a Dream" part. He had prepared and rehearsed to stick to his game plan and go with the tactical performance. But two thirds into the speech, he was urged to preach by Mahalia Jackson, so King switched to an adaptive performance. According to *New York Times* op-ed contributor Drew Hansen, the adaptive performance was a "speech that he never intended to give and that some of the other civil rights leaders believed no one but the marchers would ever remember."[14] Note that the "I Have a Dream" part of the speech, the adaptive performance, was not made up on the fly. King had used it before. He had the right adaptive performance for the right occasion, and it is today considered one of the greatest speeches in modern American history.

But switching from tactical to adaptive can also turn into a maladaptive performance. Take the first speech Donald Trump gave after he became president. He went to the CIA headquarters to give a simple speech to honor the CIA agents who had died in the service of the country and to mend the strained relationship between him and the agency. The tactical performance would have been to honor the sacrifice of the CIA agents, thank the men and women who work for the agency, and say that he was looking to have an excellent working relationship to keep the country safe. If he had stuck to this tactical performance, no one would have said anything but that he acted presidential. But President Trump engaged in an improvised performance by bringing up topics that were self-serving, such as the crowd size at his inauguration and how untruthful the media is. The result was a maladaptive performance. Trump did not allay concerns about his pettiness, and that failure became the lead story for the next few days.

The point is that when you are giving a speech, you need to work hard to give a tactical performance, but you should also plan to switch to an adaptive performance if you see that you are losing your audience. However, you should not engage in adaptive performance "off the cuff" if you have not prepared well, since it could easily lead to a maladaptive performance. And that would be sad.

Actors can't shift from a tactical performance to an adaptive performance. They are locked in with their tactical performance. As a speaker, you may be locked in before giving your speech, but you still have the option to shift from a tactical performance to an adaptive performance if necessary. But you should consider doing this only if you have prepared and rehearsed a Plan B speech to augment your performance at the last second. Actors can't do this. Only speakers can, which gives you tremendous flexibility to resonate with your audience. You can turn an average performance into a good-to-great performance.

The performance hack is the risk/reward hack; there is no way to know whether it is going to work until you have finished your performance. With the other hacks, you have some idea of whether you have good content and a solid message. With the performance hack, however, you will not know if you closed the deal (achieved your overall objective) with your audience until you have finished your speech. Your success is up to the audience. You will not need a survey; you can tell from the audience reaction during and after the speech whether you won or lost.

The Versatile Speaker versus the One-Topic Speaker

Soon with deliberate practice and motivation, you are going to become an acknowledged good-to-great speaker. You will face a choice as many actors do, which is to remain a versatile actor, such as Benedict Cumberbatch or Philip Seymour Hoffman, or to become a big adventure-genre movie actor, such as Tom Cruise or Will Smith.[15] Speaking is no different. You will have to decide whether you want to be a versatile speaker or become a one-topic "big league" speaker.

Many excellent speakers you see on YouTube, including motivational speakers, political speakers, and business speakers, are one-topic "big league" speakers. If you can command big bucks and you enjoy giving a one-topic speech, then that's fine. However, if you are trying to persuade audiences that are going to be different, then being versatile will pay off in a big way. You can speak to a wide variety of audiences. Being a versatile speaker is hard, time consuming, and uncertain, but if you enjoy speaking on a wide variety of topics, then this is the kind of speaker you want to be. I consider myself a versatile speaker, since I like to challenge myself with different kinds of speeches that I can give to different audiences.

Performance Persuades

One of the common pieces of advice you get from public speaking experts is that you have to speak to one person. That might make you feel like you are connecting to a handful of people that are in the audience; however, to persuade one or even a few, you need to get many people in the audience to react to your speech. You need to elicit an audience reaction to persuade those who might be sitting on the fence. When you are giving a speech, you are performing for many to persuade a few. Is this manipulation? Of course it is, but if you are ethical, that is not a bad thing. Since you have a very small window of opportunity for persuasion to happen, you need to manipulate your audience to get people to act.

Why do Tony Robbins and other motivational speakers always get their audience excited with loud music and wild theatrics? They want to get the crowd (mainly the diehards) into a frenzy, so that they will persuade those who are attending for the first time and thereby sell them the potential transformation that Robbins offers. It is hard to not believe when you see people going crazy and you being the only one not joining in the action. What I have found from my experience is that many of the people who attend these events or "rock concerts" are repeat customers, so they in a sense have become part of the act. They know what to expect. It is often hard to tell whether they are attending to be entertained or to be converted. Whatever the case, the entertainers do put on a great performance, and that talent has made them wealthy.

When you are giving a speech, you can tell how effectively your message is going to spread based on the audience's reaction. You have to perform to win. Consider how much Democrats had to spend in their attempts to overcome Trump's advantage in performing to crowds and the media during the 2016 presidential campaign. Performance worked for Trump in the Republican primary and in the general election.

Barack Obama was a great performer when he ran in 2008. He had a catchy slogan, "Yes We Can!" When he used it, he was creating a winning speech moment. And he would get the audience involved with the slogan "Fired Up, Ready to Go." People were persuaded to join his movement, and they came up with their own reasons to justify supporting Obama.

The same thing happened with Donald Trump in 2016. He was a terrific performer on the campaign trail, and he also had a catchy slogan, "Make America Great Again." During rallies, he would get the audience involved after saying that one way he was going to make America great was by building a wall along the Mexican border. Trump would then get the audience fired up by asking, "Who is going to pay for the wall?" And the crowd would yell, "Mexico!" It was a great show, it made people start believing that Trump was speaking to their issues, and they voted for him.

Let's address the elephant in this book: Is Donald Trump a great public speaker? Yes, as a campaigner and no as the president. Trump arguably has been one of the greatest campaign speaker/performers in American politics, since he is a great showman. He was able to create many winning speech moments at his campaign rallies. No previous presidential candidates had ever got the audience fired up the way Trump can. And that performance helped him win. But he is not an effective speaker/performer as the president, since he can no longer be a showman but has to transform himself into an explainer-in-chief. Trump has thus far failed to demonstrate that he can persuade people who are not part of his solid base who elected him and still vehemently supports him. Unless he learns really fast to become an effective speaker as the president—like Reagan, JFK, and FDR were—he will not be successful. Based on Trump's early track record, the jury is out on whether he can, or even wants to, make the necessary changes to his communication style as the president. And this change he must make if he wants to be remembered as a great president.

The last example I want to point to was Ronald Reagan in 1980. The *Nashua Telegraph* editorial staff wanted a GOP debate between the two front-runners: Ronald Reagan and George H. W. Bush. But Reagan wanted other candidates to be included, so he paid for a debate that included all the candidates. But as the debate was about to begin, the editorial staff had set only two chairs at the podium, and when the other candidates arrived, chaos ensued. At one point, the moderator of the debate tried to get a sound technician to turn off Reagan's microphone to prevent him from making an introductory statement. Reagan became angry and yelled, "I am paying for this microphone, Mr. Green!"[16] This was probably Reagan's best performance ever. The crowd loved it and helped solidify Regan as being a tough, no-nonsense leader. It helped him win the GOP nomination and the presidency in a landslide. The moment changed history. It is simply amazing how a simple phrase delivered by the right person at the right time at the right place in the right way can have such a profound impact. *That is the power of winning speech moments.*

Do not become disappointed that learning how to create winning speech moments takes time. Putting on a good-to-great performance does indeed take time. I suggest you put this time in, employing performance elements, with a single speech if you are giving that same speech often, so that you will know what is working before you use those elements in other speeches.

CHAPTER 14

The Performance Hack: Presentation Moment(s)

We are all Dugs.

— Ben Parr, in his book *Captivology*, referring to the attention-deficient dog Dug in the Pixar movie *Up*

The first thing to master in a performance hack is how to create presentation moments by integrating your content, your message, your credibility, your authenticity, your vulnerability, your voice, your body language, your controlled emotion, and your logic.

The audience expects you to be interesting and to make them feel smarter. Just because they are listening, however, does not mean they are paying attention. You need to interact with them by asking questions, or you need to get a reaction from them the way Tony Robbins does when he exhorts his audience with "Say, 'Aye'" after he makes a point.[1] And the audience always obliges; they respond with a vigorous "Aye!" Your interacting with your audience breaks a pattern of you just talking and performing, and it helps you ensure that your audience is paying attention. (But you have to do this sparingly, so it does not become gimmicky.)

You need to go through the iterative process of, first, building your content, second, developing your message, and then, incrementally, adding other elements to create presentation moments that will not only capture your audience's attention but retain that attention throughout the speech. Since you control the process, this is the performance that you can put together.

You raised the stakes of your speech by preparing hard and rehearsing well, but before you give your speech, you must now lower the stakes a little so that you enjoy the experience of giving a speech before an audience. If you don't lower the stakes and ensure that you enjoy the experience, you are likely to stiffen up and not deliver a great performance. But if you show that you are having a good time, then your audience will feel the same way; they will also have a good time. Remember, you control how the audience feels, so you have to make them comfortable.

You have be on top of your game from the start, since your audience will pick this up right away, so you must practice and rehearse the first few seconds of your speech. It is like launching a rocket. You are going to expend a lot of energy to get your speech off to a great start.

Content and Message

Using the content hack and the message hack, you have your content and your message that you want to deliver. Now it is time to integrate the other seven attributes of a good-to-great performance: credibility, authenticity, vulnerability, voice, body language, controlled emotion, and logic. But first, some words about content and message.

One of the common mistakes that many speakers make is that once they have written their speech, they think they are pretty much done. In fact, you may be only half done. Creating solid content is a good first step, but content alone won't carry the speech for you. You have to make the speech come alive in front of an audience. Best-selling authors Chip Heath and Dan Heath cite research done by Stanford University psychology graduate student Elizabeth Newton showing how difficult it is to get others to figure out what well-known song you have in mind when you are merely tapping out its rhythm.[2] As the tapper, you know how the tune goes; in fact, it is impossible for you not to "hear" the song while you are tapping. But the listener hears only a kind of bizarre Morse code. When you are giving a speech, you are the "tapper," and your audience is the "listener." Ask yourself: Can you "tap" your speech so that others get it? In Newton's experiment, "the tappers were flabbergasted by how hard the listeners had to work to pick up the tune."

You have the content and the message clearly in your mind; in fact, it is probably impossible for you not to understand your content and message very clearly, but you don't want to make your audience work hard to comprehend that content and message. The burden is on you to ensure that the content and message make sense. An effective way to "tap" your speech so that your audience gets it right away is to integrate all the elements of the presentation moments.

Crafting a speech is a skill that takes a lot of work; hence, many politicians and business leaders hire speechwriters to help them with their speeches. You, however, have to do it on your own, and then deliver it to create presentation moments. Though this requires some work, you can do it with some practice.

Many authors are not good-to-great speakers. But good-to-great speakers at least tend to be good writers. You do not want to delude yourself into thinking that just because you may be a good writer, you will be a good speaker. Writing and speaking are not the same. For example, a good speechwriter is not necessarily a good speaker, and conversely, a good speaker is not necessarily a good speechwriter. Also, in the film industry, very few actors and actresses are good screenwriters. The content of a book and its message need to be repurposed to a speech so that it can be made interesting before it can be delivered to an audience. Repurposing a book to a speech for a speaker is not much different from turning a book into a screenplay for actors. Both the speaker and the actor need to make the content shine.

Credibility

When you are speaking, 90 percent of your reason for being on the stage should be your credibility, which gives you the power to elicit belief. If the audience doesn't know you well, then you must first establish credibility, so the audience knows you and starts paying attention to you.

Often credibility is the hardest thing to establish. If you are well known, then your chances of bombing a speech are low to none. If you were a Trump or a Clinton supporter during the 2016 election, there is little that anyone would say or how he or she would say it that would make you change your mind. You have a high credibility with them. When your credibility is high, your audience often is not that hard on your content, message, or performance. Credibility has always been the most important aspect of any performance, whether it's a speech performance, an acting performance, or a musical performance.

Authenticity

As I explained in Chapter 13, when you are speaking, you are a first-party performer. Remember, you are the message, and the message is you; authenticity has to do with how well you are identified with the message. The message is a more substantial part of your speech than the speech's delivery or its content. **You are the message first, the delivery second, and the content third.**

The Mehrabian theory, named after Albert Mehrabian, professor emeritus at UCLA, is commonly referred to as the "7%-38%-55% rule": When you are communicating, 55 percent of what your audience processes is visual (how you come across, your message), 38 percent is vocal (how you sound, your delivery), and 7 percent is verbal (what you say, your content).[3] Critics have completely misinterpreted this rule and have tried to disprove it by asking you to watch a TED Talk with the sound turned off and then explain what the speaker was saying, assuming presumably (and absurdly) that you would understand at least 55 percent of the talk. But Mehrabian was merely explaining how your brain processes the information when someone is delivering a speech.

Let me explain how I interpret the Mehrabian rule. You see a movie so you can experience different artists building a product (the movie) that integrates all three elements—visual, vocal, and audio (verbal)—to create a magical experience. This is no different from looking at a sexy sports car. When you see that car in a showroom, it is just a sexy-looking sports car. You can't do much with it but admire its beauty. If you take that car outside the showroom and hear its engine revving, you probably want to get inside the car and experience it. But you can't go anywhere without enough gas in the tank. Gasoline is verbal, the revving engine is vocal, and the beautiful body is visual. When you get inside the car, you are experiencing the car, and the people who are seeing you drive by are awed by its beauty and perhaps by its revving, purring sound. The one thing people are not going to be focusing on is what kind of gas you are using, however. Gas is the least important part of a sports car, but without gas, the car can't go anywhere. Similarly, your speech without words (the content) does not work. When you are communicating, visual, vocal, and verbal are all working together.

Words are extremely important, but not when it comes to the audience processing what you are saying. Though speaking is a "full Monty" communication, the brain does not process it like that. It follows the Mehrabian rule, and you will dismiss this rule at your peril.

The one product that is hard to automate is your speech. Yes, you can automate some of the content today, but it would be very hard to automate the message and the performance. Even if the message can be automated with a sophisticated algorithm in the future, the Mehrabian rule protects you from being replaced by a machine when it comes to speech, since visual (your message) makes up 55 percent.

Again, you should be authentic so that it helps you achieve your objective. You need to craft your content and your message in a way that makes it easier for the audience to understand it. On the other hand, I don't agree with the advice given by many speech gurus that you must inevitably reveal a little private information about yourself. I suggest you do that only if it helps you achieve your objective. Remember, you are giving a speech to achieve your overall objective first. If revealing private information about yourself achieves that, then certainly do it. (More on this in the next section, on vulnerability, and authenticity and vulnerability certainly go together.)

Essentially, you are performing in order to convey your message. When you are on the stage, what you are doing is no different from what an actor does on a stage or on the screen. As part of the method acting approach, actors need to be authentic to the characters they are portraying. Before you get on the stage, you need to be authentic by actually *being* the message you want to convey. Otherwise, there will be a disconnect between you and the message, and you will likely come across looking inauthentic.

Remember, you care about your audience, your content, and yourself. You need to know what you want your audience to take away, and you can bring your personal story into the mix to enhance their overall understanding. You have to care for your audience so that they will appreciate your honesty.

Again, the bulk of what the audience perceives and processes in your speech (55 percent) is visual, which is how you come across (your message, which is you). The second largest part (38 percent) of what your audience perceives in your speech is vocal, which is how you deliver it. And the third largest part (7 percent) of what they perceive is verbal, what you are actually saying, your content. In that order.

When you are speaking, you are on a date with your audience, and you can gauge quickly how well the date is going by the way they react to you. At the end of the speech, will they want to go out with you again, or they are glad it was over? Well, if you do it right, they may even want to "marry" you. And if you continue to serve them, they will remain with you for a long time.

Is it a good idea to be yourself all the time? No. You need to be what your audience needs you to be, so they like you. If they like you, they will believe you and pay attention to you.

Vulnerability

Being vulnerable is a hard thing for speakers to do; thus, they don't take risks or give a speech in a way that inspires people. Many simply don't want to show any vulnerability when they are speaking, and as a result, the audience can't connect with them and relate to them. Having said that, there is a fine line between being vulnerable, which is good, and coming across as pitiable, which is not so good. Being vulnerable means that you are going to take chances and show something that was not pleasant and how you overcame it so others can learn, and even be inspired, by your example. But you are going from struggle to triumph, not struggle to misery. If you come across as pitiable, your audience will not be inspired; they will feel sorry for you. Between coming across as vulnerable and coming across as pitiable is a fine line, and since you are not a professional actor who can go in and out of character in an instant, you will likely discover where that line is only when you experience crossing it.

You need to practice how you show your vulnerability, since you don't want the audience to feel sorry for you. You want to lift them up so they feel that if you can do it, then they can do it, too. For example, I am not afraid to show my vulnerabilities in this book, since I have overcome a lot in improving my speaking skills through hard work. By being vulnerable, you are being transparent. It's a risk you have to take if you want to connect with your audience.

You also need a balance in your speech between being vulnerable and being confident. You use your vulnerability to show the audience that you are willing to expose yourself by moving from being confident to being vulnerable to being confident again. Show the transitions between confidence and vulnerability so that people will believe each stage and trust you; then your speech will be impactful to your audience. That is how you can create a memorable experience.

Voice

You don't need an actor's voice to give a good-to-great speech. You can do a lot with the voice you have if you use it in a calm, controlled manner. By this I mean you should sound like you normally do, but vary it to convey a feeling that you want the audience to have. If you think your voice may distract from your message, then the best thing to do is to acknowledge your distracting voice in a light-hearted manner right away so the audience can pay attention to your content. And it works! This is exactly the suggestion that author and certified speaking professional Neen James gives when she appeared on the Michael Port's podcast *Steal the Show*.[4] She acknowledges right at the start of any speech she gives the obvious: that she is short and that she has the voice of a little girl (or a cartoon chipmunk); since she addressed "the elephant in the room" right in the beginning, her audience is not distracted by her "weakness." In fact, people approach her after her speech and tell her they had forgotten all about her height and her voice. She removes what could have been distracting in people's consciousness, so they focus, instead, on her message.

The main thing to remember is that you have to do this in a humorous way. Actually, you can make your supposed weakness something to work with. For example, I coach many people who have accents, and I tell them to bring it up in the beginning. I realize that some speech experts advise against doing this, warning that you are calling attention to your weakness, and it is true that you should not say such things as "I am nervous" or "I haven't had much time to prepare." But if it is something you can't do anything about, then address it upfront, since your acknowledgment will make you more credible. Do not apologize for something you can't fix. Acknowledge it upfront, and your audience will not even care; they will focus on your speech.

Voice is a powerful tool, so you should use it fully. You need to vary it by putting emphasis on particular words, phrases, and sentences. You've got to make your voice "dance" like that of a great motivational speaker. Listen (not watch) a live performance of motivational speakers to understand what I am referring to. For example, listen to Zig Ziglar's *See You at the Top: 25th Anniversary Edition*.[5] Just listen to what he does with his voice; he really makes it dance. You just can't stop listening to him. I don't want you to listen to him on video, since you will be distracted by his body language and miss how effectively he uses his voice to communicate. Your voice is a great tool in your speaker's toolbox. Use it, master it, and perfect it.

You need to develop a speaking voice that you can control from start to finish. Identify certain parts of the speech that you want to emphasize by varying your voice. At times you want to use your voice for effect. Iterate a few times using an audio recorder until you feel comfortable with how you are integrating your voice with your content. Once you feel that you have control over your voice, you can move on to your body language (the next section of this chapter).

Avoid trying to do too much with your voice when you are speaking, however; you don't want to come off as inauthentic or phony. Now, it may help some to get some voice lessons to strengthen your voice, but accept that you are born with certain things that you just have to make the most of. Voice is one of those things. You are probably better off working with your strengths more than trying to fix your weaknesses.

One great speaker who used his voice well was Ronald Reagan. Remember that one incident in New Hampshire when he yelled, "I am paying for this microphone, Mr. Green!" That outburst worked and helped him win the nomination and the election. But you never heard him do that after he was elected. According to speech expert Merrie Spaeth, Reagan

> never labored over his words but spoke from conviction. He was measured but never unsure. His voice had a moderate, comfortable tone, not forced, that drew the listener in. This stood out from the typical politician who tends to speechify by yelling, possibly mimicking the worst type of circuit preacher or televangelist. [Reagan's] phrasing was pitch-perfect and you got the message on the first try, from listening to him. I use him as a role model every day in training business people and others.[6]

One important thing you should be aware of is how you use pauses. Use pauses not only for emphasis but also to get your audience to pay attention and even catch up to what you are saying. Suppose you made an important point and you want to repeat it. It would be a good idea to pause after you say, "Let me repeat this point again." *Pause.* And make the point again by varying your voice from the way you said it the first time.

Body Language

Once you have your voice working with the content of your speech, you next need to integrate it with the right body language: your hand gestures, your facial gestures, and your other movements. You need to practice this; remember, the visual is 55 percent of the Mehrabian rule about what your audience is going to process. You need to spend a lot of time on this, but unfortunately, most speakers ignore their body language. It is very important, though; body language can make or break your speech.

The most important body language is at the opening of a speech. I can tell very quickly how comfortable a speaker is right from the time he or she is introduced and the time he or she starts speaking. I suggest you rehearse (even choreograph) the opening well. Pause without speaking for three to four seconds, but do not extend the pause for more than seven seconds. (If you go over seven seconds without a good reason, your audience may think you are a prima donna and tune you out.)

Most of us don't have an actor's background when it comes to using gestures, facial expressions, and other body language. Make sure that you are not exaggerating some body language, that you are not making awkward movements or gestures, to make a point. The only way to see this is by looking at your video. Remember, video is your best buddy when it comes to speaking. Use it. With some practice, you should be able to correct ineffective or awkward body language. At the same time, however, ensure that whatever changes you make will make your speech better, not make it worse. You don't want to look like you are wearing a straightjacket. You want to look smooth, with your body language working in unison with your content and your voice. It has to be synchronized. But the body often communicates the most, since that is what the audience sees, so you simply can't minimize the importance of your body language.

When you are rehearsing, I recommend you make a video of your speech with you using bad body language or none at all (that is, play it stiff). View that video and then record another one, where you exaggerate your body language to the point where it is over the top. After watching the second video, record one more, this time using body language that is appropriate. I use this three-video technique when I am rehearsing my body language. Yes, it's a lot of work, but it will pay off in a big way when you give a speech.

Now that you have your content (the verbal), voice (the vocal), and body language (the visual) fully integrated, your presentation should be very good. But if you have time and want to create a great experience, then you can keep working on some additional things to supercharge your presentation moments. Read on.

Controlled Emotion

You can show emotion at some point in your speech, but it has to be controlled; otherwise, you will make your audience either feel uncomfortable or feel sorry for you. You don't want that. Your audience will remember that more than they will your content or your message. With your controlled emotion, you want your audience to understand the point that you are making. If they are feeling sorry for you, then your emotion is hurting your message. You need to understand when and how to use emotion. If it seems inappropriate or looks fake, then you are not going to be believable.

If you are speaking in a simple presentation mode—that is, aiming to include presentation moments—you are giving a good presentation but not necessarily making it memorable. Many excellent business presentations given by CEOs tend to fall into this category. They are good, but they don't have a memorable moment or a signature moment, which I cover in the next two chapters. Their speech is like the State of the Union speech, which has many presentation moments, but rarely does one ever have a memorable moment or a signature moment that people will remember days after it has been delivered. The speech tends to be long, and it is so content-rich that it exhausts the audience.

In her book *Presence: Bringing Your Boldest Self to Your Biggest Challenges*, Amy Cuddy writes about research done by a visiting student, Lakshmi Balachandra, at Harvard, on what kind of pitches by entrepreneurs were successful in getting funding from investors.[7] Her research found that those who exuded confidence, a high comfort level, and passionate enthusiasm were more successful than those who had better credentials and content of their pitches but who were deficient in confidence, comfort level, and passion.

Emotion is hot, and logic is cold. The question is, should you use one or the other or both? I still think that great speeches are great because of their logic—but that happens over time, that is what the audience will remember afterward. If you want to move an audience while you are speaking, then you need to use emotion in a controlled manner. A good example of how this works is the research that is cited in the book *Made to Stick: Why Some Ideas Survive and Others Die* by Chip Heath and Dan Heath. Researchers wanted to find out if there was any truth to what Mother Teresa once said: "If I look at the mass, I will never act. If I look at the one, I will."[8] The researchers created a meaningless survey and offered the subjects five $1 bills if they completed it. When they returned the survey, they received their money along with a letter requesting that they donate some of their money to a Save the Children charity. But there was a twist. The letter some subjects received used statistics to solicit the donation, and the letter other subjects received included a personal story of a seven-year-old girl named Rokia. Still other subjects received a letter containing statistics and the Rokia story. The letter with just the statistics generated an average of $1.14. The letter with just the story of Rokia generated an average of $2.38. The letter including both the statistics and the story of Rokia generated an average of $1.43. The experiment clearly showed that if you want to get the audience to act, appeal to their emotion rather than their logic. The logic behind the statistics aimed to help many faceless children who were suffering, but the appeal simply did not resonate with people unless it made them feel for the one child who was suffering. We are swayed more by emotion than by logic. I suggest you lead with emotion in your speech and then incorporate logic. Logic alone will make your speech fail.

Recently, I was talking with a woman at a party who, upon finding out that I coach people how to give high-stakes speeches, was very proud of how well her husband delivered a heartfelt speech at their daughter's wedding—without much preparation. And she added that her husband hardly ever gives speeches. I said to the woman that her husband certainly rose to the occasion, since many wedding speeches that I have witnessed have been unmitigated disasters. In fact, that is the part I often remember when attending weddings. If you want to give a heartfelt speech, don't expect that you will rise to the occasion without preparation.

With the speech you have to give, I recommend you spend time crafting it, practicing it, and testing it so that when you are on stage, you are delivering a well-rehearsed performance with the emotion you want to convey. Best-selling marketing author and keynote speaker Scott McKain writes what his late speech coach Ron Arden used to say: "You should never speak from the heart." Instead, Arden would advise, "You should write and prepare what you have to say from the heart. You should speak from your skill."[9]

Do not create an emotion that you didn't rehearse. What you want is controlled emotion, and you achieve that by rehearsing it. If you don't rehearse your performance, you are more likely to crash and burn and will probably be remembered for delivering a car wreck of a speech. And as you know, people don't quickly forget "car wrecks." They tell others. Today that means that your car wreck will be on Facebook, Twitter, or YouTube before you are done with your speech. Don't let that happen. Practice, practice, practice!

Viewing Your Audience As Though They Were Venture Capitalists

When you are giving your speech, you should view your audience as though they were potential investors. Your presentation should leave an indelible impression on them that is hard to erase from memory. If they see you being confident, comfortable, and passionate, then from your stage presence, they will regard you as a person who is trustworthy, credible, competent, and worth investing in. What they are investing with is their attention.

One of the most high-stakes speeches you can give is when you are asking venture capitalists to invest in your company. View your performance in every speech as though your audience were a roomful of venture capitalists. You must stay on your "A" game. Looking at it from the perspective of a venture capitalist, here are some of the questions you should ask yourself:

- **Are you buying what you are selling?** If your audience doesn't think you believe in what you are saying, then they are not going to believe it either.

- **Are you trying to impress the venture capitalist more than caring for what you believe?** If you are focusing too much on what others think, rather than showing them how much you care for what you are presenting, then you are going to sound much like other pitches. They will listen, but they will ultimately reject your pitch.

- **Are you too defensive?** It is okay to be confident, but do not be cocky. You are not expected to know everything, so don't pretend to.

- **Are you nervous?** You should be nervous, since you are engaged in a high-stakes presentation! But let this anxiety work for you, not against you.

Being in the presentation moment is making sure all aspects of your speech are integrated and working well together. If they are not, then you are not going to come across as believable, knowledgeable, or genuine. The result will be that you are not going to move people and achieve your objective.

Logic

The most moving thing in a speech is always the logic.

— Peggy Noonan, author, political commentator, and Ronald Reagan's speechwriter

Becoming an inspirational speaker is the pinnacle of all speaking. It is the kind of speaking that creates powerful movements that can be both good and bad. We know the good Winston Churchill, Mahatma Gandhi, and Martin Luther King Jr. achieved with their inspirational speaking. But we can't overlook how Hitler, Mussolini, and other dangerous demagogues throughout history have inspired people to do evil deeds.

Though if you are like most of us, you are not likely to create a large movement, you do have the power to inspire people with your speaking skills. You want to inspire people to take action toward something good. You want to inspire with a clear message, solid purpose, and authenticity. People need to know that you are a "real deal" and that you have a cause that is greater than yourself. People gravitate toward speakers when they are inspired.

The term *inspirational speaking* is used so often it would seem that anyone who speaks is inspirational. But consider three speeches that are undeniably the gold standard of inspirational speaking and good examples of great simple logic. These three speeches have framed the United States as a country. The United States has gone through three major revisions, and they each had a speech tied to its evolution. First, Patrick Henry's "Give Me Liberty or Give Me Death" speech helped create the nation, then Abraham Lincoln's Gettysburg Address reframed the nation by getting rid of slavery, and, finally, Martin Luther King Jr.'s "I Have a Dream" speech again reframed the nation with the goal of extending civil rights. These speeches didn't just move people; they changed the history of the United States. No other speech has had the kind of effect that these three speeches have had. And what made each of these three speeches work more than anything was its simple logic—a logic that anyone can understand and be moved to take action for the good. Its words and clarity touch "the better angels of our nature," a phrase Lincoln used to conclude his first inaugural address in 1861.

Do not get too preoccupied and carried away by the performance aspect of a speech. Your audience might be entertained, but soon they are hardly going to remember much, if anything. One thing that is everlasting in a good-to-great speech, but especially in an inspirational speech, is its simple logic. You can't salvage a speech that has faulty logic, that can't withstand even a scant of scrutiny. Many speakers often focus on telling stories or injecting humor in their speeches. That is a good technique for connecting with the audience, but stories or humor alone will not make your speech inspirational if you do not back it up with solid logic. Making the logic in your speech clearer should be a primary goal, not a secondary one.

A speaker in the past did not need to balance logic with entertainment; he or she could simply rely on logic. Today, however, when giving a speech, you need to constantly feed your audience, as though they were seals. The problem with entertainment is that your audience is continuously hungry. The logic in your speech is different, however. Staying with the feeding analogy, think of waiting for weeks or months to get a reservation at a restaurant that is owned by an expert chef; you will not forget the taste of the food, and you will look forward to eat there again. If your speech has a lot of stories and humor but weak logic, then you are mostly entertaining and not making your audience smarter. You are not going to be judged an inspirational speaker.

Logic Closes the Deal

You probably know that famous speech by Marc Antony in William Shakespeare's play *Julius Caesar* that begins "Friends, Romans, countrymen, lend me your ears." Antony gives this famous speech at Caesar's funeral. Caesar had been murdered in a conspiracy plot by those who were jealous of Caesar's powers. Antony's was an inspirational speech, since its logic was so clear that it aroused people to turn against the conspirators.

A speech is binary in that it has either good logic or bad logic. If a speech has bad logic, then the speaker is either an entertainer, a fool, or evil. You may not be good at telling stories or using humor, but there is no excuse for having bad logic. Bad logic means that you can't think well, or that you don't respect your audience's intelligence. Do not let this happen.

The whole point of giving a speech is to have one big idea that you want to convey in a logical manner. Once you have the logic right, then you can keep polishing your speech with stories and humor if you want to capture and keep people's attention.

Stories and humor are not necessary for your speech, but good logic is a must. You have to work on making your logic so simple that anyone can understand it. If the logic makes your audience smarter, they are going to be satisfied and more likely to spread your message and make others smarter too.

What makes a speech truly inspirational is how many people know and listen to your speech when they were not in the live audience. Today that is measured by views on YouTube and its long-term effect. A perfect example of these are the TED Talks. Many of them get a lot of views, and they change how we think and behave.

If your logic is simple, then people will remember it and will spread the message or take action. Bad logic may work in the short term, but it can't stand the test of time. The simpler the logic, the more persuasive the speech. What was beautiful about the three historical inspirational speeches that framed the United States as a country was their simple logic. Their logic led to action.

Logic is cold, and many speakers don't understand its importance, so they tend to minimize it or ignore it. Emotions are hot and often overemphasized, since the reaction is immediate. Speakers want instant feedback, and emotions achieve that. But emotions won't carry the day for long, and they gradually get cold, whereas the logic in a speech gets warmer over time. Logic's temperature does not fluctuate the way emotions' temperature does.

Let's look at the three speeches that are undeniably the gold standard of inspirational speaking—the speeches given by Patrick Henry, by Abraham Lincoln, and by Martin Luther King Jr.

Patrick Henry's Speech: Creating United States Version 1.0

Patrick Henry, a planter, politician, and Founding Father, gave his famous "Give Me Liberty or Give Me Death" speech[10] during the meeting of the Second Virginia Convention on March 23, 1775, in Richmond, Virginia. Henry was persuading the delegates to declare war against the British in order to seek liberty. I consider this a high-stakes speech, not only because it was about freedom, justice, and self-determination but also because Henry was risking his life: He undoubtedly would have been hanged if the British had prevailed in the coming war. What could be more important than this? I consider this one of the greatest speeches ever given by an American.

Henry's logic regarding freedom and slavery was straightforward.

Henry's arguments:

- Based on their past acts, the British can't be trusted.

- They are saying conciliatory things only to buy more time so they can prepare their armies and navies to crush the opposition.

Henry's call to action:

- The time for talk is over; now it's time to fight.

- Henry ends the speech with a call: "Give me liberty or give me death."

Look at the simplicity of Henry's logic. Do you want to control your destiny and fight for a new nation, or would you rather subject yourself, your children, and your grandchildren to live under tyranny? The delegates at the convention were stunned by his speech, but when they collected their thoughts, they passed Henry's resolution to go to war with the British.

Henry's logic won because his logic was simple and clarified the course of action with his oratory. Henry's speech helped the

United States to become a new nation, to become (using tech speak) what I call Version 1.0.

Abraham Lincoln's Speech: Creating United States Version 2.0

Lincoln redefined the nation by ending slavery during the Civil War, and I like to refer to his Gettysburg Address[11] as a keynote for United States Version 2.0. According to author and columnist Peggy Noonan,[12] Lincoln's speech "contained the logic of the war." It was a speech that "defined things." I consider this a high-opportunity speech, since President Lincoln was more of an afterthought for this commemoration. He used this opportunity, short though it was, to redefine the nation; his address ranks as one of the greatest speeches ever given by an American. In only 272 words it transformed the nation. That's why I emphasize that if you can't close the deal in a three-minute speech, then you can't close it if you have more time.

Lincoln's arguments:

- The Founding Fathers created America as an experiment that "all men are created equal."

- The Civil War is testing whether this experiment can still apply today.

- The people who sacrificed their lives proved that the experiment can even work today.

Lincoln's call to action:

- It is up to the living to ensure that the experiment continues and makes the nation stronger and better.

The speech was so powerful that Edward Everett, the principal orator for the event, realized that his two hours of oration barely touched the main idea that Lincoln conveyed in 272 words; here are Everett's actual words in a letter he wrote to

Lincoln after the occasion: "I shall be glad if I could flatter myself that I came as near to the central idea of the occasion in two hours as you did in two minutes."[13]

Lincoln's logic was so simple that he saw no need to add any more words. He redefined the nation in just 272 words. Even if you say those words slowly, it takes less than three minutes. If Lincoln can redefine the nation in 272 words, then what is your excuse for getting your message across with more than 272 words? Great speeches are great because their logic is simple, clear, and purposeful and can stand the test of time.

Martin Luther King Jr.'s Speech: Creating United States Version 3.0

King's "I Have a Dream" speech[14] is very logical and helped bring about the passing of the Voting Rights Act and the Civil Rights Act. I consider it a high-risk speech because of what could have happened if the crowd had become unruly and thereby undermined the overall cause by alienating some people who had been supportive of civil rights. No protest this large had ever been attempted for the civil rights cause. Notwithstanding all that could have gone wrong that day, King kept his eye on the prize and delivered one of the most memorable speeches ever given by an American.

King's arguments:

- Abraham Lincoln helped free the slaves, but African Americans still do not have civil rights in our society.

- African Americans are still not able to participate in the great American experiment that guaranteed them "unalienable rights of life, liberty, and the pursuit of happiness."

- The time has come for African Americans to be free and to be treated equally, as envisioned by the Declaration of Independence.

- Until that happens, African Americans are going to continue their peaceful protests to end the injustices and indignities they face every day.

- King's dream envisioned an America where everyone could be free to enjoy the fruits of liberty and would be judged based on the content of their character.

King's call to action:

- America must redefine itself so that civil rights become a reality rather than still being a dream for many.

That call to action succeeded—first, with the passing of the Civil Rights Act and the Voting Rights Act, laws that provided adequate protections; and, second, by gradually changing the mindsets of people all across the land.

Inspiring Your Audience with Your Logic

Speeches endure because they have good logic, and good logic leads to good solutions. Good oratory combined with good logic results in action without the need of threats or of exerting force.

There was another famous person who was able to captivate people with his excellent speaking skills, and his name was Adolf Hitler. Today, we can't remember a single speech that he gave, because his logic was not only flawed but catastrophic. He blamed the Jews, the Communists, and others for Germany's problems. Because of his propaganda machine, he was able to fool his own people and world leaders. By the time people realized what they were dealing with, Hitler had caused tremendous destruction as well as millions of deaths. In the long term, bad logic leads to bad results.

If you want to persuade people, get the logic right first, make it simple, and empower your audience. If you do that, then you will inspire people to take action and spread your message.

"Open Line Friday"

Rush Limbaugh, radio talk show host, calls his radio program on Fridays "Open Line Friday." Though I don't agree with anything he has to say, I will use this idea when I am giving a speech. Limbaugh starts the show by jokingly saying that by giving control to rank amateurs (his audience) to pick topics that would be interesting to them, he is taking a big risk in his career. He has been saying this for three decades while earning tens of millions of dollars a year. Anyway, the reason I include Rush Limbaugh as an example is that you should do the same when you are giving a speech. You have to let the audience feel that they are in control, while in reality you maintain complete control. If you can do that, you will make your audience pay attention to your message.

You need to engage your audience so they feel as though you were having a conversation with them, not delivering a speech to them. In other words, you need to prepare your speech as though you wanted to have a conversation with them. The technique is very effective, but it presents some risks, since, like what Limbaugh does, you have to give a little seeming control to get the audience more engaged, while you actually maintain complete control. If you can do that, your speech is going to resonate well with the audience and will create excellent presentation moments. One speaker who does this well is Tony Robbins; he is always engaging with his audience.

Don't Make Your Audience Work Hard

When you are giving a speech, you want to engage your audience, perhaps even challenge them, but do not exhaust them with your content or make them work hard by forcing them to do any kind of exercise. Remember, you are on stage to perform, so stay on the stage and perform. Do not share the stage with the audience. It is gimmicky when a speaker gets off the stage and starts mingling with the audience. Engage and challenge your audience with your performance rather than getting up close to them.

The audience is there to listen and learn. Do not turn your speech into a seminar or a workshop. An audience will do what you ask them, but that does not mean you should ask them that. If anyone in the audience wants to know more, then they can visit your website and possibly attend your seminar or workshop. A speech, on the other hand, is your show. And you'd better deliver what the audience is expecting. The audience is not there to do work, so don't make them. You do the work, and let the audience just pay attention. That is hard enough work in itself, so don't add more complexity to your presentation.

CHAPTER 15

The Performance Hack: Memorable Moment(s)

What makes things memorable is that they are meaningful, significant, colorful.

— Joshua Foer, journalist and author

I f you have been presenting and resonating with your audience, you are creating presentation moments, but perhaps you have not yet made your speech memorable. You may have decided to give a safe speech and are happy to be done with it; on the other hand, you could decide to take risks and then reap the reward that comes with that risk. To make your speech memorable, you have to get out of your comfort zone and take some chances. To charge your performance, you need to do something that the audience is not expecting. If during your speech you have been faithfully delivering what the audience was expecting, then at the point you choose to take a risk, they will be receptive to the change you are about to make in your performance. Speaking is like football; it's a risk/reward activity. Most speakers don't take risks and remain average speakers. They have the knowhow, talent, and motivation, but it is the lack of risk taking that is keeping them average. The difference between a good speech and a great speech is the calculated risk that you take as a speaker.

To further explain using a football analogy, assume you have the ball. You could play it safe and run the ball, or you might take some risk and throw a long pass. You know that bad things can happen when you pass the ball, but as a quarterback, you have to know when to take calculated risks. When you are speaking, you are the quarterback, and your speech is the ball you are holding. What are you going to do with it?

You need to do something that will get people's attention, that will make them remember you and your message clearly. If that something goes well, you are golden; if it bombs, you are toast. Since the audience is not expecting what is about to come next, that something is simply a risk/reward moment in your speaking performance. With an actor's performance, the audience is *expecting* changes to occur during the performance. That is not the case with your performance, however. The audience views you as a speaker, not an actor, and they are not expecting you to make unexpected changes in your performance. Such changes are risky. Many speakers shy away from taking such a risk. Or they take it when they have not adequately prepared and rehearsed the risk. And today with smartphones and social media, your speech will be viewed by many for a long time.

Note: There is a good chance that an unexpected change may not work with the audience you are speaking to, but sometimes you just have to say, "What the f*ck," and go for it.

To create a memorable moment, you are there to accomplish a mission. Your mission could be to get people to sign up for a good cause, to exercise more, to go to college, to give money to a charity, to achieve success, or any number of other inducements.

Once you have your mission, you need to either tell a story or an anecdote or use humor to make your point both entertaining and so clear that there is no difference between the way you see your mission and the way your audience sees it.

Do the Right Thing

By doing the right thing, you have a personal stake in what you are about to say. Not only are you saying it, you are living it. You are willing to expose yourself in front of people, because you believe in what you are saying, and you are there to do what's right, no matter what others think. You are willing to show them who you are, so there is no doubt between you as an actor, you as a performer, and you as a person. They are all merging into one, since that's how strongly you feel about what you are communicating.

Your objective can be one or more of the following missions, which you need to identify during the performance hack:

- **Help people.** You are there to help someone make a transformation.

- **Get justice.** You want to correct something that is unfair or unjust.

- **Tell the truth.** You want to let people know about some difficult personal experience about yourself so that your story will help others who may be going through what you went through.

- **Have a cause.** You are more likely to persuade if you have a conviction about anything.

- **Be generous.** You want to win with generosity, preferably without any expectations.

- **Show you care.** You care about something that is important to you. (For example, celebrities and athletes often associate themselves with a cause to raise money or to bring visibility.)

- **Gain support.** You have an idea, and you want to get others to spread it or adopt it.

Keep It Simple

Though the need to keep a speech simple may seem obvious, many addresses still remain hard to understand and impossible to remember. According to research conducted by cognitive scientist Carmen Simon, people remember only 10 percent of a speech.[1] The problem is you don't know which 10 percent they are likely to remember!

C. Peter Giuliano, chairman of Executive Communications Group, explained what made Ronald Reagan such an effective communicator, attributing Reagan's communication success to his simplicity:

> He kept his messages short and clear. His speeches were not laden with more facts and data than people could quickly and easily absorb.[2]

Reagan was a simple man, and one of his favorite quotes, which he repeated often with the Russians was the Russian maxim taught him by writer Suzanne Massie: "Доверяй, но проверяй" ("*Doveryai, no proveryai*," meaning "Trust, but verify"). At one White House event with former Soviet leader Mikhail Gorbachev he used it, to which Gorbachev commented that the president repeated that at every meeting. Reagan replied with a smile, "I like it." He disarmed Gorbachev with his wit and charm, developing a trust that ultimately led Gorbachev to break up the Soviet Union.

Had Gorbachev and Reagan not liked and trusted each other—as had been the case between previous U.S. presidents and Soviet leaders—I don't think they could have worked together to find common ground.

Tell a Story

One of the best ways to do the right thing is by telling a story, preferably a personal story. The more personal the story, the more relatable you will be with your audience. A personal story is more powerful, since only you can tell it the way it affected you. Telling such a story can be hard, since you are going to be vulnerable; however, if you want to give a good-to-great performance, you must be willing to take some risk. A story that can capture your point does two things:

- You are telling something you know well.

- You are making it easier for your audience to process the information you are sharing.

One of the speakers who loved telling stories was Ronald Reagan. In a typical speech, he would make an important point and then follow the point with "which makes me think of a story—everything makes me think of a story."[3] The remark would get the audience laughing and wanting more. If you want to be an effective speaker, learning this technique from Reagan will help you better connect with your audience.

A word of caution on using stories, though. They are not always as effective as many speaking coaches proclaim. There are many reasons offered for this, but it basically is a matter of credibility. Why are you telling a story? How does your audience know whether your story is true? What if the story is not good, or what if you are bad at telling the story? What if your story is so

261

good that it stomps on your overall objective? How do you convince the audience that you are not manipulating them? Anytime you add anything to your speech's content and message, the result is not always positive. In fact, the result can even be a big negative, detracting from rather than supporting your main message. You need to weigh the pros and cons if you are using a story.

None of the three great speeches in our nation's history that are undeniably the gold standard of inspirational speaking—Patrick Henry's "Give Me Liberty or Give Me Death" speech, Abraham Lincoln's "Gettysburg Address," and Martin Luther King Jr.'s "I Have a Dream" speech—have a story in them. Yet they are considered the three greatest American speeches, each one changing the direction of the United States.

Stories are effective when you share the audience's experience and when the audience knows you really well. For example, if you are a sales professional speaking to a technical audience, you may have a great customer story, but if the story is not relevant to the technical people's experience, the speech will bomb. Still, if you are famous or if people have paid a lot of money to come listen to you, then you'd better tell great stories. This is exactly what you saw when Zig Ziglar spoke and you see when you attend Tony Robbins's events. Also, there is a famous speech that Steve Jobs gave at Stanford (cited in Chapter 17), where he told the audience that he had three stories to tell. It was very effective, since people knew Jobs and what he had accomplished. They wanted a message, which was amplified with three well-thought-out personal stories.

However, if you are speaking to an audience that don't know you well, you should err on the side of getting your speech done fast. If you can't sell your message without a story, then telling a story is akin to putting lipstick on a pig. People are not going to be fooled. Furthermore, it is not automatic that even great stories will work. The following are two famous examples of great storytelling that were big flops.

Coca-Cola

A famous ad was aired during the 1979 Super Bowl telling a story of the great Pittsburgh Steelers' "Mean" Joe Greene, injured, angry, and walking toward the locker room.[4] A kid sees that Greene is hurt and offers him a bottle of Coke. Greene is in no mood to talk to anyone, let alone a kid with a Coke, but he rethinks and accepts the kid's offer. After he guzzles down the bottle, Greene is feeling a little better, and he throws his sweaty football jersey to the kid, who is ecstatic.

Everyone loved this ad. Viewers to his day talk about the ad. Coke's bottlers loved it. Coke's marketers from all over the world wanted the ad translated for their local markets. So what could possibly go wrong?

The ad did not result in people buying more Coke. Sergio Zyman, marketing czar at Coke, explained:

> I had a strategic goal—which was to get more people to buy more Coke. What would have been a big waste of money is to have kept buying airtime for something that wasn't getting people to do that.[5]

Apple Macintosh

Many of us have seen the famous ad[6] by now (on TV or the Internet) that was aired during the 1984 Super Bowl with the tagline "Why 1984 Won't Be Like 1984," which played on George Orwell's dystopian novel *1984* with the message for the viewers to free themselves from the technology of "Big Blue" (IBM), move to the Apple Macintosh, and unleash their creativity. It was a clever ad, and it told a great story, but it failed.

Many bought into the ad's message and purchased Macintosh, but the product lacked the vast software that purchasers could use for both personal and business needs. The sales sputtered and led to one of the most famous executive firings of all time: Steve Jobs. Macintosh was a great computer for personal use but not for businesses, and it could not end the rule of the IBM PC.

An Excellent Method for Telling Stories

When Thom Winninger, author, speaker, marketing strategist, was a guest on my YouTube show, he offered an excellent tip on how to tell stories:[7] When you tell a story, you should have three levels of relationship with the content for it to be effective and for people to pay attention.

Level 1: You were affected. For example, my belt buckle of a nice leather belt, which I had purchased from Nordstrom more than eighteen months ago, broke. I brought it to the store, and they replaced it with no questions asked. I was the recipient of that great customer experience.

Level 2: That experience happened to one of my friends or relatives. I know someone that was affected.

Level 3: This excellent customer experience from Nordstrom happened to a friend of someone I was sitting next to.

The levels describe your relationship to the content. The highest impact is level 1, then level 2, and then level 3. In your stories, use more level-1 experiences than level 2, and only sparingly use level 3. The content loses its relevance when you have no personal relationship, since you have no way to verify it.

Why do you think people attend games and shows or go to interesting places? They want a level-1 experience so that they can tell others or write about it. When you are telling your story, you need to bring a level-1 experience into it for it to resonate with your audience. According to Carmen Simon, "One of the best and easiest ways to include perceptive details and activate our audience's senses is to share personal experiences."[8] She adds that personal stories are very effective in convincing others, since it is your story that you remember in detail. Also, you know the backstory of your own experience, a knowledge you don't have when you are relaying a story that you only heard or read. To capture your audience's attention, lead with your own story.

Use Humor

Humor can be quite effective, especially if it is self-deprecating humor. People like a speaker who uses humor; it makes him or her more relatable, and it makes the audience feel smarter. But humor is tricky; many people are not good at it and completely bungle it. If you want to use humor, you need to practice this harder than any other technique, since you don't want to be remembered for falling flat with your humor. I suggest you play it safe if you want to use humor, or just avoid it entirely. If it goes bad, you are done, so you need to be very careful. If you do want to use humor, though, record yourself and get feedback before you use it in a speech.

One of the things that made Ronald Reagan deserving of the title Great Communicator was that he injected humor effectively to convey his message. A good example of this is when he was invited to speak at Moscow University in 1988. He wanted to attack communism, but he didn't want to offend his host, Mikhail Gorbachev, by mocking communism directly. So he decided to use a parable that made the point by focusing on how communism perpetuates bureaucracy. In this parable, a woman confronts a government official who was "chairing" a meeting at her village:

> There is a folk legend where I come from that when a baby is born an angel comes down from heaven and kisses him on part of the body. If the angel kisses him on the hand, he becomes a handyman. If she kisses him on his forehead, he becomes a scholar. And I've been trying to figure out where the angel kissed you that you should sit there so long and do nothing.[9]

The students laughed, since they could easily relate to the story, considering the bureaucracy they had to deal with.

The best way to use humor is to make it situational, something that everyone in the audience is experiencing. A great example of this is when John F. Kennedy gave his famous going-to-the-moon speech at Rice University on a hot day. At one point in his speech, he used the following bit of humor as he was describing how hot the capsule would get on its return from the moon,

> reentering the atmosphere at speeds of over twenty-five thousand miles per hour, causing heat about half that of the temperature of the sun—*almost as hot as it is here today...*[10]

This kind of humor is very effective and should be used. But I would avoid humor if there is a chance that there are some in the audience who can't relate to what you are saying.

Quote Famous People

One of the techniques that has proven to work well in many situations is to quote someone famous—if you genuinely believe the quote helps to convey how you feel. A great speaker who did this well was—you guessed it!—Ronald Reagan. As you can see, I consider Reagan one of the greatest speakers of our time. You may not agree with his views or policies, but he did everything well when he was giving speeches: He used all the winning speech moments.

Reagan biographer James Rosebush described how Reagan used quotes:

> He would frequently repeat quotations from historic thinkers, patriots, or writers to make certain his audience understood the import of his message.... [It] added power and import to his speeches—to depend on other thinkers who might enjoy the broad support that history sometimes bestows.[11]

Rosebush added that politician Reagan quoting others was no different from actor Reagan using the words of a screenwriter to make people believe the character he was playing. However, when he was giving a speech, not only was he performing to convey a message, but he was also using other people's words that reflected his views.

Quoting other people is a powerful technique, which is very effective in conveying your message. In fact, Les Perelman, former professor of writing at MIT, showed that it helped high school students get good grades on the essay portion of the SAT test.[12] Based on Perelman's findings, some colleges have made the essay portion on the SAT optional. Nevertheless, it does show the power of the words attributed to famous people in helping you get your message across. People tend to pay attention when you are quoting someone famous. I think it is a good idea to include a couple of quotes in your speech.

Repeat the Message

Why do we keep seeing the same advertisements over and over? Marketers know that the only way to get their message into people's heads is through repetition. And when you are giving a speech, it should be no different. Repeat as often as you have to, but in different ways, so that people get your message. All great speakers, such as Abraham Lincoln, Ronald Reagan, and others, have used repetition effectively.

Take Risks

During the 2016 Democratic National Convention, there were plenty of outstanding speeches given from such speakers as First Lady Michelle Obama, former President Bill Clinton, Senator Cory Booker, Vice President Joe Biden, President Barack Obama, presidential candidate Hillary Clinton, and others. But the two I still remembered a week after the convention was over were those given by Senator Tim Kaine and Khizr Khan, the Gold Star father of a soldier who had been killed in action in Iraq in 2004. The reason those two were memorable was because each did something in his speech that *made* his speech memorable. They took risks—and it worked. But taking risks does not always work, so you need to decide whether you want to play it safe or go for it.

Tim Kaine did a poor imitation of Donald Trump by repeating "believe me" several times to drive home the point that Trump could not be trusted.[13] Even though his speech was bland, and his attempting to do a Donald Trump impression was terrible, it was still quite memorable. It worked, at least for me.

Khizr Khan was joined by his wife, Ghazala, to pay tribute to their son Humayun, who died a hero in Iraq in 2004. Khan was there to point out that they are Muslims whom Trump is trying to ban from coming into this country strictly because of their religion. At one point Khan asked Donald Trump this question, "Have you even read the United States Constitution?"[14] And then he pulled it out of the pocket of his suit and said he was willing to lend it to him. It was very effective and was considered by many to be one of the most memorable speeches ever given at a political convention.

Taking a risk can yield big rewards, but it can make you flame out too. That's why you have to take a risk knowing that you may bomb. And that is exactly what happened to Clint Eastwood when he gave a speech at the 2012 Republican National Convention, when he used an empty chair to represent an invisible President Barack Obama. Eastwood took a risk and it was unexpected, but it left people confused, since it was over the top. The caper "was campaign malpractice that the Romney managers sent out a dithering, clueless Clint Eastwood."[15] Here was a great actor who was incoherent and looked like he was dying on stage in front of thousands in the convention hall and millions watching him on television. When you take a risk, the reward can be terrific, but it can also be tragic.

Examples of Two Famous Memorable Moments

Reagan's Memorable Moment That Won Him the Reelection in 1984

According to many political pundits—if you believe them—Ronald Reagan won the 1984 reelection during his second debate against Walter Mondale, former vice president under President Jimmy Carter, by using a memorable moment when the issue of age came up.

There was considerable behind-the-scenes intrigue that resulted in that game-changing debate performance by Reagan. According to all political analysts and media at that time, Reagan had had a disastrous first debate performance against Walter Mondale. Reagan appeared old and didn't have his "fastball" at the debate. Age had suddenly become a major issue in the presidential campaign.

The Reagan campaign's brain trust was struggling with what to do. That is when political media manager Roger Ailes asked Michael Deaver, Reagan's closest adviser, for access to the president. Ailes said to Deaver, "If you give me that… he'll win. If you don't, he'll lose."[16] Ailes could be so confident, since he had faith in Reagan's communication skills and knew what to do to turn things around quickly. Ailes explained to Reagan that there were five strategies that he could follow for the second debate: attack, defend, counterattack, sell, or ignore. He told Reagan that he had played defense in the first debate and had lost. If he used the same strategy, he would lose again.

Based on what Ailes believed the public expected of Reagan, he offered the president the following advice:[17]

> You didn't get elected on details. You got elected
> on themes. Every time a question is asked, relate it
> to one of your themes. You know enough facts,
> and it's too late to learn new ones now, anyway.

Furthermore, for both the mock debates and the real debate, Ailes told Reagan, "[Go] back to your instincts. Just say what comes to you out of your experience."

Ailes's strategy of "Let Reagan be Reagan" worked well in the mock debates, but when the preparation for the real debate was over, there remained one thorny issue that still had not been broached: age.

Ailes asked Reagan how he planned to respond to the age question, which was surely going to come up during the debate. Reagan said he was planning to use a certain old line he had used before; after hearing it, Ailes was convinced that the old Reagan whom people were used to seeing was back.

During the debate, when the age question did come up, Reagan masterfully delivered the famous line that has been credited with helping him win the election:

> I want you to know that I will not make age an issue of this campaign. I am not going to exploit for political purposes my opponent's youth and inexperience.[18]

Everyone laughed, including Mondale, and the next day the press led with that quote. Reagan was proclaimed the winner of the debate, people were assured that the "Gipper" was indeed back, and they rewarded him with a second landslide win.

We can all learn from Roger Ailes on how to adroitly handle the age issue: attack with humor to defuse it, so you can focus on the job. It worked for Reagan, and I am sure it can work for you. All the preparation paid off, but it had to be executed to perfection with controlled emotion, humor, facial gestures, voice, and authenticity. Reagan had his memorable moment that helped him win the election in a landslide. Does anyone even remember what else he said during the rest of the debate?

Mark McGwire's Unfortunate Memorable Moment

Memorable moments are not always good. Sometimes they can define you in a negative way for the rest of your life. A good example of this is baseball great Mark McGwire, whose career reached its peak when he broke Roger Maris's home run record in 1998. When Major League Baseball learned that he had used steroids, the record was stricken. McGwire had to appear before the House Government Reform Committee to discuss the use of steroids in the majors. He put on a bad performance, since he was determined not to tell the truth. Instead, as he kept on answering each question with the following response, he sounded like someone who had something to hide:

> I am not going to go into the past.... I am here to make a positive influence on this.[19]

This bad memorable moment will probably keep him out of the Baseball Hall of Fame in Cooperstown, New York, since he looked not like a hero but like someone who was lying. Though he did come clean that he had used steroids, the damage had been done. Had he come clean when it mattered, he might have reduced the long-term damage to his reputation. He would have faced short-term consequences for taking steroids, but he would have rehabilitated his image if he had come clean and showed genuine contrition. People tend to be forgiving when you admit you made a mistake, apologize, take full responsibility, and accept the punishment that's due.

What made McGwire's testimony so memorable is that sports athletes are revered and are eventually forgiven if they tell the truth. But when they don't, they are never forgiven. Pete Rose, one of the greatest baseball players of all time, is still not in the Hall of Fame, because he lied, denying that he had bet on baseball games while he was coaching for the Cincinnati Reds. If he had come clean when he was caught, apologized, and took his punishment of being banned from baseball, I think he would have been in the Hall of Fame today. Now I doubt if he'll ever get into the Hall of Fame, though he deserves it based on his performance as a player.

CHAPTER 16

The Performance Hack: Signature Moment

My ambition is to further create a signature sound, a signature spirit, that makes some kind of contribution to music in general.

— David Lee Roth, famous rock star with the band Van Halen

The signature moment not only charges your performance but supercharges it and defines you and your speech. I feel this should come after you are deep into your presentation moment(s) and have moved into your memorable moment(s) and can end your speech with the signature moment.

So, what is a signature moment? Simply put, it is what your audience will remember after your speech, if not forever. You know these famous signature moments: "I have a dream," "Mr. Gorbachev, tear down this wall," "Ask not what your country can do for you, ask what you can do for your country," and so on.

People's attention span is getting shorter because of all kinds of distractions, so it is important for you to get people's attention. Today attention is currency. Whoever gets attention wins in just about anything, including the presidency. The importance of attention to wealth creation has shifted the price of "real estate" today: The most expensive real estate in the world is people's short-term memory, the second most expensive real estate is people's long-term memory, and the third most expensive real estate is the Internet.

To get into people's brain, you need to get into their short-term memory, which unlocks their long-term memory; then they can go to the Internet (or the Cloud) to get more details. Your speech should be structured so that your audience can remember your signature moment, since without that signature moment, your speech will not be remembered, nor is it likely that your message will spread to others.

Think of a signature moment as the key that you are giving people to remember the memorable moments, the message, and even some of the content. Without your providing it, your audience will not have a key (your speech's signature moment) stored in their short-term memory, with which to open up what they might have stored about your speech in their long-term memory. Consider how relational databases work. Someone who wanted to access some personal information about you would need a unique "key," such as your social security number. If the information is not in the random-access memory (short-term memory), then the key could help in accessing it from the hard disk (long-term memory). If the information is not on the disk, the key would enable retrieval from archival storage (the Cloud). Hence, the signature moment embodies the key in people's brain that will help them unlock your speech and its main message.

The hallmark of a signature moment is the way you can challenge your audience. Best-selling authors Matthew Dixon and Brent Adamson discuss how you need to teach, tailor, and take control.[1] You need to teach your audience, making them at least feel smarter; you need to tailor your speech to show them a better future; and you need to take control, so you create that magical moment, your signature moment, where you and your audience see the situation the same way. If you can do this, then you will have created not only a magical moment but a winning speech moment.

Chapter 14 discussed some of the stylistic techniques you can use for a persuasive presentation. There are many techniques, but when you use them at the right point in the speech, the result can be a signature moment.

People generally do not go back to look at their home movies, but they do go back to look at their individual pictures. After seeing it once, they don't see an entire movie again, but they might review clips of memorable scenes. People don't see the replay of an entire game; they review the memorable plays only. Your success in any presentation is going to be remembered not for your entire performance but for the memorable part in that performance. But once you make your performance memorable, you can take it to the next level and create a signature moment.

The signature moment is the climax of your speech, where you take risks and made your audience understand both you and your message. This moment can happen at a specific point during the speech, and if you miss that, then your attempt will appear awkward.

Four Examples of a Signature Speech Moment

When you are delivering your speech (whether one on one, in a small group, or at a podium before many people) and have done everything to win your audience over, but you sense that you have not closed the deal with them, the final thing you can do is to create a magical signature moment. A story, an anecdote, a metaphor, or an analogy can crystallize your thoughts or ideas in a simple way that your audience is more likely to agree with you and later justify their agreement with facts and arguments. You can use this technique during a job interview, a business meeting, or even a speech before a live audience.

The following are four examples that show how this was done by Eric Schmidt of Alphabet, Steve Jobs, Bill Clinton, and John McCain.

Eric Schmidt's Signature Moment to Get Sheryl Sandberg to Join Google

Technology executive, activist, and author Sheryl Sandberg described a famous job interview she had that included a defining moment. Sandberg liked Google but was not sure if it was the right move at that time in her career. She was weighing the decision using a spreadsheet with pros and cons between joining Google and joining a top management consulting firm. When she shared her quandary with Eric Schmidt, Google's CEO, he said something that was the defining moment that clinched the deal for her. He put it to her straight: "If you're offered a seat on a rocket ship, you don't ask what seat. You just get on."[2] After hearing that, Sandberg made up her mind "that instant."

In any high-stakes situation, you need to create a defining moment that will close the deal. If someone has made it with you this far, then you know that a candidate has to be interested and you have to close it out. The best way to do it is by hitting them on the head with a proverbial two-by-four, so they don't think too hard; they just say "yes!"

Bill Clinton's Signature Moment to Get Funding

Bill Clinton's presidential campaign was in deep trouble in 1992 after he lost the New Hampshire primary. The campaign was bleeding money and needed $90,000 to fight another day. One of Clinton's staff members called movie producer Peter Guber to help raise that sum by getting many people to donate the $1,000 maximum that was allowed by the campaign finance rules. Peter Guber wrote about this in his book *Tell to Win*.[3] Before he started calling people for money, Guber wanted to know whether Clinton had a chance to win.

To allay Guber's concerns, Clinton himself got on the line and said, "Hello, Peter, this is Bill." After a long pause, Clinton asks, "Have you ever seen the picture *High Noon*?" Clinton knew that Guber, as a movie producer, would be familiar with this classic western from 1952. It is about a sheriff who prepares to fight a notorious gang that was due to arrive by train at noon. The only person who stood by him to take on the gang against all the odds was a young boy.

Clinton did not need to explain the story; he just said, "Peter, this is *High Noon*." Guber immediately understood. Clinton was looking for Guber to support him like that young boy (Johnny–Town Boy) in the movie against all the odds, to put his credibility on the line to solicit $1,000 donations to help save the day. And it worked! Guber called his Hollywood A-listers and asked if they knew the movie *High Noon*. All of them did, so he said to them, "Well, this is *High Noon* for Bill Clinton." By late afternoon, Guber called Bill Clinton's chief of staff and was happy to tell him, "It's *High Noon*, and you've got your money. Now take on the bad guys and win."

To convey a sense of urgency, Clinton knew that he had to use the right metaphor that would resonate with Guber. Clinton knew a movie producer would immediately get it if he used the movie *High Noon* as the metaphor. Clinton went on from New Hampshire to win the South Carolina primary and eventually the Democratic nomination and the presidency. Without knowing how to use metaphors effectively, it is hard to succeed in just about anything.

Steve Jobs's Signature Moment to Get John Sculley to Join Apple

In any lengthy job interview for an important position, where you have had several meetings and the candidate is still not making a commitment, this technique can work. At this point, you need to create a defining moment where you have to close the deal. According to best-selling biographer Walter Isaacson, Steve Jobs was impressed with John Sculley, who was a rising marketing star at PepsiCo. Sculley liked Jobs but was not sure if he wanted to leave PepsiCo and join Apple. Sculley wanted to be Jobs's friend, and he said, "Anytime you're in New York, I'd love to spend time with you." Jobs did not want a friend; he wanted a commitment from Sculley to join Apple. Jobs, in a memorable defining moment, said to Sculley, "Do you want to spend the rest of your life selling sugared water, or do you want a chance to change the world?"[4] How can anyone refuse when it is put like that, especially by Steve Jobs? The defining moment is a sales moment, but it can work only when you reach a point where you have to make a go/no-go decision.

John McCain's Signature Moment in the 2008 Presidential Campaign

During the 2008 presidential election, a woman confronted candidate John McCain at a Minnesota town hall event with her racist concerns about Barack Obama: "I can't trust Obama. I have read about him and he's not, he's not uh… he's an Arab. He's not—"[5] McCain immediately took the microphone from her and replied:

> No, ma'am. He's a decent family man [and] citizen that I just happen to have disagreements with on fundamental issues and that's what this campaign's all about. He's not [an Arab].

John McCain has accomplished great things in his life, but he will always be known for this signature moment, when he did not vacillate or pander to the audience but did the right thing. McCain could have stoked fear about Obama, but he did not go there. And based on what we saw in the 2016 election, McCain probably could have won if he had played the race and religion cards. McCain did not hesitate, however; he had decided that he would rather lose with dignity than win with disgrace. That day McCain showed that not only was he a war hero and a public servant, but he was also a decent man.

* * *

The most effective winning speech moment is generally closer to the end of your speech. For example, when you watch a sporting event live or on TV, you are more likely to remember a memorable game based on who made the winning shot in the closing seconds in basketball, scored the winning touchdown in football in the last two minutes, or made the winning birdie putt on the seventy-second hole. If you leave your audience with that signature moment at the end, then that is what they are going to remember. And even if that moment is all the audience remembers, then you are more likely to achieve your objective.

The "Smash-Mouth" Public Speaking Approach

The Seattle Seahawks were losing to the New England Patriots by the score of 28–24 in Super Bowl XLIX. But the good news was that Seattle had the ball on New England's one-yard line with the strong running of their tailback Marshawn Lynch. Seattle had two more downs to run the ball in for a certain touchdown and a sure win with one minute left in the game. If Seattle were to get a touchdown, they would become repeat Super Bowl winners. But Seattle Seahawks head coach Pete Carroll decided to pass the ball on the next down, and the ball was intercepted, giving New England a Super Bowl win. According to both football experts and fans, Carroll's decision to pass was the worst call in Super Bowl history.[6]

Now, in football, you can see the score, but often when you are giving a speech, there is no scoreboard. You don't know what "play" to run to win the game. You decide to tell a joke or a story when all you should do is ram the message to the audience and get off the stage fast, not only with an applause from an audience, but with a likely win. My suggestion to you is not to be too cute when the stakes are high. You must focus on the win.

I used the football analogy in the beginning of Chapter 15, to assert that you have all kinds of tools available to deliver a good-to-great high-stakes speech. Humor and stories might be appropriate for other kinds of speeches, where the stakes are not high, and you have the latitude to try different things, but not when you *must* win. I suggest you use the "smash-mouth" speaking approach and get a win.

The word "smash-mouth" is used in football for a style of offense where a team is constituted to run the ball mainly and pass the ball sparingly—that is, smash the other team in their mouths by constantly running the ball right at them. The other team's defense knows what's coming but still can't stop it. Though this style of offense is simple and considered old-school, it still wins games at all levels of play.

So, what is "smash-mouth" public speaking?

Offensive linemen are the content. They are in front to open up holes for the message to penetrate the defense. The running back is the message. He has to get in the end zone. The guy who is performing a drive is the quarterback. But It is the quarterback's performance that controls everything. The success and failure depends on the quarterback's performance to drive the message forward through the content. Using football analogy, you see how content, message, and performance help make a winning speech.

In short, a "smash-mouth" pubic speech is where you have well-organized content, a solid message, an understated performance, and a signature moment. That is what great speeches have looked like throughout history and even today.

Abraham Lincoln's Gettysburg Address, Martin Luther King Jr.'s "I Have a Dream" speech, John F. Kennedy's inauguration speech, and Ronald Reagan's "Tear Down the Wall" speech—to name a few famous historical speeches—used the "smash-mouth" approach.

Note: The speeches, however, don't have to be historical. They can even be in sports. People still remember football coach Herm Edwards's rant "You play to win the game" and former basketball player Allen Iverson's famous rant: "We're talking about practice.... We ain't talking about the game!"[7]

One of the most memorable speeches ever given in sports was by Lou Gehrig when he retired from the New York Yankees because of amyotrophic lateral sclerosis (ALS).[8] It is known as the "The Luckiest Man" speech. It was short and simple with a great opening,

> Fans, for the past two weeks you have been reading about the bad break I got. Yet today I consider myself the luckiest man on the face of the earth.

And he ends it with a great closing:

> So I close in saying that I may have had a tough break, but I have an awful lot to live for.

Today there is a lot of emphasis on using humor, stories, PowerPoint slides, and audience participation. I do not advocate this for high-stakes speeches, though. Woody Hayes, a great coach of Ohio State University football, was once asked why he does not like to pass the ball? His answer: "Three things can happen when you pass and two of them are bad [incomplete and a loss of down, or an interception]."

There are only three things that can happen when you try to be too cute with your speech, and two of them are bad: Your speech will not achieve anything, or it will be remembered for the wrong reason. Before you add anything to your speech, you have to ask yourself if it is going to make much difference. I say it probably won't, and you should leave it out. Getting the content, message, and performance right is a lot of work. You don't want to add more complexity into your speech.

Lastly, why do I include "smash-mouth" approach to public speaking when the common advice you get today is to include humor and stories, to make your speech more entertaining than informative? Personally, if I am investing my time to get smarter, I'd better get smarter. If I want to be entertained, I will see a movie, a play, a sporting event, or stand-up comedy. Entertainment is not my purpose for investing my time attending a speech where my *main* goal is to get smarter in the shortest time possible. I will be prepared, so I don't want you to waste my time telling me a story that I may not relate to and that will make me think you don't value my time and don't know what's important to me. If you are telling stories, it will hurt your credibility with me.

Having said that, however, I do expect you to be interesting. You do have to think carefully about your choices in crafting and delivering your speech and how your audience will react to them. I suggest you include stories if you are well known and that is what the audience is expecting from you.

CHAPTER 17

Wow Your Audience

You have to inspire me!... Tell me what we have to gain!

— Travis Kalanick, cofounder of Uber

I n this chapter, I focus on how your speech can create a great experience for your audience. No matter whom you are speaking to, you want to try to create an experience that they won't soon forget. You may not always succeed, since an audience is unpredictable, but your intention for giving a speech should be to provide a great experience. You have to view yourself as a professional, even though you may not be getting paid to give your speech.

Your speech is all about how your audience perceives you, your message, your purpose, and your authenticity. You need to be an artist who is in command, yet vulnerable, since you are putting it all on the line. You are not going to hold back, since you may never get another shot. You are willing to take the risk to get the reward. You will approach the speech with a winner's mindset. You will learn from the experience, no matter what the outcome is. You want to be on stage, and you enjoy speaking in front of an audience. You are like NBA great LeBron James when you are on the speaking stage. You need to psych yourself out, since no one else is going to do that but you.

To create a great experience, you need to craft a speech, create a message, and deliver a performance that results in your audience spreading your message, making a change, or taking an action. You are creating a great experience for one purpose: You want to achieve your objective for giving a speech.

I know you want to help and serve your audience, but you are also selling when you are speaking. That means that you must have a simple "ask." If you don't ask, you will not get. It is okay to serve your audience, but it is also perfectly acceptable to ask them to buy, by showing them how and what to buy. By this I don't mean asking them to buy a product or service as though you were a salesperson, but asking them to "buy" your ideas, your insights, and, most important, you. If your speech does not achieve your objective, then, in my definition, it was a waste. And you should not ever want your speech to be a waste.

If you are giving a high-stakes speech, you don't want to be "one and done" with your audience. You want to put on the best performance you possibly can, a performance that not only makes your speech memorable but also makes people spread your message and take action.

To create a great experience for your audience, you have to combine three hacks: the content hack, the message hack, and the performance hack. You start with the content hack to put a speech together quickly. If you have time constraints, this is all you will use to put a good speech together. But if you have time, you should develop a message with the message hack and create a performance with the performance hack, using all the moments (presentation moments, memorable moments, and signature moment), thereby creating a winning speech moment.

You may be saying this sounds too simple. Conceptually it is simple, but it takes practice: The more you do it, the better you will be in hacking a great experience. If you use this method, you will be a pro at delivering a great experience in any situation you find yourself. Always remember this: When you are interviewing for a job, you need to know how to get the job first. But to get the job, you need to have the skills to engage, connect, influence, and persuade. To put it bluntly, you need to "wow" your interviewers.

I was once rejected from getting a job at a big company. I felt hurt by the feedback I received from the hiring manager (through a recruiter): I had not "wowed" her. Answering questions had not been sufficient. She was looking for more. Though her feedback hurt, I was glad that it had been honest. I had not created an experience for her to want to hire me. Since it was not "Hell, yes!" it was an easy "No."

Now I want the kind of experience that hiring manager wanted when I am working with someone, so I work hard to provide that experience with the clients I serve. And that principle of excellence applies to speech giving, too. Your audience is like that hiring manager. That is how an audience views experiences today; they want the experience to be good to great.

There is no difference when it comes to social situations. You can't get a second date unless you create a good first-date experience. Also, on a much bigger "dating" scale, you can't be the president of the United States unless you create a good experience for the voters, since people have to put up with a president on TV and social media for the next four years.

A person running for president had better wow the country to get the job. The last three former presidents (Clinton, Bush, and Obama) and the current president, Donald Trump, did exactly that and won. The one stat that media often cites on electing presidents is the beer test, which asks people which candidate with whom people would enjoy having a beer. And the one who comes out on the top in this test usually wins the presidential election. It is a likability test. You have to be likable in anything you do, especially when you are giving a speech. If you are likable, then the audience will pay attention to your content. To sum it up, no matter what job you want in life, you first need to get the job before you get to do the job. And to get the job, you must learn to perform and create a memorable experience. Unless you are working to create a great experience that wows your audience, you are less likely to succeed.

Anyone can create a great experience. You can be young, old, educated, uneducated—whatever. You don't need to be a great actor to create a really memorable experience. You just need to be yourself and serve the audience in way that achieves your objective. If you can do that, you can get your message across to anyone, anytime, anywhere, whether it is one on one, in a small group, or in front of a large audience.

But for many of us who give a lot of speeches, we need a method that is fast, effective, and successful. When the stakes are high, you need to put these three hacks together to deliver a great experience that achieves your objective and does not take too long. That is a tall order, but I know this method works, since I and many others use it when they have to give a speech.

Here is one of the things I tell people I coach for a job interview: Let the interviewer know that what you are looking for, above all, is having a good experience. By saying this, you are letting the interviewer know that he or she had better perform, since you are looking for them to be on top of their game, too. And it works. I have coached people who had no confidence but ended up getting six-figure offers!

People have used this method for interviews, meetings, coaching, sales calls, and formal presentations. Giving a speech is a highly stressful activity. Do not use up a lot of energy on preparation (deciding what to say). Instead, use most of your time for practicing as though you were giving the real speech, so that when you are giving that speech in front of your audience, you can do it flawlessly. The integration of content hack, message hack, and performance hack will help you get energized and to be ready to deliver a good-to-great performance that will create a winning speech moment.

The linchpin of this method is the entrepreneurial philosophy of "iterate fast and release often." You are going to iterate and test until you are comfortable and feel that it will help you achieve your objective. A speech is too important to deliver on a wing and a prayer. The stakes are just too high.

Your Speech as a Startup Product

You can use such traditional frameworks to write your speech as numerical, chronological, problem solution, compare and contrast, modular (break a speech up and isolate around themes), and others. But the framework I think that is most effective is the one that helps you craft a good-to-great experience iteratively and incrementally and improve it based on the feedback or reaction you receive when you test it. This process may take some time at first, but as you keep using it, you will reduce the time it takes in hacking an experience for any situation. This process is essential if you want to take advantage of many high-stakes and high-opportunity situations.

Think of your performance as a startup product that you want customers to buy. In your case, you are using your speech to start some conversation with one person, a few people, or many people. You hope that they like your "product" and will buy it again and also that they will spread the word to others so that they will buy it, too. Think of your speech as a packaged product of ideas that you are going to try to sell to others so they understand it, endorse it, and/or adopt it. If you can't sell your product, you will have wasted a lot of time.

At the least, you want your speech to help you be seen as a thought leader. If you regard your speech as a product that can lead to something big, then you need a methodology that will help you build your speech faster, better, smarter, and cheaper; otherwise, you will not be able to create more speeches and make them better.

Craft your speech performance in three-minute increments, so it is easy to develop and test. For most speeches, this is more than enough time to get your message across. After all, political candidates have to make their arguments during debates in ninety seconds on some of the most complex issues we are facing.

However, if you do have to give a longer speech, you can easily stitch together your short performances into a longer performance—just like they do in the movies. You are both a speech writer, a performer, and a director. When you are giving a speech and want to put on a good-to-great performance, you have to do it all; hence, you need a method that shows how to do it.

"Productize" Your Speech

When you are starting out in anything, product trumps everything. Product trumps any detailed plan. Your speech is your first, and probably the most important, product. We recently saw an evidence of this in the 2016 presidential election. Donald Trump had no discernible detailed plan like what Hillary Clinton had, but it didn't matter. Why? Trump had a solid product—his speech and a great message, "Make America Great Again." He won, defying all predictions by experts prior to the election.

Was it as simple as that? I believe so. *New York Times* journalist, author, and three-time winner of Pulitzer Prize Tom Friedman said it well:

> I'm a big believer [that] people don't listen through their ears. They listen through their stomach. You connect with them at a gut level. They're not interested in the details. [If you] don't connect with them at a gut level, you can't show them enough details.[1]

According to the outcome of the 2016 election, Trump got people in key states to think with their gut. If you can get people to think with their gut when you are speaking, you are more likely to win.

Also, speeches that have stories are very effective as a sales tool. "Stories are products; they can be monetized," according to actor and author Doug Stevenson.[2] In his Google Talk, he told the story about how the founders of Google were able to monetize their story of developing a new search engine: In 1995 Sergey Brin and Larry Page met at Stanford. They soon started to collaborate, and in 1996, they created their first search engine called BackRub. They kept working on it, and a year later, they renamed it Google and discovered that they had an amazing technology. To turn their vision of developing a search engine technology that could find anything anywhere on the web, they needed funding from venture capitalists. They met with Andy Bechtolsheim, one of the cofounders of Sun Microsystems, and after telling him their vision, they walked away with a check for

$100,000. Was their story a product? Yes. That story subsequently gave them the start that eventually made them two of the richest guys in the world.

If you are going to treat your speech as a product, then you have to think like a product manager. Entrepreneur, investor, online marketing guru, and startup enthusiast John Rampton has outlined how a product manager thinks about a product so that it achieves its objectives, especially in light of who are going to be the "customers" of your speech.[3]

- **Start with a clear vision.** What do your customers want to experience from listening to your speech?

- **Understand core drivers.** How are you going to measure the success of your speech? You need to work on your speech until it meets the speech metrics.

- **Get customer feedback.** What are your customers saying about your speech? You need to seek constructive feedback to make the product, your speech, better. You need to focus on the problems that customers are facing. Your speech should define the problems and offer solutions.

- **Brainstorm.** You need to discuss your product with others and get their help to improve it.

- **Set goals.** You need to test all the decisions you are making regarding your product as far as the key message, the opening, the closing, the "tweetables" to include in your speech, and so on.

Unless you think of your speech as a product, you will not view the audience as customers who are looking for a solution to their problems.

Examples of Speakers Who Wowed Their Audience

I will give three famous examples on the three moments (presentation, memorable, and signature) that create a terrific experience. Those moments are why these three speeches get so many views. You should use what they do well when you are speaking in front of a live audience. You want the audience to remember you, your message, and the experience you created.

Amy Cuddy's TED Talk: "Your Body Language Shapes Who You Are"

A great example of how to deliver a great performance is social psychologist and author Amy Cuddy's TED Talk.[4] I don't know how long she worked on this talk, but I would think it must have been close to three hundred hours. I will dissect it to show you what made this a great performance. It is one of the most popular TED Talks ever given—and that is going up against some great talks.

Let's break up her performance into three parts. Her delivery up to the sixteen-minute mark was very good, but that was not something new to her, since she is a tenured Harvard professor who is in her element talking about her research. If she had started concluding her speech at that point, the speech would still have been excellent though not one of the top TED Talks ever given. She was confident in delivering her content and her message that your body can affect your brain on how confident you feel. Her voice was good. Her gestures were good. She was in command and control, and she was passionate about the subject. She seemed authentic. But then the speech changed at the sixteen-minute mark in a way that made it memorable.

There are a lot of great TED Talks, so why does this one stands out? Up to that sixteen-minute mark, it was a fairly

291

functional talk about some research she wanted to describe. She did a good job but not something that would put it into the TED "Hall of Fame" category. What changed? Why is her speech so exceptional?

At the sixteen-minute mark, she began telling a moving personal story for the next three minutes, a story that brought this talk from good-to-great to even inspirational. She even had a signature moment in the speech when she said, "Fake it 'til you become it." It is from that tagline that people know this talk. It made this speech one of the most popular TED talks, and it has transformed Amy Cuddy from being some obscure Harvard professor to a household word for those who are paralyzed by fear when they have to perform, speaking one on one, in a small group, or in front of a large audience. She hit a nerve with the audience, a nerve that only she could hit with her authenticity and credibility. Each audience member was left saying, "She is talking about me."

She was doing this with three things: her story, her controlled emotion, and her authenticity to be vulnerable. Her performance communicated her message. She showed vulnerability, and yet she had a control of her story and the audience with what she was saying. It was one amazing performance.

Amy Cuddy speaking was nothing new. She was a tenured professor who had spoken in front of an audience many times. What made her speech into a performance with a signature moment was what she did at the sixteen-minute mark and went from her being a confident Harvard professor to becoming a vulnerable woman telling her story. And at the end of the three-minute story, she achieved the signature moment with "Fake it 'til you become it." That was an example of a great speaking performance. She was performing, since she was out of her element.

It is like jumping off the plane with a parachute, and for the time being you are free falling and not sure if the parachute is going to deploy and let you have a soft landing. She was brave to get on the plane, put on the parachute, take the leap, and then deploy it, and the result was a soft landing.

Presentation moments from start to finish:

Cuddy was in a "presentation moment" explaining her research of how our nonverbals affect us. She went into explaining how power or the lack of power affects two hormones: testosterone and cortisol.

She was in the presentation moment, presenting the research in an interesting way. If she had concluded at around the sixteen-minute mark, it would have been an excellent speech, but I doubt it would have been one of the top TED Talks.

The memorable moment: From the sixteen-minute mark to the nineteen-minute mark:

She went into her personal struggle to gain the confidence of speaking in front of people.

The signature, or defining, moment: The 19:31 mark:

"Fake it 'til you become it."

What made Amy Cuddy's speech so great?

If I told you that you need to watch this professor from Harvard named Amy Cuddy talk about her research on how nonverbals can influence you, I am sure you would not be too excited to see her live or even watch her video. You would think that she was going to throw all kinds of science at you in a boring way. But you would be wrong.

What made her experience so great for the audience was that she used seven particular techniques: the promise, humor, information, a personal story, a signature moment, a reward, and an ask.

- **A promise.** She started her speech by promising the audience that she was going to show them a no-tech life hack that they could do for two minutes, but she was saving that till the end. If you were an audience member, you would be hooked.

- **Humor.** She then proceeded to use humor to relax the audience, not only demonstrating that she was in command and also making her more likable. People who use humor make others comfortable.

- **Information.** She then went on to take close to fifteen minutes explaining the research on how your body influences your brain. She did this in an interesting way. Now, she could have ended her speech right after explaining the science, but she did not.

- **A personal story.** She then pivoted from what her research was all about to her "why." Why was this research so important to her? She tied her personal story to her research and how it had personally affected her. It was the highlight of the presentation, and she could have ended her talk after that, but she did not.

- **A signature moment.** She proceeded to create the signature moment of her talk when she said, "Fake it 'til you become it." Now she had given the audience the tagline of her speech, something they would not forget. But she did not end the talk yet, because she had not rewarded the audience with the no-tech hack.

- **A reward.** She rewarded the audience by showing them that by doing a simple power pose for two minutes, they could influence their brains to feel more confident whenever they might be in evaluative situations.

- **An ask!** Now that she had rewarded the audience, the last thing she did was to ask them to share this with others who had no access to this information, people who might be suffering from all kinds of anxieties when they were going to be judged. There was nothing more she could do.

The speech was a good speech until she started telling her personal story, and she kept on elevating from good until it moved into the inspirational category; this speech has remained one of the top TED Talks for years. Learn it, study it, and use it. It works!

Steve Jobs's Commencement Address at Stanford University in 2005

Steve Jobs had never given a commencement address in his life, but when he received an invitation from Stanford University to give one, he accepted.[5] Since he was turning fifty and was battling cancer, he was in a reflective, contemplative mood.

But what to say? He sought help from the producer Aaron Sorkin, but then one night, he wrote some personal things he wanted to tell the students. He put something together in a single night, bouncing a few ideas off his wife. What he came up with was simple. He was going to tell the students three stories: First, dropping out of college, second, getting fired from Apple, and third, being diagnosed with cancer. All three stories had a larger message in them. The speech has become a modern classic due to his enduring life lessons. According to Jobs's biographer Walter Isaacson, other speeches

> may have been more important, such as George Marshall's at Harvard in 1947 announcing a plan to rebuild Europe, but none has had more grace.[6]

Presentation moments:

Jobs's entire presentation was to tell three stories to teach an important lesson that he had learned. When Jobs was launching an Apple product, he spoke without notes, but for this formal occasion, he used his written speech, since I think he wanted to follow the words closely. He was probably not that comfortable behind a lectern, but he did a terrific job.

Memorable moments:

There were three of them.

- **One:** The first story was about connecting the dots.

  Lesson: "You can't connect the dots looking forward; you can only connect them looking backward."

- **Two:** The second story was about love and loss.

  Message: "You've got to find what you love. And that is as true for your work as it is for your lovers.... Don't settle."

- **Three:** The third story was about death.

  Lesson: "Your time is limited, so don't waste it living someone else's life."

The signature moment:

"Stay hungry. Stay foolish."

What made Steve Jobs's speech so great?

It is simple. He started by saying to the audience: "Today, I want to tell you three stories from my life. That's it. No big deal. Just three stories." He proceeded to do just that. Since this was a commencement speech, the graduates expected a reward, which in this case was three lessons from his personal life.

Jobs started each lesson with a personal story that he used to teach a life lesson. He ended his speech with his signature moment, "Stay hungry. Stay foolish." The model Jobs used was a little different from Amy Cuddy's; his speech was made up of three memorable moments that included three rewards. It was a simple model, but what made it effective was its honesty and vulnerability in telling personal stories that Jobs had not before discussed publicly in front of a large audience. The speech moved people, and it still moves people and is considered one of the best commencement speeches given in recent history. But when you break it down, the model is very simple and can be used by anyone in any similar setting—even you.

Sheryl Sandberg's TED Talk: "Why We Have Too Few Women Leaders"

Another excellent speech that you can learn a lot from is the one Sheryl Sandberg gave for her TED Talk.[7] I consider Sandberg one of the best business speakers today. In this speech she was masterful in balancing both emotion and logic. In the end, she conveyed a message that was very persuasive.

Presentation moments:

Sandberg started the speech by telling mostly American women that they were lucky to be living in a country that respected civil rights. Then she moved into the problem: "Women are not making it to the top of any profession anywhere in the world."

She told a story about a business meeting she had, where the men there had no idea where the ladies' restroom was, indicating that there had been very few women who had ever been in a high-powered business meeting at that location before.

She then said directly what the purpose of her talk was:

> My talk today is about what the messages are if you do want to stay in the workforce, and I think there are three. One, sit at the table. Two, make your partner a real partner. And three, don't leave before you leave.

Memorable moments:

Sandberg told a lot of stories in her speech, stories that were balanced with the stats she provided to argue her main points. She used stories really well to make her points clear. She weaved stories with stats so that her audience benefited from the emotion of her talk, which helped them pay attention to the stats she provided. Her personal stories helped her connect with her audience. She did something quite clever: She *was* the message!

The signature moment:

Sandberg did not have the same kind of signature moment that Amy Cuddy and Steve Jobs had. But she did have an excellent closing. She ended the speech with the following:

> I want my son to have a choice to contribute fully in the workforce or at home, and I want my daughter to have the choice to not just succeed, but to be liked for her accomplishments.

What made Sheryl Sandberg's speech so great?

Sheryl Sandberg is a great speaker. She had a message and she knew how to get that message across to people in a way that was entertaining, informative, and persuasive. She did so many things well in her speeches that I urge you to study and model your speech the way she put it together.

In her TED Talk, she could have easily gotten bogged down into different areas, but she cleverly avoided them and focused on her main message: why women are not getting to the top and what they can do to fix this. She even mentioned a couple of times in her talk that she was going to stay away from anything that would distract from her main message. The hallmark of a great speaker is someone who can both entertain and make you smarter.

How Much Time Should You Devote to Create a Memorable Experience?

The time you should spend on your speech depends on the stakes involved. If you use this system, then you know that you are taking each speaking opportunity seriously. When you have high stakes, you need a proven method to put your speech together even if you have no access to a speaking coach.

If you are not sure what the stakes are, then the content hack alone will be an excellent way to prepare for an informal speaking opportunity. The content hack takes the least amount of time to get your speech ready. If you need to deliver a persuasive message, then the message hack will help you. If you have a high-stakes or high-opportunity speaking opportunity where you have to perform, then the performance hack will help you prepare for the event. When you put all three together, then you are likely to create a great experience for your audience.

Here are some quick formulas to determine which hacks are appropriate for the speech you are giving:

- **Low stakes or no stakes:** content hack

- **Medium stakes:** content hack + message hack

- **High stakes:** content hack + message hack + performance hack

Evaluating Speeches on the Internet

As you no doubt have noticed in this chapter and the earlier ones, I view a lot of speeches on YouTube. YouTube is a great tool not only for watching speeches but for watching them again and again to learn what the great speakers were doing (and what they were not doing).

In this chapter I took three speeches and broke each of them down, explaining what I think made them work. You can do the same. Another thing I often do is mimic parts of a YouTube speech and see if I can do it as good or even make it better. You need to watch the videos several times, since you must focus on so many elements in a speech, such as the content, the message, the presentation moments, the memorable moments, and the signature moment. Once you start analyzing speeches in depth, you will also be able to start incorporating many of those techniques in your speeches.

Another place to turn to learn how to deliver good speeches are movies. They are perfect speeches. They have to be, since they are professionally done with armies of people. The good thing is that most speeches in the movies are short. They have to be short, so they don't lose people's attention. By watching them, you can learn how to make your speeches crisp, clear, and compelling.

PART FOUR:

The Speech

CHAPTER 18

Assessment and Feedback

It is what we know already that often prevents us from learning.

— Claude Bernard, French physiologist

Y ou need to assess yourself every three to six months, so you know where you are with your goals of becoming and remaining a good-to-great high-stakes speaker and what specific things you need to work on to increase your win ratio.

Remember, the higher you go or the more money you are making, the bar on your speaking skills also gets higher, so you can't afford to get lackadaisical. And as I said earlier in the book, today with YouTube, you can't afford to give a bad speech. You need to be on your "A" game—all the time.

Here are some questions I ask during my quarterly assessment:

- Where are you with your high-stakes public speaking goals?

- What is the "60/30/10" of the improvement you need to make with your public speaking skills? You use the

303

60/30/10 rule so you have three things to focus on, in order of importance and weight.

- Can you confidently speak to anyone, anytime, anywhere and raise the stakes?

- Are you seeing tangible results?

- Are you increasing your win ratio?

- Are you having fun?

You can come up with other specific questions.

You may want to keep this exercise simple, and it may help if you do it with a person whom you have chosen to keep you accountable. Performing this assessment exercise may seem tedious, especially if you are busy, but without it, you may be wasting a lot of time and not make faster progress. But keep your eye on the prize, and constantly evaluate whether you are actually achieving your goals.

Feedback

It's very important to have a feedback loop. Constantly think about how you could be doing things better and questioning yourself.

— Elon Musk, PayPal cofounder, SpaceX founder/CEO, Tesla Motors cofounder/CEO

Feedback is so fundamental to your improvement that I believe you need to learn the skill of obtaining and using feedback before you can improve to being a top-gun speaker. Navy fighter pilots become top-gun pilots not only from constant practice and precise training but also because of the feedback they receive.

Similarly, if you want to become a top-gun speaker, you are going to spend a lot of time on feedback.

Has any colleague or manager ever pointed out to you that you need to improve your speaking skills? I doubt it, since we don't like hurting people's feelings. Unfortunately, we don't have a great boss at work like Sheryl Sandberg, who cares about the people who work for her and is not afraid to use some candor, brutal honesty, and "tough love" with them.

When Sandberg was at Google, she once took Kim Scott, author, entrepreneur, and former executive at Google, for a walk and told her that she needed to improve her communication skills, as described in Scott's blog post titled, "Radical Candor—The Surprising Secret to Being a Good Boss."[1]

Sandberg was clear and direct; she said to Scott,

> You know, Kim, I can tell I'm not getting through to you. I'm going to have to be clearer here. When you say 'um' every third word, it makes you sound stupid.

It worked. It got Scott's attention, and Google got her a speaking coach to improve her communication skills.

To get good at receiving feedback, you have to first become good at giving feedback. Then you have to watch how a person receives your feedback. Receiving feedback is not as simple as it might appear. According to corporate consultants Douglas Stone and Sheila Heen, there is a clash of two human needs.[2] At one end, we want to learn, grow, and achieve, but at the other end, we also want to be accepted, be respected, and feel safe. For feedback from others to help you, you need to first give permission to others, you need to listen, and you need to be willing to get out of your comfort zone. Feedback is very tricky, but it is essential.

But before I give you all the ways you can give and receive feedback, I have to give you my seven rules for feedback so you know this is a critical but rare skill.

The Seven Rules of Feedback

You need to understand that for you to improve, you need to get good feedback. Now, this sounds simple, but it's hard to get good feedback. People are generally not good at this skill. Most of them can't give you feedback that will help you improve; rather, they merely give you their opinion or outlook, which is presented as feedback. They are looking at the situation only from their point of view, rather than evaluating precisely what you need to do to incrementally improve. Most people who give feedback don't understand this, so they can lead you astray if you are not careful.

Note: You can get better only incrementally, so when someone wants you to make a big change, realize that they are giving you their opinion. The following are my rules for feedback, which will help you better understand how to get feedback that is valuable.

Rule number one: Don't give anyone unsolicited feedback, and don't ask anyone for feedback. Instead, learn to become good at giving yourself objective self-feedback. After you become adept at giving solid self-feedback, then you can ask others for feedback if you like.

Rule number two: Avoid asking anyone close to you for feedback, since they are going to be either too critical or too praising. Instead of asking for their feedback, ask for their support. Once you start giving speeches, you will have enough data to know what you are doing well and what you need to improve.

Rule number three: You should ask only for feedback that helps you achieve your overall objective. In fact, ask yourself the following question: How will this feedback help my overall objective? Can you be more specific? How would you do it?

Rule number four: Most people are not good at providing feedback, so you need to be very specific about the feedback you are seeking. Remember, you control the process. What people may often give you is not so much feedback but their opinion or outlook. Feedback is incremental, so solicit feedback that is quickly actionable.

Rule number five: Feedback should help you make your speech better than before. Unless someone can specifically show you how they would make it better, you should politely thank them and ignore their feedback.

Rule number six: The person you are soliciting feedback from needs to put in a lot of time to give you valuable feedback. That is the only way someone can provide the specificity you are seeking so that you can improve.

Rule number seven: Pay for feedback. One of the reasons people get coaches is to get professional feedback from someone who can deliver results. A good coach is worth the investment.

Now that you know my seven rules, let's see how you can make feedback work for you.

Different Ways of Seeking Feedback

Don't Ask, Just Observe

I often prefer this approach, since people often don't have time to give you valuable feedback. Instead of asking for feedback, you can get a lot from how they are reacting to your talk, what kind of questions they are asking, and whether they are engaged. If they are not engaged, then either they are not interested or you are not engaging them. If they are engaged, then they, not you, will drive the conversation. If you have this kind of engagement, then you have done a good job with your speech.

Asking people to tell you at a high level whether your speech was good or not is referred to as *observational feedback*. You can use this method of feedback with anyone, anytime, anywhere. It is the simplest and most direct. You can try to correct your delivery midstream, but it is hard. If you can't correct your speech, then at least learn what you can do better next time. You need to experiment and try different things, to see what works and what you need to change. By giving more speeches, you will keep getting better. You can even ask what the people who are giving you feedback got out of your speech.

Do Self-Feedback

One of the hardest things to do—but something that you need to master if you want to improve—is to *be* your biggest critic. You may want to be open to constructive criticism, but you need to know that assessment first before you hear it from others. According to world-renowned personality expert Tomas Chamorro-Premuzic,

> when you are your own worst critic, you stand a much better chance of developing competence than when you are your biggest fan.[3]

You need to learn to provide feedback to your own speech objectively as best you can so you can improve. But one thing you want to be very careful about is not to aspire to be "perfect"; remember what Voltaire is quoted as saying: *"Le mieux est l'ennemi du bien"* ("The perfect is the enemy of the good").[4] You need to put your speech product out there, and then you can learn from it and make it better. You do have to "ship" the product. If you wait for it to be "perfect," then you will be working on it forever.

When you are giving a talk, the one thing you don't want your audience to say to themselves or to the person sitting next to them, "I have no idea what that speaker is talking about." You'd better ask this yourself, or get feedback from others, before you give your speech. And reassure your listeners that you are open to feedback by asking them to tell you if you are not making much sense. It is better not to make sense when you are preparing than when you are in front of a live audience and the stakes are high.

One thing you need to self-evaluate is the overall flow of your speech. That is, can you discern the outline of the speech from viewing a recording of it? If you can, then you have organized your speech in a way that is easy to understand.

Listen to Yourself

You want to become a good-to-great listener, but do you ever listen to yourself. Before you can become a good listener, you should practice this on yourself. Do what I do, which is to record my ideas on an audio recorder. You can use your smartphone if you don't want to carry a separate device. After recording, listen to what you recorded. You will be amazed how smart you are. You will develop confidence in your thoughts, and you will learn to think better and communicate effectively whether it is with one or many. I recommend this as one habit that can pay off big time for you, and it is easy. You can do it right now before proceeding.

Solicit Appearance Feedback

Consider asking people who you believe may not give you good feedback on the content to focus only on your appearance, such as your body language, your vocal variety, your hand gestures, your intonation, the main idea of your speech, and so on. Do not ask them to give you feedback on anything else. Since you are the one in control and you are the one who needs to do the work to improve, you need to stick to these limits in your request for feedback. If they insist on providing more feedback than you are soliciting and you don't want to upset them, accept the excess feedback politely but ignore it.

Ask Questions

One way to get good feedback from yourself and from others is to ask questions. The questions that some companies want their employees to ask about goals and plans include "Why...?" "What if...?" and "How might we...?" You can adapt this same idea to your speeches.

- You can ask such "why" questions as the following:

    Why am I giving this speech?

    Why am I going with the structure of the speech?

    Why is this topic important to the audience?

- You can ask such "what if" questions as the following:

    What if I showed more controlled emotion?

    What if I repeated things twice that I think are important for the audience?

    What if, instead of doing a Q&A, I ask at the end of my speech what the audience learned?

- You can ask such "how might I" questions as the following:

    How might I increase my presence on the stage?

    How might I sound more in control?

How might I tell stories that resonate with the audience?

To improve as a confident speaker, you need to grab the bull by the horns and ask tough questions. If you want to keep getting better at developing your public speaking skills, you need to be the best student, the best teacher, and the best coach.

Be the "Yes" Person

After you have recorded your speech, or after you have delivered it, look for things that you did well, since you are the only one who can answer that. As organizational theorist Karl Weick said, you need to "argue as if you are right and listen as if you are wrong."[5] If you don't think you did anything well, then you are going to believe people who will tell you what you did wrong. You have to dissect your speech the way a PGA champion golfer can review every shot he or she hit in a round of golf when talking to reporters after winning the championship.

But be the "yes" person if anyone has any suggestions on what you could have done better. Instead of dismissing their thoughts or opinions, check out what they have to say and how they would have done it better. You want to listen to all opinions and thoughts if they can help you become a better speaker, but it is unlikely that they are going to pick up as much as you can from your speech.

Solicit Content Feedback

From those who you feel are familiar with the content of your speech, you may want to ask the following questions: Does the content makes sense? Is it well organized? Did you get your point across in a way that they can take something away? Is the content actionable? What is missing that should have been included? What will the audience be looking for that is not included? What kind of questions will it generate?

Solicit Expert Feedback

Experts are the people who are in the arena getting their butts kicked like you are. You want to give them some latitude in giving you feedback. But first, you need to let them know that you are looking for feedback that will help you make your speech better. It is not enough to tell you what you could improve if they do not show you how they would do it.

In the end, you own your feedback process. You need to decide what you are going to consider and what you are going to ignore, since it is you who has to make the improvement. Again, don't try to be "perfect"; you need to "ship" your art. Until you put it out there, you can't make it better. As best-selling novelist Jodi Picoult once said about writing: "You can't edit a blank page."[6] Similarly, you can't make a speech better until you have had others give you some feedback. If you don't like the feedback, then sit on it awhile before you decide to take any action.

Though someone may be an expert, they are not you. Only you can know what is good for you for achieving your overall objective. Never forget that; otherwise, you will be thrown off your game.

Solicit Negative Feedback

Elon Musk gives good advice about his amazing success in such different fields as e-commerce, automobiles, energy, and space. Besides thinking counterintuitively, he said to "pay attention to negative feedback, and solicit it, particularly from friends." He added that "this may sound like simple advice, but hardly anyone does that, and it's incredibly helpful."[7]

How to Receive Feedback

You need to be ready to receive feedback from others. I have adopted ideas on this from *Forbes* blog contributor Kevin Kruze.[8] Even if the feedback is not what you were looking for, still take it, since you often can't expect people to be good at giving feedback. People often mean well but don't have sufficient tact in providing feedback. Hence, you have to be ready for what they may say. You have to ask questions, so you can determine whether they had given a lot of thought to the feedback they are giving you.

Listen As Though You Could Be Wrong

When you create, you have to act as though you were right. But when you are receiving feedback, you have to act as though you were wrong, so that you will listen actively.

Never Argue, Just Say Thanks

You can't expect people to be always good at giving feedback, or that they will agree with you, so all you can do is listen and end it by saying "thank you."

Evaluate It Later

You may get a lot of feedback when you ask for it. You should write it down and then evaluate later whether it is something you should consider. You should allow some space, so you don't have a knee-jerk reaction and dismiss the feedback right away.

Pay Particular Attention to Negative Criticism

We all like positive criticism, but the feedback that can help you the most is negative criticism, since often your critics may see things that you are not seeing. If you want to improve, do not dismiss this criticism. If your critics have a suggestion for your improvement, that is all to the good.

Be mindful:

Everyone has an opinion, so do not become disappointed if people are being brutally honest with you. You should also reassure your potential critics that you will consider all feedback, so they are free to give you their honest criticism. Since you asked for feedback, you'd better be able to receive it. Also, do not forget to follow up with the people who gave you the feedback so they feel part of the process and feel invested; that way, you can go back to them again for future feedback.

Negative criticism is better than no criticism:

Some people are going to criticize you no matter what you do. You have two choices: listen to them or ignore them. It is hard to ignore these people, since they get such pleasure in criticizing others. If they are so worked up about your speech, then at least they are paying attention. But what is often hard to take are those who are ignoring you. You can ignore your critics, but what do you do when people are ignoring you?

Getting Good Feedback from Reviewing a Video Recording

In real life, you get only one shot to make a good impression, so you need to be on top of your game. A good way to make sure your speech successful is to get good feedback when you make a recording.

When I am asked to provide feedback of a video recording, I do it in three passes. You can listen to just the sound (to the flow of the speech) in one pass, to just the visual (with the sound muted) in the second pass to review your body language, and then review the complete video in the third pass.

Focus on Only One Aspect at a Time

One of the things I have learned is that you don't get good feedback if you are not specific on what kind of feedback you are looking for. If you are lucky to have two people who can provide you feedback, then you need one person to focus only on what you did well and the other person to focus only on what you could improve in. The reason for this is that it is difficult for a person who is giving feedback to do a good job with both.

If you only have one person who can give you feedback, then you probably should focus on what you can improve in. The reason for this is that people are more attentive when they are criticizing. Also, you probably already know what you did well.

The 10-Percent Feedback Approach

If you are at the level of public speaking this book is intended for, the feedback you are looking for will make a very small improvement. I like to refer to it as the 10-percent improvement. But first let me review the a rule that I use when it comes to success: the 60/30/10 rule, which I introduced in Chapters 5 and 6 and am now applying to feedback.

Everyone has some rules they follow for success. I have found that success in anything usually comes down to the 60/30/10 rule. By this, I mean that for anything you do, you need to focus on no more than three things to succeed, and they are not weighted equally. I weigh the first one at 60 percent, the second one at 30 percent, and the third one at 10 percent. This rule has always worked for me, so I am sharing it with you to see if you find it useful.

Many leaders often insist that there is only one thing that matters. But I don't think it is a good idea to get fixated on a single story, just as it is not a good idea to have so many things to think about that you can't make sense out of them. The 60/30/10 principle reconciles the two ways of looking at any problem. I think you will find that 60/30/10 works for just about anything.

The best way to explain a 10-percent improvement is to give you an example of how I gave feedback to an executive whom I had asked to record a three-minute video. Though she is highly successful, she had never before used a video to request feedback on her speech. I asked her to self-evaluate and answer the following two questions: (1) *What did you do well?* and (2) *What could you have done better?*

Here is the answer I got back from the executive for the first question:

> First and foremost, it was a huge step recording the video. I believe I covered a lot of the key issues and did a decent job of transitioning them. I also tried to be relaxed, since I believe it is super important to speak confidently about what I do.

Her answer to the second question was the following:

> A little more confidence, better positioning in terms of where I'm sitting, perhaps make the message a little more compelling, and a solid call to action at the end.

I provided feedback by taking two things that she did well and make that my 60 percent and my 30 percent, respectively, and then I add something new, which she should improve, as the 10 percent. I have found that when the person is confronted with all three things, each of them different, he or she will not do anything. I am interested in 10-percent improvement. Here is my feedback based on the 10-percent incremental approach:

1. Congratulations on taking a huge first step. Now that you recorded the video, it gets easier. You can't stop—no matter how awful you think your first video was. *This feedback makes up the 60 percent.*

2. You did get more relaxed as you got into the speech, and I saw no hesitation or that you were losing your train of thought as you were speaking. You said what you wanted to say in a way that made you look knowledgeable, confident, and likable. *This feedback makes up the 30 percent.*

3. Now that you are strong with the first two, I suggest that you record the next video with the following structure: (A) introduction, (B) problem, (C) solution, (D) outcome, and (E) call to action. *This would make up the 10-percent improvement.*

Then I gave her feedback on how I would do it, so the feedback was specific and actionable:

A. **Introduction:** I am Jay Oza, founder of Hire Smart, where I help companies hire smart (*or something similar to that*).

B. **Problem:** *Get to the point right up front with questions.* Have you hired someone who just did not work out, someone who was negatively affecting your business? *Something that would make the person nodding "yes." (It could be two questions, but no more than two, since then it would come across as though you were an attorney.)*

C. **Solution:** *Talk about one of the areas that could mitigate a bad hire. You could quote some famous CEOs whom you cite in your blogs.*

D. Outcome: *Talk about some personal stories where you helped make a difference based on your experience, knowledge, and insight.*

E. Call to action: Today, you win through Hire Smart. I am Jay Oza. If you would like to learn more about how we can help you hire smart, please check out my blogs, and let's figure out how we can work together.

The executive found the feedback very helpful, and her second video was much better and needed only one more take to get it right.

Why is 10-percent feedback effective?

Some people can't handle negative feedback, so you have a dilemma: You want to help, but you can't help unless they listen to you. According to the behavioral scientist Francesca Gino, people tend to move away from critics who provide negative feedback, especially if it makes them feel bad about themselves. "They do not listen to their advice and prefer to stop interacting with them altogether."[9] People tend to focus on their positive attributes and discount negative ones. But this can be quite costly. "Being aware of your weaknesses and shortcomings—whether you like it or not—is critical to your improvement." So how do you give and receive feedback that is going to help?

Feedback, as I have indicated, is hard, both the giving and the receiving of it. You have to be delicate in how you do it. When receiving, you have to educate yourself how you want it, and when giving, you should focus on the 10-percent approach. You are giving them 90 percent praise, confirming what they already like about their speech. After you agree with what they did well, indicating that that is 90 percent of your assessment, they are more likely to listen to the 10-percent tweak you are asking them to make. It is much easier for people to accept the 10-percent change if you praise 90 percent of what they did. Unfortunately, if you are asking them to make a 100-percent change, then not only are they going to ignore what you are telling them, but they will even stay away from you. In fact, you are going to be blacklisted for feedback. (If you don't agree, ask yourself, whom do you always ask for feedback, and what you think of them afterward?)

Reviewing Your Recorded Speech from Different Perspectives

I provide the following feedback tip to those who are going to be giving the same speech to a different audience. Before you give the speech, you should try to arrange ahead of time how your speech is going to be recorded. You want your speech recorded from the front, with the camera focused on you, but you also want a different perspective, which you rarely ever see: the speech recorded from behind you, with the camera focused on the audience.

You can later review the two perspectives of your speech, preferably in a split screen, showing you what the audience saw and also showing you what your audience did while you were speaking. By looking at the split screen like a football coach analyzing the game film with players, you can see what worked with your speech as you had planned it as well as what did not work with the audience you were speaking to. This is something you should do as part of your post-speech analysis to improve. Otherwise, you'd better be a great speaker, or you will not be an effective high-stakes speaker. You (or you with your speech coach) need to go through this the way football coaches do to compete and win. The plays in football are successful because the players studied films of what they were doing. Similarly, you can win with a high-stakes speech by reviewing your speech performance, viewing both yourself and your audience.

Self-Coaching

I coach people so they can win and not to make them dependent on me. I usually coach people who are performing but are not yet winning. I believe that before you look for a coach, you have to learn to self-coach. Unless you are already performing, getting a coach is likely going to waste your time, money, and energy.

There are ten simple steps you can use to coach yourself to become a good-to-great high-stakes speaker: knowing, saying, having, doing, repeating, learning, improving, executing, performing, and winning. I use myself as an example related to public speaking, a skill that I am constantly working to improve.

- **Knowing:** I know what I have to do to become a good-to-great high-stakes speaker, which I cover in this book. Since I wrote the book, I can confidently say I know what I am doing.

- **Saying, or understanding:** Since I wrote the book, I understand what I have to do to improve, so there is no gap between knowing and saying for me.

- **Having, or possessing**: Do you have the basic skills to become a good-to-great speaker? I have many of the skills based on my experience, but I could use voice and acting lessons. But I am not sure how much better it will make me as a speaker, so those lessons are not on my priority list right now.

- **Doing:** I have ample proof that I am practicing speeches by recording on YouTube. I record many speech-tip videos, and I do a weekly YouTube show called *Speech Talk Live*.

- **Repeating:** Public speaking has become a habit, so I am certainly repeating it.

- **Learning:** I am constantly learning by practicing, speaking, mentoring, and coaching. I am also reading books, viewing videos, and interviewing many professional speakers.

- **Improving:** Through deliberate practice, I strive to improve my public speaking skills.

- **Executing:** Today I don't have a problem executing without an audience or in front of a safe audience. I practice this by doing many videos.

- **Performing:** I can perform in front of an audience. In fact, as I have gotten better, I look forward to speaking in front of an audience. I have developed sufficient confidence through practicing that I can perform in front of an any audience, anytime, anywhere.

- **Winning:** I have increased my win ratio as I have become more focused. The thing I am working on is speaking in front of a larger audience and in a corporate environment.

These are the ten steps you have to focus on to self-coach yourself in public speaking or in just about anything. You don't need a coach to do these ten steps. You can do it yourself. In fact, you should do this before you know what kind of targeted coaching you might need and how a coach can help you win. Then you should work with the coach incrementally. Avoid any coach who has a dependency coaching practice. You are coachable only if you can coach yourself well but have hit a wall in your performance.

I think a coach can help you only if you are executing but not performing, which I call level-1 coaching. Level-2 coaching will take you from performing to winning, and level-3 coaching will take you from winning occasionally to winning consistently. Hence, level-3 coaching is the ultimate in coaching. A good example of this was Butch Harmon, Tiger Woods's coach when he was so dominant that his ranking distance in points was greater to the second-ranked player than that player was to the one-hundredth-ranked player. That is sheer dominance that we are unlikely to see in golf for the foreseeable future. Another coach who has done that in team sports is Bill Belichick of the New England Patriots in the National Football League (NFL). Coaching is needed to increase your performance and winning to remain competitive in just about anything, especially in public speaking.

CHAPTER 19:

It's Speech Time!

The reporter asked, "Why did you play so hard?"

"Because there might have been somebody in the stands today who'd never seen my play before and might never see me again."

— Joe DiMaggio, one of the greatest baseball players, who played for the New York Yankees

You have worked long and hard to get on the stage. You have prepared well for this speech. It's just you and the audience now. Your first job is to capture and keep your audience's attention; your second job is to achieve your objective. If you can do both, you win.

You probably don't feel you are ready, but that's okay. At some point, you have to say **"Done is better than perfect."** You are never going to be completely satisfied with your speech. You are just going to run out of time. The deadline has been set. You can't get out of it. You have to deliver it. It's time to psych yourself out and have fun. This chapter is to help you get your speech done. To help you, I provide a checklist that you can use to start preparing your speech from start to finish. I would recommend you review the checklist before working on the speech.

According to Amy Cuddy, whenever you have an opportunity to speak to someone, to a group, or to a large audience, you should take it. If you don't capitalize on it, you may not get another opportunity.[1] That one moment comes and goes fast. You need to be prepared and ready to deliver. If you aren't prepared and ready, only you are going to know that you did not take the shot that was available to you. You can rationalize, but the fact is that you whiffed when you had a chance. Here is one stat that is hard to argue with: You have a zero chance of making the shots you don't attempt, and that is true in sports, relationships, friendships, business—anything. Giving a speech is no different.

The difference between success and failure in pulling off a speech hit comes down to how you accomplish a lot in the little time you have. You need to follow the 80/20 rule—also known as the Pareto Principle, which states that 80 percent of the effects come from 20 percent of the causes—so you focus on what is important that will generate the biggest payoff.

Perhaps you just don't have time to write a good speech and practice a lot. You may be busy and have other things that are taking priority over working on a speech; therefore, your speech will achieve little, if any, of your overall objective. The speech is not ready for prime time, but the only person who often does not know this is, sadly, you, the speaker.

Suppose you came to me and say, "Jay, I have a speech to give in a week. What should I do?" First, if you just have a week, and if the speech is a high-stakes, a high-opportunity, or a high-risk speech, then you need to focus only on this speech and nothing else. If you don't prepare hard and well, then the speech will be a high waste of time for you and for your audience.

- A **high-stakes speech** is one where you are going to either win or lose. This could be a sales presentation, an ad pitch, or a job interview.

- A **high-opportunity speech** is one where you are not going to lose anything, but it could lead to a huge opportunity. This could include an informative speech at a conference, an impromptu speech, or an interview.

- A **high-risk speech** is one where you are not going to win anything, but you could lose a lot if you don't do it well. The most common high-risk speech is one that you give in private, such as a speech at a wedding or a private meeting.

- A **high-waste-of-time speech** is, unfortunately, one where you don't care and are just going to wing it. The audience will notice how bad it is, but out of politeness they will often not tell you that you gave a terrible speech.

Second, to handle the stressful situation of giving a speech, you need a checklist to make sure that you and your speech resonate with the audience. I have a short checklist if you are time-constrained and a long checklist if you have plenty of time. If you are time constrained, then you should go through the first eight items on the list; however, if you have a lot of time, then go through the entire list to be well prepared and well rehearsed.

The following is the complete checklist that I use for delivering a speech. It contains a lot of items, but you can decide which ones are important to you after the first eight (and the result of your paring down would be the "short checklist"). I credit two sources for the idea behind this checklist: Atul Gawande's *Checklist Manifesto*[2] and Chris Vander Mey's *Shipping Greatness*.[3]

Speech Checklist

☐ **Ensure that you can make a six-year-old understand your speech.** If you can't make a six-year-old understand your speech, you are in trouble. People have a very short attention span. This exercise will show how well you understand your speech. I cover this in more detail in Appendix A.

☐ **Write a press release of your speech ahead of time.** Your press release should address the following items: What is the speech titled? When are you giving it? Whom is it for? What is the big idea? What evidence supports the big idea? What do you want the audience to say about your speech afterward? A press release is a crisp summary of what, when, and why from the audience's perspective. You can write this press release after writing an outline, but make it no more than four or five short paragraphs (or about five hundred words).

☐ **Write a sales letter of your speech.** You will have to sell your speech. I suggest you use the "PASTOR" method advocated by communications strategist and best-selling author Ray Edwards.[4] The acronym breaks down this way: P is for problem, A is for amplify (the result of not solving the problem), S is for solution, T is for transformation, O is for offer (in your speech this is your key takeaway), and R is for response (in your speech this is your "ask").

☐ **Create a "Frequently Asked Questions (FAQ)" list.** You include in this list every question that comes to your mind as you are preparing for your speech. This is something I do for each speech, blog, or book that I am working on.

☐ **Determine what job the audience needs done with your product (your speech).** While you are preparing your speech, the "jobs theory" question described by Clayton Christensen et al.[5] will make you ask what outcome the audience is hiring your speech for. What progress do they want to make? By addressing this question, you won't overshoot what the audience needs in your speech.

☐ **Raise the stakes pre-speech; lower the stakes during the speech.** To give a good-to-great performance, you need to raise the stakes during your preparation and rehearsal but lower the stakes and expectations during the speech itself. You have done everything to do a great job, but now it is out of your control, so go have fun and enjoy the experience.

☐ **Anticipate the five regrets of not achieving your overall objective (your "pre-mortem").** You'd better know ahead of time "why your speech failed," so you can avoid it actually failing. (1) You did not practice or rehearse well. (2) You did not know the audience well. (3) You did not focus on your performance. (4) You did not exude confidence. (5) You did not play to win.

☐ **Take chances to avoid being boring.** People will forgive you for a lot of things, except one: being b-o-r-i-n-g. If your content is not to their liking, your audience had at least better be entertained. That will make them stay till the end. But being boring will not, and it shouldn't.

The foregoing are the only eight things you absolutely need to address (the short list), but the following items should be reviewed if you are not time constrained and want to cover additional aspects to increase your chances of winning.

☐ **Ensure that your speech will make your audience feel good about themselves.** Happiness is tied to this item, since you must make the audience feel good. If they feel good, then they will come up with all kinds of reasons to like you, your message, and your content.

☐ **Determine your "WHY."** *New York Times* best-selling author Simon Sinek explains: "By WHY I mean what is your purpose, cause, or belief?"[6] So answer this question first, so you know it before you go any further with your speech.

☐ **Determine your overall objective.** You need to know the endgame for giving a speech. Here is the coaching advice that TED speakers receive: **Start with the end.**

☐ **Determine your "ask."** You need to ask it either in the beginning or at the end, or both, but you *must* ask, preferably with a purpose.

☐ **Determine your target audience.** You need to know who your audience is so you can tailor your message and predict their response with high accuracy. If you don't know your audience well, then your speech is not going to resonate with your audience and result in a win.

☐ **Determine the 10 percent you want your audience to remember.** Focus on the 10 percent you want people to remember from your speech, since according to research, they will forget 90 percent of your speech, and—unless you take care of this—the 10 percent they do remember may not be what you want them to remember.

☐ **Plan to speak to your audience's experience.** You need to know your audience's experience so you can resonate with them. For example, if you are a male speaking to a female audience, you may want to avoid excessive football metaphors unless you know for sure that the female audience loves football.

☐ **Determine what your BIG idea is.** You need to be clear on this, since this is something the audience should take away from your speech. You should have a tagline for the speech that you can repeat as needed throughout.

☐ **Determine why the audience should listen to you.** Often credibility is 90 percent of the game, and that's why great speakers are so successful. Establish your credibility early in the speech so the audience pays attention to all of it.

☐ **Determine why the audience should care about your speech.** What is in your speech for the audience to care about? You need to appeal to their self-interest. Will they want to make a change as a result of what you say? Will what you say help them make the change? You need to answer these two questions.

☐ **Determine what you want the audience to do.** You'd better have someplace for the audience to get more information, spread the message, or take some action.

☐ **Anticipate some objections to your content and message and be able to address them.** You need to know the opposing view so you can be proactive in handling questions during a Q&A session. You may not want to address objections during the speech itself, though, since your job in a speech is to show why you are right.

☐ **Determine what the key takeaway is for the audience.** Know the one thing you want the audience to remember at the end of your speech.

☐ **Determine what your opening, transitions, and closing sound like.** You need to get off to a good start so your audience will pay attention. You need to end strong, since often the last thing you say leaves a lasting impression. Lastly, make sure that your transitions are smooth.

☐ **Know the dress code for the event.** Though this is a no-brainer, you need to know the event's dress code. If you can't find out ahead of time, it is better to overdress.

☐ **To ensure success, determine the ultimate question you want to ask your audience.** If your speech is a persuasive speech, the ultimate question would be: Was the speech persuasive? Yes or no? If the speech is informative, the ultimate question would be: Did the speech make the audience smarter? Yes or no? By answering either question, you are doing a pre-mortem; you want to know ahead of time so you can make fixes rather than doing your fixes during a post-mortem, when it is too late for this speech.

☐ **Determine how you would rate your speech if you were in the audience.** Self-evaluate your speech. What do you like about it? What do you need to improve?

☐ **Ask yourself if you are excited with the opportunity to give a speech.** Let your audience know—by showing rather than telling—how happy you are to be speaking in front of them.

☐ **Know your stuff cold.** All bets are off if you don't know your material cold. The first advice Gary Vaynerchuk offers on his blog is to "stick to what you know," adding: "As long as you stick to your personal experience and expertise, you can have the confidence to go up and talk about your insights."[7]

☐ **Do not overthink your speech structure.** Just use Aristotle's technique: you tell the audience what you are going to tell them, you tell them, and you tell them what you told them. Why? This technique will show that you have your stuff together and that you can get stuff done—that you can pick a structure that will make your speech clear to your audience.

☐ **Plan to finish your speech five minutes before the allotted time is up.** Suppose you are allotted forty-five minutes. When you practice, try to make your speech about thirty-five minutes long, since you are likely to go over.

☐ **Romance your points.** This tip comes from Brian Tracy, famous self-development author and motivational speaker.[8] Instead of cramming a lot of information in your speech, tell stories and give examples on a few points. Do not exhaust your audience. You want to leave with them wanting more, not stuffed.

☐ **Remove stuff.** This is another great tip from Brian Tracy. You get to decide what your audience needs to know. This is addition by subtraction. Err on the side of taking things out. (Your audience will not know that you removed stuff.)

☐ **Get your audience to act before, during, and after your speech.** You are in the business of winning a speech, not giving a speech. To accomplish this, you need to get the audience to act at least three times. First, before they come to your speech. This could be having them watch a short (or long) video. Second, you need to get the audience to do something during your speech, such as trying to guess something or write down something important. Third, you need to get them to do something after you give the speech. This could be going to your website to get your checklist or a short guidebook on your topic. It is better to get the audience to act than to just listen. Listening to your speech is good, but getting them to act is better.

☐ **Feel good, look good, and smell good.** You need to look good, meaning wear good clothes. I like to wear a blue jacket, which I can always take off if the temperature gets a little warm. You need to smell good, meaning take a shower, put on a nice cologne, and, lastly, make sure your breath smells good. How many times have you gone to a speaker after their speech and they have bad breath? If the person has bad breath, that is the only thing you are going to remember. Also get a lot of rest, so your energy is high during the speech and a short time after the speech so you can engage with some of the audience members.

The following are areas that you should focus on during the speech:

☐ **Be excited.** If you are not excited, your audience will also not be too excited to listen to your speech. Get them on your side right away.

☐ **Be energetic.** People may hate your speech, but if you show some energy, they will at least say that you were very energetic throughout the speech. Make sure you are under control, however, since you don't want to look like an energizer bunny.

☐ **Look as though you have done it before.** Though you may not be a pro, once you are on the stage, you belong there—so act like it. Say thanks and get to the speech.

☐ **Make sure your audience knows you before your speech.** Record a short ninety-second video and make it available to the event coordinator and put it on YouTube and your website before the speech. Make sure you have control over the content of what the person introducing you says, and don't assume that the introduction will be done well.

☐ **Breathe and enjoy the experience.** Take a few deep breaths so you have your breath under control before you begin speaking. Do a power pose if it loosens you up and gives you confidence. You also may want to listen to some upbeat music or some stand-up comedy routine so you go in with a good frame of mind.

☐ **Make sure your voice is under control, and speak clearly. And don't forget to take strategic pauses.** When people are nervous, they tend to speak faster and raise their voice up as much as an octave. You can vary your speech, but make sure your voice is under control throughout the speech. And breathe.

☐ **Show that you are having fun and that you want to be there. Show it with your words, with your body language, and, most important, with your smile.** If you are tense, your audience will become tense. You need to show that there is no other place you would rather be than in front of the audience, since you have something important to say.

☐ **Remember President Lyndon Johnson's famous quote before you start: "Power is where power goes."**[9] You've got the power. Be powerful. Be the CEO of the stage. The audience is ready to follow, so lead them to where you want to take them.

☐ **Don't forget to tell the audience where they can get more information and can stay in touch with you.** Your speech may be over, but now you have to turn the audience into your followers. Don't be in a hurry to bug out after a speech. You want to stay and meet with people. Also, you have to shift to marketing by providing ways they can get more information about you.

Here's what you need to do after your speech:

☐ **No more than ten to fifteen minutes after the end of your speech, do a quick self-evaluation.** You need to do this soon after you are done speaking, so it is fresh in your mind.

☐ **Document your experience in developing and delivering the speech, so that you can learn from it.** Documenting is important, so you have a history of something you want to be good-to-great at.

☐ **Determine whether you achieved your overall objective.** What was your expectation of the speech? What was the outcome? What do you need to do to have a better outcome?

☐ **Save the checklist that you used for assessment.** You should fill out the checklist for every speech you give, so you can use it to learn and assess your speaking skills. You want to get better every time you give a speech.

☐ **Celebrate and reward yourself.** Congratulations! You created winning speech moments!

CHAPTER 20

We Are All "Professional" Speakers Today

This is the big leagues. These are the best in the world. Everyone is prepared, and everyone can hit.

— Aroldis Chapman, 105-mph pitcher for the New York Yankees

Before I close this book out, I want you to think of yourself as a professional speaker. And if you develop and master your speaking skills, you are more likely to become a highly paid professional speaker. And if you offer high value when you are speaking and want to unshackle yourself from a steady corporate paycheck, then you can even go out on your own and become a paid speaker.

Though you and I may never make the kind of money that is made by Barack Obama (now that he is former president) when we give a speech, nevertheless, we all are professional speakers. You may not think of yourself as a professional speaker unless you are being paid a big fee to give a speech. But think about it now: What do you do mostly at your job? When you interview for a job, you are hired because you can speak the job, not because you can do the job. Companies will not know whether you can do the job well for some time. Did people elect Donald Trump because he can do the job or because, better than any other candidate, he spoke about his doing a great job? If you don't speak the job well, you will not get a chance to do the job, even if you would have been good at doing the job. Conversely, if you *do* speak the job well, you will have the best chance to do the job, even if you are not good at doing the job. How do you think so many incompetent people get good jobs?

If speaking is not that important to your job, then you can easily be replaced by machines. Machines don't get many jobs, however, because they cannot speak the job. To be relevant, you have to think of yourself as a professional speaker, meaning that your employer is going to pay you a good salary because you speak well and a lot. If you speak well, then your employer and others will give you the benefit of the doubt that you can do the job well too.

Here is Daniel Pink's expanded definition of sales: "Like it or not, we're all in sales now."[1] I agree that we all are selling something, though we may not carry the title of salesman or saleswoman. Likewise, I will here expand the definition of a professional speaker. If we are all in sales now, then you can't be successful without speaking well. **You speak to sell, and you sell to win.** Therefore, you are a professional speaker now—and you'd better think that way to be successful.

Rush Limbaugh, Megyn Kelly, Oprah Winfrey, Tony Robbins, Dr. Phil McGraw, Michael Strahan, the Kardashians—all are professional speakers, because they get paid a lot of money to speak.[2] They all make money because of their speaking skills. We see or hear them only when they are speaking. There are others who probably help them prepare, but no one knows who these people are, since we don't see them speaking on radio or TV.

Your success in whatever you do is predicated on how many people are interested in listening to you.

Athletes need to speak well to do pregame and postgame interviews, as well as to secure endorsements. Retired athletes who speak well typically earn more than those who don't. Speaking opens up all kinds of opportunities for them. The late great golfer Arnold Palmer was an excellent example of an athlete who pioneered how athletes could leverage their fame to make millions, even after they retire. Michael Strahan is another great example, considering how well he has done after retiring from football; he is now a cohost on ABC's *Good Morning America*. Musicians have to speak well to get people to attend their concerts. Actors have to speak well to get people to see their movies or TV shows. Are they all professional speakers? They'd better be, since if they can't sell, they are not going to be making millions.

Media companies don't put people on radio and TV and pay them tremendously high salaries unless they are generating a lot of revenue through advertising. Rather than emulating only TED Talks or Google Talks speakers, you should also follow these successful radio and TV professional speakers. They are very good at speaking, and they know how to make a point quickly, often in an entertaining way.

How Can You Become a "Professional" Speaker?

Today you have so many tools to become a "professional" speaker. You can do a YouTube show, for example. In the beginning, your recorded speech may not be that good, but not only will you get better and focused, but you will start gaining a following. Still, you have to be patient and hone your skill. I don't make money from my YouTube show, but it helps me produce content, and I use it to market my speaking, consulting, and coaching business. Hence, my show is very important, enabling me to grow both personally and professionally.

Google has made it easy for you to create your own show on YouTube. Just open a Gmail account. You can then go into YouTube and either start a Hangout live or schedule one. You can create an agenda and start the broadcast. My show lasts between forty-five and ninety minutes. You can determine how long you want to talk on the Hangout. After you end the broadcast, Google will place the recording on your YouTube channel. You can then edit it with annotations, cut out portions of it, or create additional videos. Once you have the videos, you can then promote them on social media. Then you can prepare for the next show. With your Gmail account, you can record videos for free using Google Hangout, or you can upload your videos. Today there are no excuses to not develop and master your public speaking skills.

You will then be the star of your own channel! You will be a "professional" speaker. Take a look at one of the episodes of *Speech Talk Live* to see what I have done. As you can surmise, there are just two chickens and a pig in Idaho watching my show right now, but I can say that I have my show on YouTube. I am the star of my show.

Next time someone asks you what you do, if you are a professional speaker, you can proudly say, "I speak for a living." And you would be right!

Does giving a lot of speeches make you a better speaker?

Many speech experts say that if you want to get better, you should give a lot of speeches. I do not subscribe to this theory. Yes, giving a lot of speeches will make you more *confident*, but it is not necessarily going to make you a good-to-great high-stakes speaker. A good-to-great high-stakes speaker presents some insight that captures the audience's attention, makes them smarter than before, and moves them to action.

Typically, when you give a lot of speeches, they tend to become routine, sort of like the stump speech a politician gives when he or she is running for office. The bar is often so low that if you are a confident speaker, you may not have to be that good at speaking. However, sooner or later your mediocrity will catch up with you. To remain a pro, you have to practice a lot in private. Most great professional athletes or entertainers are probably performing 1 percent of their time and practicing and rehearsing 99 percent of their time. I didn't realize how much the great ones practice till I came across what put Jerry Rice, who played wide receiver for the San Francisco 49ers, into the Pro Football Hall of Fame.

What Makes Someone a "Professional" Speaker?

Someone is a pro because not only can he or she get the job done, but he or she can do it better, cheaper, faster, and smarter than others. But it takes years to become a pro at anything. I learned this the hard way by playing two sports that I never became good at. One was tennis. I was a very good practice player but a terrible game player. Why? I did not have a good second serve. So I gave up tennis and moved to golf. I didn't become good at that either. Why? I could not make the putt between four feet and eight feet of length with a higher percentage to lower my score. So I lost interest and gave up golf.

When it comes to public speaking, there is an amateur way and a professional way. A real good amateur will spend time on his or her speech as follows:

- **Content:** 60 to 100 percent

- **Message:** 0 to 30 percent

- **Performance:** 0 to 10 percent

But a professional speaker does something completely different. A pro has been working on his or her craft for a long time so when preparing a speech to give, he or she spends time as follows:

- **Performance:** 60 percent

- **Message:** 30 percent

- **Content:** 10 percent

A pro spends little time on the content because he or she will give similar speeches with slight changes to the content to keep it fresh but will rarely start a new speech on a completely new topic. A pro is unlikely to take too many risks especially if he or she is getting paid. If the pro is a politician or a business leader, then he or she is probably going to have speech writers and coaches for assistance. Dealing with a new topic, of course, the pro will allocate plenty of time for all three hacks for that first speech. As you get mastery, you will know how much time you need to spend, but you need to measure this; otherwise, you could end up wasting a lot of time.

The pro knows that winning is all about performance. When you are watching a great actor or a TV personality, think about how much time they are they spending on the content, how much on the message, and how much on performance? They are on TV or stage mainly because they are good-to-great performers.

While you are developing your skill, you will naturally follow the 60/30/10 distribution like an amateur; however, as you develop mastery and are giving a lot of speeches, you will follow the 60/30/10 like a pro.

To be a good-to-great high-stakes speaker, you need to be a student, a teacher, and a practitioner of speaking. You need to be a speaking athlete. Sports athletes spend most of their time practicing and less time playing. You have to do the same when it comes to speaking. Without that constant practice, dedication, and discipline, you are not going to grow as a speaker.

Be a speaker athlete! Grow stronger every day!

CONCLUSION:

Let the Journey Begin!

Some say it takes a village to raise a child, but in my case, it took a village just to get the child out of me.

— Sheryl Sandberg, COO of Facebook

If I got this far, it means I did it. I am a first-time author. Along the journey, I learned an important thing that makes this project worthwhile: When you create something, you start feeling younger and more relevant. You will start feeling good if creation is your ultimate reward.

When I started thinking about this book, my objective was to learn about public speaking, since it is so fundamental to our success in life, love, and business. The one thing we don't measure in life and at work is how much money we save or make, or how much we enjoy life, because of good communication. I want you to start paying attention to this, since you could lose a lot of money, or not enjoy your life as much as you should, because of bad communication, whether one on one or with many.

Many people don't succeed, because they have not developed and mastered their public speaking skills. To make matters worse, they don't even know the reason for their lack of success, and they continue to struggle, they become frustrated, and they eventually give up. But after spending several years learning, teaching, coaching, practicing, and assessing public speaking, I decided that I had to share my ideas about public speaking and my method with others so they can benefit and start their own speaking journey, if they haven't already.

I hope that you now know how to create winning speech moments with anyone, anytime, anywhere. You first have to become a confident speaker by mastering the content hack. And then you can move to the message and performance hacks to become a good-to-great high-stakes speaker. And through deliberate practice, you will be able to easily create winning speech moments when you speak—all the time. This is a long journey, but you are on your way, and if you persist, I know you are going to get there soon.

Writing this book has been both fun and painful, and I am a little sad that I have come to the end of this book's journey. Since I love learning, that part was a lot of fun. But when you are learning, you start thinking. And thinking means you have to put your thoughts into words that make sense to others. And that can be draining. After getting to this point in my first book's journey, I have a deep respect for those who write books. Soon I will find out what it feels like being a published author. For now, I am happy to be finished with this book. At some point you have to say what Mirjana Lučić-Baroni, professional women's tennis player, said in a courtside interview after she made it to the quarterfinals at the 2017 Australian Open:

> F*** everything and everybody who ever tells you can't do it. Just show up and do it with your heart.[1]

I am done here, but I hope you are inspired to speak well and perhaps even write a blog or a book about public speaking or anything else. Remember, you are "uniquely unique," and there are people out there only you alone can reach with your voice and passion. What are you going to do to help them? I look forward to seeing you on Instagram, LinkedIn, Twitter, YouTube, and my website.

If this book has helped you in any way, then all I want from you is a brief mention of *Winning Speech Moments* in your book, your blog, your Facebook postings, and, of course, your great Amazon review. That will be my greatest reward from you. If you got this far, then you are definitely concluding your speaking journey successfully. Since we both have to get back to our speaking career, I will close with what I think *Toy Story*'s Buzz Lightyear would say if he had written this book: "To creating winning speech moments... *and beyond.*"

Good luck!

Learn to Deliver Your Speech to a Six-Year-Old

If you can't explain it to a six-year-old, you don't understand it yourself.

— Albert Einstein

In the movie *Margin Call*, a risk analyst discovers that the Wall Street firm he is working for is so heavily leveraged that it is likely to get wiped out if the markets turn against the company's current positions. The situation is so dire that the company executives had to set up an emergency meeting in the wee hours of the morning to come up with a game plan. During the meeting, the CEO, played by Jeremy Irons, wants to understand what is going on and asks the risk analyst a very important question that we can learn from when we are trying to explain what is complex:

> Maybe you could tell me what you think is going on here. And, please, speak as you might to a young child or a golden retriever. It wasn't brains that got me here, I can assure you that.

Okay, you may say this is just a movie. But who do you know that makes a six-year-old understand better than anyone? Yes, you probably guessed it: Donald J. Trump. One of the main reasons I believe Donald Trump has been so successful in politics is that he can make a six-year-old understand him better than anyone. And if a six-year-old can understand you, then you can be assured that any member in your audience will understand you. Bringing his speech down to a six-year-old's level worked in Trump's case. Trump keeps his speeches so simple for his supporters that it makes them feel as though he were one of them—even though he has very little in common with them.

I want you do this simple exercise before you work on your speech. It is simple, but it's one of the most important exercises you will do in this book. You don't need to prepare for this simple exercise.

As you know when you are speaking, it is all about your audience. You have to take yourself out of the equation and focus on making others smart. The following exercise will help you make others smart:

1. Pick something complex that you want to talk about. It could be just about anything—big data, quantum computing, a Supreme Court decision, a negotiating tip, a sports strategy, a marketing or sales principle—whatever.

    You can think about it for few minutes if you need to.

2. Explain the complex topic to a fictitious or, perhaps, even a real-life six-year-old so that he or she understands what you are saying and can explain it to others. If you can explain something to a six-year-old, then you can explain it to a C-level executive when the stakes are very high.

This simple exercise is all about ensuring that your audience understands you and can make others understand you through them. After you explain the topic, you are out of the picture. You have taken the training wheels off your idea so that people feel confident that they can make others understand it. If you can make your audience feel smart, then you will have succeeded.

Why Do This Exercise?

The foregoing exercise can save you when you are giving a speech. Here is a simple reason.

When you are giving a speech, you know your stuff cold, so you lose track of the fact that your audience may not know the topic the way you do, or that they may know little to nothing about what you are talking about. You might then create and deliver a speech that will impress them on how smart you are, but the speech will not make your audience smart. Hence, they will not spread the message or act.

If you can't explain your idea, no matter how complicated it is, to a six-year-old, then you may be wasting both your time and your audience's time. You must nail this exercise first.

Why Does This Exercise Work?

The reason this exercise is so effective is that you are moving people from uncertainty to certainty and from certainty to strong certainty. When your audience understands you explaining something they did not know well, they are empowered. Their understanding makes them tell others, thereby spreading the message and even taking action.

It is too early to tell what kind of president Donald Trump will turn out to be, but there is one thing he knows he can do anytime:

He can make his supporters and the conservative media more certain by citing facts as he understands them, by repeating over and over again the same thing even if it is false, by getting his supporters to defend him, and by saying his message simply and with ease. When you add it all up, he makes more people certain that not only did they make the right decision supporting and voting for him, but also that he—and only he—can "make America great again."

One of the best tools you can use to explain something complex to a six-year-old is simple drawings. According to best-selling author Dan Roam, "The conversation today is visual. Draw like your world depends on it."[1] Drawing is the oldest technology for communication, and one thing six-year-olds are good at is drawing to communicate. You should draw whenever you want to get something out of your brain and into other people's brains.

People today are so overwhelmed with information that no matter how smart we think we are, we favor those whom we can understand. When we can understand something, we feel smart and are susceptible to be persuaded. The power to persuade key decision makers needs to go through a six-year-old. Go find that six-year-old and let him or her determine how well you will do when you take that message to grown-ups.

Being an expert is good when someone likes you, but not when you are trying to persuade people who may not like you or who are neutral. To inoculate yourself from being viewed as an expert, you need to stay several grade levels below the average grade level of your audience.

Now, this means you have to use short sentences and simple language. You certainly need to avoid jargon. Though there may be people in your audience who may be impressed with your intellect, they are unlikely to act if you don't make them feel smarter. And the only way to do that is to speak several levels below their grade level.

The Power Business Presentation

A brand for a company is like a reputation for a person. You earn reputation by trying to do hard things well.

— Jeff Bezos, founder, chairman, and CEO of Amazon

Though we enjoy watching both Google Talks and TED Talks, they are not that effective for a power business presentation that you need to give. Why? The purpose of a business presentation is not to teach but to elicit a go/no-go decision among decision makers in the audience and influence those whose counsel decision makers will seek.

The format that I believe is effective for today's business presentation (but unfortunately, not generally used for most business presentations) is a slight variation of a what a typical U.S. president uses at a formal White House press conference. The only difference from what a president does is that you should give a solid summation at the end—something presidents never seem to do. Presidents usually end their press conferences by taking one last question from the White House correspondents and then, after answering that question, leave as fast as they can.

If you need to deliver a business presentation before a small group, put yourself in the audience's shoes. What would you be interested in? Sitting through a boring thirty-minute presentation filled with PowerPoint slides? Listening to another story? Probably not. You may love showing off your PowerPoint slides and telling your heartwarming stories, but they often don't work; in fact, they can hurt your effort to achieve your objective.

Again, the purpose of your business presentation is to win. For you to win, you must have complete control over the presentation's format. A solid format will make it easier for those in the audience to decide. However, if you confuse them with irrelevant stuff, they are not likely to make a decision—and that is an outcome worse than a "no-go" decision, because you will probably need to expend more time, money, and resources. Why? You will have become a victim of the "sunk-cost effect"— that is, you will have invested too much time and effort to quit.

The following procedure is what I would highly recommend you start practicing and using with your future business presentations. Of course, you should be ready to go into details if they are needed (for example, in step 6), but that should happen only if the decision makers ask questions that prompt your going into details. You can modify the procedure based on the way the decision makers are processing your presentation. But do not assume that your audience wants to be educated. You are presenting to win the business, not to educate.

The following procedure will help you win anytime you are giving a business presentation:

1. Give a brief five-to-seven-minute opening statement, which highlights all that the attendees need to know. If you are prepared, you should be able to do this between five and seven minutes. You should not go on too long with this opening, since, as I like to say, "more words you use,

more people you'll lose," and you can't afford to lose key decision makers in this or in any presentation.

2. Engage in Q&A for fifteen to twenty minutes. If the attendees are well prepared, they will ask relevant questions during the Q&A. You are giving them control, so you can address anything that the key decision makers in the room bring up.

   Note: You need to know your stuff and how to be crisp, clear, and accurate. You must be well prepared and well rehearsed. You should expect just about anything they might throw at you, and you need to maintain your composure when you are answering their questions. You are being judged not only on what you are saying but on how you are saying it.

3. Give a three-to-five-minute summation. You can address any objections that might have been raised during the Q&A, and you should give them reasons why they should make a go rather than a no-go decision.

4. Provide the call to action. Let the attendees know what you want them to do, and explain what's in it for them.

5. End your presentation five minutes early. That is, if you had thirty minutes set aside for your presentation, finish it in twenty-five minutes. (Be sure to let everyone know that you just gave them five minutes. It may not be a big deal, but people notice when you give them time, since it happens rarely, especially in business meetings.)

6. Reserve time for offline discussion, if necessary. You don't want to leave quickly afterward. You should stay to answer the few questions that attendees could not ask due to time constraints.

Since you have a limited amount of time, you need to be focused. Quantified Communications, a company that uses data to understand what kind of speeches resonate with an audience, had reviewed thousands of speeches given by businesspeople, and its CEO and cofounder, Noah Zandan, determined that business leaders such as Elon Musk resonate with their audience by focusing on three things:[1]

- They talk about the present rather than the future.

- They keep it simple.

- They want their vision to get in the heads of their audience.

If you give a power presentation that is under thirty minutes and do what successful business leaders do, you will also resonate with your audience by looking knowledgeable, competent, and confident. People tend to judge you by what they see. If decision makers see you appearing confident and competent, you are moving them from uncertainty to certainty, or even to strong certainty. The facts you provide in digestible form will be used as their justification to support you.

Another reason I am a big advocate of this approach rather than giving a longer presentation is that you often can't control who is going to be in the audience. It is risky to assume that the key decision makers and influencers all think, process, and decide the same way. According to the book *The 5 Paths to Persuasion: The Art of Selling Your Message*,[2] there are several personality types you are going to have to satisfy: the charismatic, the thinker, the skeptic, the follower, and the controller.

- **Charismatics** are people who want the big picture.

- **Thinkers** are people who want details and process.

- **Skeptics** are people who want you to establish your credibility.

- **Followers** are people who want proof.

- **Controllers** are people who want to feel like they are in control.

Can you possibly give a presentation that will satisfy all five types in the limited time you have? No. You want to give a brief statement that will elicit questions. Based on the questions that the audience members ask, you will be able to know their personality and decision styles. If you can't answer their questions completely, you can follow up with them later to satisfy them.

The mistake you don't want to make is to think that everyone in the audience thinks alike or, worse, that they think like you. You have to be prepared to be flexible on demand. You have to use the low-risk strategy that is more likely to result in a win. You should start the presentation with what is it that you want and what you want them to do. You will have to say this three times: in the beginning, in the middle, and at the end.

Remember, you are not there to dazzle them with details. You are there to flush them out to know where they are, what they think, and what you still need to do. They are not going to make a decision right then and there, so to increase your chances of a win, you need to obtain as much information as you can in order to address any questions or issues right in the meeting, in front of everyone present. You can certainly do a "deep dive" later, in a smaller setting with those who still have further questions.

Your job is to control time and attention.[3] If you start losing that, then you are losing the frame. You need to keep their attention during the twenty minutes that they are going to be attentive.

For Q&A, do not open it up to everyone after you are done with your opening statement. You want to ask the most important decision maker first, since he or she will set the overall mood. For example, if you are in a meeting with the CEO, then you ask the CEO, "So Mr. CEO, what do you think? Do you have any questions or concerns with what I've presented?"

One thing you don't want to do is detail dumping. You should do it only for those who are interested in getting into the details. The reason for this is that you are likely to lose people who just want the big picture.

You now have a presentation approach you can use for any high-stakes situation and win.

The Skills Needed to Become a Great Speaker Today

There are always three speeches, for every one you actually gave. The one you practiced, the one you gave, and the one you wish you gave.

— Dale Carnegie

Many authors spend a lot of time teaching you how to become a good-to-great speaker, but they don't tell you what specific skills you need in order to achieve that. I have narrowed the skills down to five.

- **Purpose.** Purpose is your most important reason for giving a speech. Why should the audience listen to *you*? Why should the audience care? You need to address this quickly, so the audience does not tune you out.

- **Leadership.** Speaking is leading. You got on the stage. Now you need to lead them toward your thinking. You need to have some leadership skills to command the audience to pay attention to you and take action.

- **Writing.** You don't have to be a good writer to be a good speaker, but you need to be able to at least write blogs. Writing will make you think and will help you put those ideas on paper, ideas that you can then repurpose into a speech. Writing will help you develop your research skill to make your content rich.

- **Marketing and sales.** You need to know what your audience will get out of your speech and why they should care. You need both marketing skills and sales skills, but this does not mean you have to be a sales or a marketing guru.

- **Acting and performing.** If you can have a conversation with a person, you are already acting. You just have to do the same with your audience.

Coaching and Speaking

This appendix describes the coaching and speaking services I offer.

Coaching Individuals One on One to Deliver Results

I have provided everything you need to craft and deliver a winning good-to-great high-stakes speech. However, some of you may have an important speech to give soon—in particular, for a job interview—and you don't have ninety days. If it is a speech you want to win, then you should consider hiring me as your coach. I can't guarantee that I alone can make you win, but if you are coachable and want to win, then I can guarantee that you will go into any situation with competence and confidence, which is something you control. And you will have a better shot at winning.

Here is one thing you will get by working with me: **Great experience**. You get to work with someone who not only knows what he is doing but also knows how to work with you, so there is mutual trust, respect, and understanding. You are probably doing many things well, but you still want to get better and you probably need some guidance to achieve a major breakthrough.

You already have all the tips, techniques, and exercises from this book. But the book cannot customize that knowledge to your specific situation, to make you successful. If experience is important to you in anything you do, then you should get in touch with me.

All the clients I work with need to be referenceable; that is, I have a detailed testimonial of their success so others can hear from their words how they succeeded working with me. I follow a simple rule: If I can't make you successful, then I will let you know rather than wasting your time. Coaching is about generating results for those who can execute but who need some guidance with performance and winning.

If you would like to schedule a free exploratory call, please contact me by e-mail at joza@winningspeechmoments.com. During that call, we each will likely be able to determine whether we can win together.

Note 1: Doing an exploratory call is very expensive for me, considering the time I need to prepare for the call. Still, I believe you need to have total confidence in the coach you are working with before you make a commitment.

Note 2: If group coaching is what you are looking for, then please let me know, since I do offer group coaching when I have a few students who are interested. This is a great way for small companies to develop these critical skills among their employees, skills that not only are affordable but also produce results. See the next section.

Coaching Companies to Supercharge Their Performance

You are in business to win. To win, you need to improve the performance of your employees. One of the most effective ways to do that is through improving your employees' communication skills, especially their public speaking. You can save money, make money, and have more fun if everyone in your company has excellent communication skills.

If you agree, then you have probably considered either sending your employees to training or bringing the training onsite. Unfortunately, this usually does not work, because employees are hired to get a job done, not to learn. You don't become a good cook by going to a restaurant; you become a good cook faster if someone comes to your house and helps you prepare meals. Likewise, you learn speechmaking better by practicing it with a coach so you can later do it yourself. Similarly, relevant training needs to be customized and ongoing so that it is integrated with the way your employees work.

If you want to learn how this approach will help you increase your employees' performance, please contact me at joza@winningspeechmoments.com.

Speaking

If you would like me to speak at your school, office, or event or to conduct a seminar or workshop, please contact me at joza@winningspeechmoments.com. I speak to a wide range of audiences who are interested in winning through high-stakes public speaking.

Speech Checklist

Before preparing a speech, I go through the checklist I provided in Chapter 19. I am making that available as a separate free pdf document that you can download at
www.winningspeechmoments.com/resources/checklist

Note: Please provide your e-mail so I can update you twice a month about questions readers have raised about the book, future projects I am working on, and free stuff that I create that I believe will help you develop your speaking skill and succeed. At any time if you are overloaded or don't find any value in what I am sending you, then before you unsubscribe me, please let me know how I can provide value to you. I always want to know how you might improve on what I am doing, so I can learn from you. Not only do I want to get better at developing my speaking skill, but I want to improve my serving skill, too.

Questions and Answers

As you know, no book is ever complete, and at some point, I need to stop writing the book and ship it. I am sure, as you are reading it, you are going to have questions. Please send me your questions at joza@winningspeechmoments.com. If I have not previously addressed that question, then I will either post it as a blog or make a video so that others can benefit from your questions and from my (hopefully) insightful answers. You can find them at www.winningspeechmoment.com/resources/Q&A

I will not have all the answers, but I am always willing to learn from you, so please let me know what you are doing that is helping you achieve your objective when you are speaking one on one, in a small group, or in front of a large audience. If I think what you are doing is teachable to others, then I may even ask you to come on my show if you are interested. Let's help each other out to improve this difficult skill so we can all get better, succeed, and help others improve.

Acknowledgments

Imagine being on a rocket ship all by yourself. You know that either you are going to return safely or you will crash and burn at any time. For you to succeed in the mission, you require help, support, and prayers from a lot of people. Though writing a book is not the same as being sent on a mission into space, when it's your first book, it sure feels like that.

I could not have written this book without my family. My wife, Bhavna, and my children, Gopi and Hersh, had to put up with my being away from home on many weekends since I began working on this book. Through their love, support, and encouragement, they had the most to do with my finally realizing my dream of writing a book.

Next, I have to thank my parents and my siblings. My father not only let me use his office but was available to listen to my ideas that made their way into this book. My mother helped me by providing love and encouragement throughout the journey. My sister and brother were always there to provide encouragement, feedback, and support.

For any long project to complete, you need one person who is going to make sure you get your book done and not get bogged down in trying to make it "perfect." Julie Wu Finkelstein was that person for me. Julie and I both mentor the Coursera public speaking courses, and she was also my cohost on more than fifty episodes of the YouTube show *Speech Talk Live*. To improve the book, she was always generous with her input, comments, and suggestions till the very end.

When you are working on a book, you need that one person who is your most ardent supporter. Fabiana Matano was that person for me. She read all my drafts and informed me that she was learning a lot. Her saying that made me know that I had to finish the book so that others could benefit, too.

We always need that one friend who is going to support you through good times and bad times. For me that friend was Mike Fleurant. Mike was always forthcoming with his time to read various drafts of the book, and he helped me think clearly. I knew that if Mike understood what I was saying, then I was on the right track.

A book needs a good content editor, so that it starts making sense to others the way it made sense to me. For me that editor was Kristin Clark Taylor, who helped me make the content of the book more focused and easier to understand.

In baseball, for a team to win, you need an excellent closer. Similarly, to get a book published, you need an excellent substantive editor to get the book done. I was highly privileged to work with Allan Edmands of The Wordsman Editorial Services (www.thewordsman.com). When he took on this project, he told me he was going to be tough yet fair, so the book would be easier for the readers to comprehend. He has done an excellent job in being such a strong reader's advocate. I want to thank him for all his commitment and hard work on this project. I not only got my book completed, but along the way I learned a lot from Allan about good writing.

The ideas for a book do not come in a dream. You have to learn from a wide range of sources to come up with ideas, synthesize them, and test them so you know they really work and are replicable by others. I was able to do this by getting the opportunity to mentor students who took the online public speaking courses from Coursera. I want to thank Dr. Matt McGarrity of the University of Washington for creating and delivering the content in an engaging way on the videos that make the courses one of the best online/offline that I have ever taken.

I want to thank Sowmyan Tirumurti, a Coursera mentor for the public speaking course and for participating on many *Speech Talk Live* shows. I learned quite a bit from him, since he always brought his unique perspective on improving one's public speaking skills from his vast knowledge and experience. I want to thank the Coursera students all over the world whom I have had the opportunity to mentor one on one as well as through videos and the discussion forum. I have been enriched from the experience.

I would be remiss if I didn't thank many authors from whom I have learned so much. Also, I would like to thank many podcasters who produce such excellent content from which I learn something new every day. Finally, I am so thankful of YouTube, where anyone can view so many good-to-great speeches and learn how the great speakers do it.

If you like this book, all the credit goes to people who helped, taught, supported, and prayed for me. If you don't like the book, then I am the only one to blame. If I could not help you become a good-to-great high-stakes speaker, I hope to learn from your comments, and I promise to make the book better in the next edition.

About the Author

J ay Oza enjoys speaking, coaching, and mentoring people to become good-to-great winning high-stakes speakers so they can achieve their overall objective with anyone, anytime, anywhere.

He is a great guide to help others, since it took him a long time before he overcame his fear of public speaking. He worked hard by attending a Toastmasters International club, taking courses, and practicing. Gradually he learned to better manage his fear of public speaking through preparation, practice, and purpose.

Jay has a bachelor's degree in electrical engineering and computer science from Rutgers University and a master's degree in computer science from New Jersey Institute of Technology. He worked at AT&T Bell Labs as a software consultant and in sales positions at Oracle, IBM, and Sungard. He has been a Coursera mentor for several years, mentoring students for Coursera's online public speaking courses. Lastly, he is extremely proud of the work he has done as a volunteer for Hire Heroes, helping military veterans get good jobs by teaching many of the techniques covered in this book, which is the distillation of his knowledge, experience, and insights as a speaker, coach, and teacher. He can be reached at joza@winningspeechmoments.com.

Author Photo by Lifetouch Portrait Studios Inc.

Selected Bibliography

Abrahams, Matt. "Tips and Techniques for More Confident and Compelling Presentations." *Stanford Business*, March 2, 2015, https://www.gsb.stanford.edu/insights/matt-abrahams-tips-techniques-more-confident-compelling-presentations

Adams, Scott. *How to Fail at Almost Everything and Still Win Big: Kind of the Story of My Life*. New York: Portfolio/Penguin, 2013.

Agard, Chancellor. "Seinfeld, Rock, Chappelle, Schumer, and Ansari Share 'Night to Remember.'" *Entertainment*, January 12, 2017, http://ew.com/tv/2017/01/12/seinfeld-rock-chappelle-schumer-ansari-comedy-cellar/

Ailes, Roger, with Jon Kraushar. *You Are the Message: Getting What You Want by Being Who You Are*. New York: Currency and Doubleday, 1988.

Altucher, James. "What I Learned from Spanx Founder Sara Blakely: How to Get a Billion Dollar Idea." *The James Altucher Show* (podcast audio), episode 211, http://www.jamesaltucher.com/2017/02/sara-blakely/

American Rhetoric: Top 100 Speeches. "Martin Luther King Jr. 'I Have a Dream,'" http://www.americanrhetoric.com/speeches/mlkihaveadream.htm

Ansari, Aziz [*see* Pappu, Sridhar].

Antisubliminal. "Apple—1984." *YouTube*, uploaded June 19, 2006, https://www.youtube.com/watch?v=R706isyDrqI

AP Archive. "President Ronald Reagan Address an Adoring Crowd at the [1988] Republican National Convention." *YouTube*: 2:44 minute mark, July 31, 2015, https://youtu.be/j0-PuZDfiuc

"Art of the Lie." *The Economist*, September 10, 2016, http://www.economist.com/news/leaders/21706525-politicians-have-always-lied-does-it-matter-if-they-leave-truth-behind-entirely-art

Associated Press. "McCain Counters Obama 'Arab' Question." *YouTube*, October 11, 2008, https://youtu.be/jrnRU3ocIH4

Baer, Drake. "Warren Buffett Used to Throw Up before Public Speaking—Here's How He Mastered It." *Business Insider*, December 12, 2014, http://www.businessinsider.com/how-warren-buffett-learned-public-speaking-2014-12

Baldwin, Grant. "Heroic Public Speaking, with Michael Port." *The Speaker Lab with Grant Baldwin// Public Speaking/ Motivational Speaking/ Entrepreneurship* (podcast audio), episode 7, January, 19, 2016, http://thespeakerlab.libsyn.com/007-heroic-public-speaking-with-michael-port

Bellino, Ricardo. *You Have Three Minutes! Learn the Secret of the Pitch from Trump's Original Apprentice.* New York: McGraw-Hill, 2006.

Benson, Todd. "Trump Takes a Meeting, Now Backs a Resort in Brazil." *New York Times*, May 19, 2004, http://www.nytimes.com/2004/05/19/business/trump-takes-a-meeting-now-backs-a-resort-in-brazil.html

Berlinger, Joe [*see* Team Tony].

Bernoff, Josh. "Your Outlines Are Useless. You Need a Fat Outline." *Without Bullshit*, November 24, 2015, https://withoutbullshit.com/blog/fat-outline

Berns, Gregory. *Iconoclast: A Neuroscientist Reveals How to Think Differently*. Boston: Harvard Business Press, 2008.

Blay, Zeba. "What the Viral Fame of the 'Cash Me Ousside' Girl Says about Us." *Huffington Post*, March 8, 2017, http://www.huffingtonpost.com/entry/what-the-viral-fame-of-the-cash-me-ousside-girl-says-about-us_us_58c01d90e4b0ed718268bea3?q630ykjqub22tvs4i&2

Bradner, Eric. "Conway: Trump White House Offered 'Alternative Facts' on Crowd Size." *CNN politics*, January 23, 2017, http://www.cnn.com/2017/01/22/politics/kellyanne-conway-alternative-facts/

Bregman, Peter. "Jeff Pfeffer—*Leadership BS*." *The Bregman Leadership Podcast* (podcast audio), episode 23, May 23, 2016, http://peterbregman.com/podcast/jeff-pfeffer-leadership-bs/#.WLNAdPnythE

———. "You Need to Practice Being Your Future Self." *Harvard Business Review*, March 28, 2016, https://hbr.org/2016/03/you-need-to-practice-being-your-future-self

Brooks, Mike, and Dino Dogan. "How Bryan Kramer Went from Reinventing Himself to TED." *Road to TED* (podcast audio),

July 1, 2015, http://roadtoted.com/how-bryan-kramer-went-from-reinventing-himself-to-ted/

Brynjolfsson, Eric, and Andrew McAfee. "The Jobs That AI Can't Replace." *BBC News*, September 13, 2015, http://www.bbc.com/news/technology-34175290

Burton, Richard, translator. *The Arabian Nights*. San Diego: Canterbury Classics, 2011.

Bush, George W. [*see* McCaleb, Ian Christopher].

Carlson, Nicholas. *Marissa Mayer and the Fight to Save Yahoo!* New York: Twelve, 2015.

Carnoy, David. "Watch Steve Jobs Introduce the iPhone 10 Years Ago Today." *CNET, The Verge*, January 9, 2017, https://www.cnet.com/news/watch-steve-jobs-introduce-the-original-iphone-10-years-ago-today/

Caro, Robert. *The Power Broker: Robert Moses and the Fall of New York*. New York: Vintage, 1975.

Carroll, Pete [*see* La Canfora, Jason].

CBC News. "Canadian Prime Minister Justin Trudeau Schools Reporter on Quantum Computing during Press Conference." *YouTube*, April 15, 2016, https://www.youtube.com/watch?v=Eak_ogYMprk

Chamorro-Premuzic, Tomas. *Confidence: How Much You Really Need and How to Get It*. New York: Hudson Street Press, 2013.

Charney, Noah. "Jodi Picoult on Writing, Publishing, and What She's Reading." *The Daily Beast*, April 3, 2012, http://www.thedailybeast.com/articles/2012/04/03/jodi-picoult-on-writing-publishing-and-what-she-s-reading.html

Christensen, Clayton M., Taddy Hall, Karen Dillon, and David S. Duncan. *Competing against Luck: The Story of Innovation and Customer Choice.* New York: Harper Business, 2016.

Chua, Amy. *Battle Hymn of the Tiger Mother.* New York: Penguin Books, 2011.

Chua, Amy, and Jed Rubenfeld. *The Triple Package: How Three Unlikely Traits Explain the Rise and Fall of Cultural Groups in America.* New York: The Penguin Press, 2014.

Clear, James. "The Ivy Lee Method: The Daily Routine Experts Recommend for Peak Productivity." *Huffington Post*, June 2, 2016, http://www.huffingtonpost.com/james-clear/the-ivy-lee-method-the-da_b_10257938.html

Clinton, Bill [*see* Democratic National Convention, 2012; Georgetown University; Guber, Peter].

CNN, All Politics. "Mondale's Acceptance Speech, 1984: Walter Mondale Throws Down Gauntlet in Run against Reagan." *Chicago 96 Facts*, http://www.cnn.com/ALLPOLITICS/1996/conventions/chicago/facts/famous.speeches/mondale.84.shtml

Colonial Williamsburg Foundation Center for History and Citizenship. "Give Me Liberty or Give Me Death," http://www.history.org/almanack/life/politics/giveme.cfm

Colvin, Geoff. *Humans Are Underrated: What High Achievers Know That Brilliant Machines Never Will.* New York: Portfolio/Penguin, 2015.

———. "The Skills of Human Interaction Will Become Most Valuable in the Future." *New York Times*, March 9, 2016, http://www.nytimes.com/roomfordebate/2016/03/09/does

-alphago-mean-artificial-intelligence-is-the-real-deal/the-skills-of-human-interaction-will-become-most-valuable-in-the-future

Covey, Stephen R. *The 7 Habits of Highly Effective People: Powerful Lessons in Personal Change.* New York: Fireside, 1989.

Cowen, Tyler. *Average Is Over: Powering America beyond the Age of the Great Stagnation.* New York: Dutton, 2013.

Cuban, Mark [*see* Kharpal, Arjun].

Cuddy, Amy. *Presence: Bringing Your Boldest Self to Your Biggest Challenges.* New York: Little, Brown and Company, 2015.

———. TED Talks (One of 1,000+ TED Talks), "Your Body Language Shapes Who You Are | Amy Cuddy." *YouTube*, October 1, 2012, https://youtu.be/Ks-_Mh1QhMc

Dalfonzo, Gina. "Remember When Actors Wanted to Be Versatile? Benedict Cumberbatch Does." *Atlantic*, May 21, 2013, https://www.theatlantic.com/entertainment/archive/2013/05/remember-when-actors-wanted-to-be-versatile-benedict-cumberbatch-does/276061/

Decker Communications. "Mark McGwire Testifying to Congress (Poorly)." C-SPAN recording of U.S. House of Representatives Government Reform Committee, March 17, 2005, *YouTube*, uploaded October 19, 2009, https://youtu.be/up_eQUuiDN0

Democratic National Convention, 2012. "President Bill Clinton at the 2012 Democratic National Convention," September 6, 2012, https://youtu.be/lFUtEyh20Ok

Democratic National Convention, 2016. "Khizr Khan at DNC 2016." *YouTube*, July 28, 2016, https://youtu.be/Ery-Zgo5ALs

————. "Senator Tim Kaine at DNC 2016." *YouTube*, July 28, 2016, https://youtu.be/Fis6X19Y6eU

Dershowitz, Alan. *The Best Defense: The Courtroom Confrontations of America's Most Outspoken Lawyer of Last Resort—The Lawyer Who Won the Claus von Bulow Appeal.* New York: Vintage, 2011.

Dixon, Matthew, and Brent Adamson. *The Challenger Sale: Taking Control of the Customer Conversation.* New York: Portfolio/Penguin, 2011.

Doshi, Neel, and Lindsay McGregor. *Primed to Perform: How to Build the Highest Performing Cultures through the Science of Total Motivation.* New York: Harper Business, 2015.

Duarte, Nancy, TEDxEast Interconnectivity. "Nancy Duarte Uncovers Common Structure of Greatest Communicators" (Ted Talk on *YouTube*), November 11, 2010 (uploaded December 10, 2010), https://www.youtube.com/watch?v=1nYFpuc2Umk

Duarte, Nancy, and Patti Sanchez. "Illuminate." *Talks at Google*, July 14, 2016, https://youtu.be/iUoiKidIbxU

Duckworth, Angela. *Grit: The Power of Passion and Perseverance.* New York: Scribner, 2016.

Duhigg, Charles. *The Power of Habit: Why We Do What We Do in Life and Business.* New York: Random House, 2012.

————. *Smarter Faster Better: The Secrets of Being Productive in Life and Business.* New York: Random House, 2016.

Eastwood, Clint [*see* Sabato, Larry J., et al.].

Easty, Edward Dwight. *On Method Acting: The Classic Actor's Guide to the Stanislavsky Technique as Practiced at the Actors Studio.* New York: Ivy Books, 1981.

Edwards, Ray. *How to Write Copy That Sells: The Step-by-Step System for More Sales, to More Customers, More Often.* New York: Morgan James, 2016.

Egan, Timothy. "The Eight-Second Attention Span." *New York Times*, January, 22, 2016, https://www.nytimes.com/2016/01/22/opinion/the-eight-second-attention-span.html

Face the Nation. "Ronald Reagan at 1980 GOP Debate: 'I Am Paying for This Microphone.'" *YouTube*, February 11, 2016, https://youtu.be/KVHlHR5RcSg

Feinstein, Ashley. "Why You Should Be Writing Down Your Goals." *Forbes*, April 8, 2014, http://www.forbes.com/sites/ellevate/2014/04/08/why-you-should-be-writing-down-your-goals/#60f2fe7e2f14

Finkelstein, Sydney. *Superbosses: How Exceptional Leaders Master the Flow of Talent.* New York: Portfolio/Penguin, 2016.

The First Round Review. "Radical Candor—The Surprising Secret to Being a Good Boss," http://firstround.com/review/radical-candor-the-surprising-secret-to-being-a-good-boss/

Friedman, Thomas L. *NBC News: Meet the Press*, January 29, 2017, http://www.nbcnews.com/meet-the-press/meet-press-01-29-17-n713751

———. "Owning Your Own Future." *New York Times*, May 10, 2017, https://www.nytimes.com/2017/05/10/opinion/owning-your-own-future.html?_r=0

———. *Thank You for Being Late: An Optimist's Guide to Thriving in the Age of Accelerations*. New York: Farrar, Straus and Giroux, 2016.

Friedman, Thomas L., and Michael Mandelbaum. *That Used to Be Us: How America Fell Behind in the World It Invented and How We Can Come Back*. New York: Farrar, Straus and Giroux, 2011.

Gawande, Atul. *Checklist Manifesto: How to Get Things Right*. New York: Henry Holt and Company, 2009.

Gehrig, Lou [*see* National Baseball Hall of Fame].

Georgetown University Berkeley Center for Religion, Peace & World Affairs. "Bill Clinton on Overcoming Evil in Oklahoma City Bombing Memorial Speech," April 23, 1995, https://berkleycenter.georgetown.edu/quotes/bill-clinton-on-overcoming-evil-in-oklahoma-city-bombing-memorial-speech

Gimein, Mark. "The Fallacy of Job Insecurity." *New Yorker*, June 29, 2016, http://www.newyorker.com/business/currency/the-fallacy-of-job-insecurity

Gino, Francesco. "Research: We Drop People Who Give Us Critical Feedback." *Harvard Business Review*, September 16, 2016, https://hbr.org/2016/09/research-we-drop-people-who-give-us-critical-feedback

Giridharadas, Anand. "Donald Trump Breaks with Tradition, and It's Paying Off." *New York Times*, March 14, 2016, https://www.nytimes.com/2016/03/15/us/politics/donald-trump-surprise-over-substance.html

Giuliano, C. Peter. "What Made Ronald Reagan 'the Great Communicator.'" *The Public Relations Strategist*, Summer 2004, http://ecgcoaching.com/library/Strategist_S04.pdf

Godin, Seth. *Icarus Deception: How High Will You Fly?* New York: Portfolio/Penguin, 2012.

———. *Linchpin: Are You Indispensable?* New York: Portfolio, 2010.

——— [*see also* Port, Michael].

Gokadze, Ilya. "Martin Luther King, Jr., I Have a Dream Speech." *YouTube*, published August 28, 2013, https://www.youtube.com/watch?v=3vDWWy4CMhE

Gordievsky. "Iverson Practice!" *YouTube*, uploaded April 15, 2006, https://www.youtube.com/watch?v=eGDBR2L5kzI

Grant, Adam. *Originals: How Non-Conformists Move the World*. New York: Viking, 2016.

Guber, Peter. *Tell to Win: Connect, Persuade, and Triumph with the Hidden Power of Story*. New York: Crown Business, 2011.

Hansen, Drew. "Mahalia Jackson, and King's Improvisation." *New York Times*, August 27, 2013, http://www.nytimes.com/2013/08/28/opinion/mahalia-jackson-and-kings-rhetorical-improvisation.html

Heath, Chip, and Dan Heath. "The Curse of Knowledge." *Harvard Business Review*, December 2006, https://hbr.org/2006/12/the-curse-of-knowledge

———. *Made to Stick: Why Some Ideas Survive and Others Die*. New York: Random House, 2007.

Henry, Patrick [*see* Colonial Williamsburg].

"The Highest-Paid Show Hosts of All Time." *Forbes*, 2017, https://www.forbes.com/pictures/gjdm45eded/the-highest-paid-show-ho/#1f992c715992

The History Place: Great Speeches Collection. "Ronald Reagan, 'Tear Down This Wall,'" http://www.historyplace.com/speeches/reagan-tear-down.htm

Hogshead, Sally. *How the World Sees You: Discover Your Highest Value through the Science of Fascination*. New York: HarperCollins, 2014.

"How an AI Algorithm Learned to Write Political Speeches." *MIT Technology Review*, January, 19, 2016, https://www.technologyreview.com/s/545606/how-an-ai-algorithm-learned-to-write-political-speeches/

Huffington Post Canada. "Chip Wilson, Lululemon Founder: 'Some Women's Bodies' Not Right for Our Pants," November 6, 2013, http://www.huffingtonpost.com/2013/11/06/lululemon-chip-wilson-womens-bodies_n_4228113.html

Humes, James C. *The Sir Winston Method: The Five Secrets of Speaking the Language of Leadership*. New York: William Morrow and Company, 1991.

Ibarra, Herminia. *Act Like a Leader, Think Like a Leader*. Boston: Harvard Business Review Press, 2015.

Isaacson, Walter. *Steve Jobs*. New York: Simon & Schuster, 2011.

Iverson, Allen [*see* Gordievsky].

James, Neen [*see* Port, Michael].

Jensen, Keld. "Intelligence Is Overrated: What You Really Need to Succeed." *Forbes*, April 12, 2012, http://www.forbes.com/sites/keldjensen/2012/04/12/intelligence-is-overrated-what-you-really-need-to-succeed/#41a851096375

Jiang, Jia. *Rejection Proof: How I Beat Fear and Became Invincible One Rejection at a Time*. New York: Harmony, 2015.

Jobs, Steve. Stanford University. "Steve Jobs' 2005 Stanford Commencement Address." *YouTube*, May 7, 2008, https://youtu.be/UF8uR6Z6KLc

———— [*see also* Carnoy, David].

Joel, Mitch [*see* Port, Michael].

Johnson, Boris. *The Churchill Factor: How One Man Made History*. New York: Riverhead Books, 2014.

Kaine, Tim [*see* Democratic National Convention, 2016].

Kallet, Brad. "Eighteen Years Later, Lučić-Baroni Returns to a Major Quarterfinal. *Tennis*, January 23, 2017, http://www.tennis.com/pro-game/2017/01/mirjana-lucic-baroni-australian-open-wta-tennis/63604/

Kelly, Megyn. *Settle for More*. New York: HarperCollins, 2016.

Keltner, Dacher. *The Power Paradox: How We Gain and Lose Influence*. New York: Penguin Press, 2016.

Kennedy, John F. [*see* NASA.gov Video].

Kennedy, Robert [*see* NPR Special Series].

Khan, Khizr [*see* Democratic National Convention, 2016].

Kharpal, Arjun. "Mark Cuban: Robots Will 'Cause Unemployment and We Need to Prepare for It.'" *CNBC*, February, 20, 2017, https://www.cnbc.com/2017/02/20/mark-cuban-robots-unemployment-and-we-need-to-prepare-for-it.html

King Jr., Martin Luther [*see* American Rhetoric; Gokadze, Ilya; Hansen, Drew].

Klaff, Oren. *Pitch Anything: An Innovative Method for Presenting, Persuading, and Winning the Deal.* New York: McGraw-Hill Education, 2011.

Kruse, Kevin. "How to Receive Feedback and Criticism." *Forbes*, August 12, 2014, https://www.forbes.com/sites/kevinkruse/2014/08/12/how-to-receive-feedback-and-criticism/#691f41dd7c3f

La Canfora, Jason. "Super Bowl 49: Pete Carroll's Decision Astonishing, Explanation Perplexing." *CBS Sports*, February 2, 2015, http://www.cbssports.com/nfl/news/super-bowl-49-pete-carrolls-decision-astonishing-explanation-perplexing/

Lamott, Anne. *Bird by Bird: Some Instructions on Writing and Life.* New York: Anchor Books, 1994.

Lane, Andrew M., Peter Totterdell, Ian MacDonald, Tracey J. Devonport, Andrew P. Friesen, Christopher J. Beedie, Damian Stanley, and Alan Nevill. "Brief Online Training Enhances Competitive Performance: Findings of the BBC Lab UK Psychological Skills Intervention Study." *Frontiers in Psychology*, March 30, 2016, http://journal.frontiersin.org/article/10.3389/fpsyg.2016.00413/full

Leonard, Kelly, and Tom Yorton. *Yes, And: How Improvisation Reverses "No, But" Thinking and Improves Creativity and Collaboration—Lessons from* The Second City. New York: Harper Collins, 2015.

Levy, Francesca, and Christopher Cannon. "The Bloomberg's Job Skills Report 2016: What the Recruiters Want." *Bloomberg*, February 9, 2016, https://www.bloomberg.com/graphics/2016-job-skills-report/

Levy, Mark. *Accidental Genius*. San Francisco: Berrett-Koehler Publishers, 2010.

Lewis, Michael. *Flash Boys: A Wall Street Revolt*. New York: W.W. Norton & Company, 2015.

Lincoln, Abraham [*see* Yale Law School].

LoBianco, Tom. "VA's McDonald Apologizes for Disney Waiting Line Comparison." *CNN politics*, May 24, 2016, http://www.cnn.com/2016/05/24/politics/bob-mcdonald-veterans-affairs-disney/

Luntz, Frank. *Words That Work: It's Not What You Say, It's What People Hear*. New York: Hyperion, 2007.

MacCrory, Frank, George Westerman, Erik Brynjolfsson, and Yousef Alhammadi. "Racing with and against the Machine: Changes in Occupational Skill Composition in an Era of Rapid Technological Advance." *Thirty-Fifth International Conference on Information Systems*, Auckland, NZ, 2014, https://pdfs.semanticscholar.org/164e/93f0d99852a2b8474c9c0c902eb00807a379.pdf

Machiavelli, Niccolò. *The Prince*. Translated by W. K. Marriott. Ballingslöv, Sweden: Wisehouse Classics, 2015.

Mangelsdorf, Martha E. "The New World of Work." *MIT Sloan Management Review*, March 16, 2015, http://sloanreview.mit.edu/article/the-new-world-of-work/

Martin, Jonathan, and Amie Parnes. "Obama Not an Arab, Crowd Boos." *Politico*, October 10, 2008, http://www.politico.com/story/2008/10/mccain-obama-not-an-arab-crowd-boos-014479

McAfee, Andrew, and Erik Brynjolfsson. "Where Computers Defeat Humans, and Where They Can't." *New York Times*, March 16, 2016, https://www.nytimes.com/2016/03/16/opinion/where-computers-defeat-humans-and-where-they-cant.html

McCain, John [*see* Martin, Jonathan, and Amie Parnes].

McCaleb, Ian Christopher. "Bush Tours Ground Zero in Lower Manhattan." *CNN.com/U.S.*, September 14, 2001, http://edition.cnn.com/2001/US/09/14/bush.terrorism/

McCullough, David. *The Path between the Seas: The Creation of the Panama Canal, 1870–1914*. New York: Simon & Schuster, 2001.

McGarrity, Matt. "Introduction to Public Speaking." University of Washington Coursera course, https://www.coursera.org/learn/public-speaking

McGwire, Mark [*see* Decker Communications].

McKain, Scott. *ALL Business Is STILL Show Business: Create Distinction and Earn Standing Ovations from Customers in a Hyper-*

Competitive Marketplace. Las Vegas, NV: Distinction Press, 2017.

Mey, Chris Vander. *Shipping Greatness: Practical Lessons on Building and Launching Outstanding Software, Learned on the Job at Google and Amazon.* Sebastopol, CA: O'Reilly Media, 2012.

Miller, Robert B., Gary A. Williams, and Alden M. Hayashi. *The 5 Paths to Persuasion: The Art of Selling Your Message.* New York: Hachette Book Group, 2004.

MIT Human Resources: Performance Development. "SMART Goals," http://hrweb.mit.edu/performance-development/goal-setting-developmental-planning/smart-goals

Mondale, Walter [*see* CNN, All Politics].

Morgan, Nick. *Power Cues: The Subtle Science of Leading Groups, Persuading Others, and Maximizing Your Personal Impact.* Boston: Harvard Business Review Press, 2014.

Morris, David Z. "Google's AlphaGo AI Runs the Table on Asia's Go Champs." *Fortune,* January 7, 2017, http://fortune.com/2017/01/07/google-alphago-ai/

Mosbergen, Dominique. "South African CEO's 'Bitch-Switch' Comment Prompts Firestorm." *Huffington Post,* April 28, 2016, http://www.huffingtonpost.com/entry/south-africa-ceo-women-bitch-switch_us_57218b15e4b0b49df6aa3452

Musk, Elon. TED Talks. "The Mind behind Tesla, SpaceX, SolarCity… | Elon Musk." *YouTube,* March 19, 2013, https://youtu.be/IgKWPdJWuBQ

NASA.gov Video. "President Kennedy's Speech at Rice University," September 12, 1962. *YouTube*, published May 18, 2013, https://youtu.be/WZyRbnpGyzQ

National Baseball Hall of Fame. "Luckiest Man," http://baseballhall.org/discover/lou-gehrig-luckiest-man

Noonan, Peggy. *Simply Speaking: How to Communicate Your Ideas with Style, Substance, and Clarity.* New York: HarperCollins, 1998.

NPR Special Series: Echoes of 1968. "Robert Kennedy: Delivering News of King's Death," April 4, 2008, http://www.npr.org/2008/04/04/89365887/robert-kennedy-delivering-news-of-kings-death

Ofri, Danielle. "The Conversation Placebo." *New York Times*, January 19, 2017, https://www.nytimes.com/2017/01/19/opinion/sunday/the-conversation-placebo.html?_r=0

Oza, Jay. "Conversation with Thom Winninger." *Speech Talk Live*, episode 61, *YouTube*, uploaded January 20, 2017, https://youtu.be/fKUC7m1tLAU?list=PLOySikLQ9FUgOrojDaZ_zIxjlwjF1xhJN

———. "My First Blog Post: It Starts Today." *5ToolGroup*, August 2, 2011, http://www.5toolgroup.com/blogs/first-post

———. *Speech Talk Live*, https://www.youtube.com/playlist?list=PLOySikLQ9FUg2tG4roh7l6R0URm3-yF_j

Pappu, Sridhar. "Aziz Ansari Is Still Searching." New York Times, June 8, 2017, https://www.nytimes.com/2017/06/08/fashion/aziz-ansari-master-of-none.html?_r=0

Paradi, Dave. "Are We Wasting $250 Million per Day Due to Bad PowerPoint?" *Think outside the Slide,* http://www.thinkoutsidetheslide.com/are-we-wasting-250-million-per-day-due-to-bad-powerpoint/

Pfeffer, Jeffrey. *Leadership BS: Fixing Workplaces and Careers One Truth at a Time.* New York: HarperCollins, 2015.

———— [*see also* Bregman, Peter].

Picoult, Jodi [*see* Charney, Noah].

Pink, Dan. *To Sell Is Human: The Surprising Truth about Moving Others.* New York: Riverhead Books, 2012.

Port, Michael. "The Business of Speaking for Women, Business Models for Speakers, and Much More with Neen James." *Steal the Show* (podcast audio), episode 70, http://stealtheshow.com/podcast/business-of-speaking-for-women-neen-james/

————. "Creative Path to Successful Speaking with Mitch Joel." *Steal the Show* (podcast audio), episode 67, http://stealtheshow.com/podcast/creative-path-to-successful-speaking-mitch-joel/

————. "Seth Godin on Public Speaking and Performing during High Stakes Situations." *Steal the Show* (podcast audio), episode 57, http://stealtheshow.com/podcast/seth-godin-public-speaking/

————. *Steal the Show: From Speeches to Job Interviews to Deal-Closing Pitches, How to Guarantee a Standing Ovation for All the Performances in Your Life.* New York: Houghton Mifflin Harcourt, 2015.

———— [*see also* Baldwin, Grant].

Pressfield, Steven. *The War of Art: Break through the Blocks and Win Your Inner Creative Battles*. New York: Black Irish Entertainment, 2002.

Rampton, John. "The Secrets to Building a Product Roadmap." *Inc.*, May 1, 2015, http://www.inc.com/john-rampton/secrets-to-building-a-product-roadmap.html

Reagan, Ronald. "Remarks at the Annual Conference of the Council of the Americas," May 21, 1985. *The American Presidency Project*, http://www.presidency.ucsb.edu/ws/?pid=38669

——— [*see also* AP Archive; *Face the Nation*; History Place; Reagan Foundation].

Reagan Foundation. "Moscow State University: President Reagan's Address at Moscow State University—5/31/88." *YouTube*, uploaded April 21, 2009, https://youtu.be/1lutYGxMWeA

Ries, Eric. *The Lean Startup: How Today's Entrepreneurs Use Continuous Innovation to Create Radically Successful Businesses*. New York: Crown Business, 2011.

Roam, Dan. *Draw to Win: A Crash Course on How to Lead, Sell, and Innovate with Your Visual Mind*. New York: Portfolio/Penguin, 2016.

Robbins, Apollo. "The Art of Misdirection." *TED*, September 13, 2013, https://youtu.be/GZGY0wPAnus

Robbins, Tony. "Why We Do What We Do." *TED Ideas Worth Spreading* (subtitles and transcript) posted June 2006, https://www.ted.com/talks/tony_robbins_asks_why_we_do_what_we_do/transcript?language=en

———— [*see also* Team Tony].

Rosebush, James. *True Reagan: What Made Ronald Reagan Great and Why It Matters.* New York: Center Street, 2016.

Rubin, Jennifer. "Who Flunks—and Who Passes—the Beer Test?" *Washington Post,* April 15, 2015, https://www.washingtonpost.com/blogs/right-turn/wp/2015/04/15/who-flunks-and-who-passes-the-beer-test/?utm_term=.0de009b175a3

Saatchi, Maurice. "The Strange Death of Modern Advertising." *Financial Times,* June 22, 2006, http://www.ft.com/content/117b10ee-014b-11db-af16-0000779e2340

Sabato, Larry J., Kyle Kondik, and Geoffrey Skelley. "Romney, Ryan, Republicans and… Eastwood?" *University of Virginia Center for Politics: Sabato's Crystal Ball,* August 31, 2012, http://www.centerforpolitics.org/crystalball/articles/romney-ryan-republicans-and-eastwood/

Salemi, Vicki. "Good Grades Are Meaningless in the Modern Workplace." *New York Post,* March 21, 2016, http://nypost.com/2016/03/21/good-grades-are-meaningless-in-the-modern-workplace/

Sandberg, Sheryl. TED Talks. "Why We Have Too Few Women Leaders | Sheryl Sandberg." *YouTube,* December 21, 2010, https://youtu.be/18uDutylDa4

Sandberg, Sheryl, with Nell Scovell. *Lean In: Women, Work, and the Will to Lead.* New York: Alfred A. Knopf, 2013.

Sanders, Tim. *The Likeability Factor: How to Boost Your L-Factor and Achieve Your Life's Dreams*. New York: Crown Publishers, 2005.

Schmidt, Eric, and Jonathan Rosenberg. *How Google Works*. New York: Grand Central Publishing, 2014.

Simmons, Gene. *Me, Inc.: Build an Army of One, Unleash Your Inner Rock God, Win in Life and Business*. New York: HarperCollins, 2014.

Simon, Carmen. *Impossible to Ignore: Creating Memorable Content to Influence Decisions*. New York: McGraw-Hill Education, 2016.

———. "The Neuroscience of Memorable Content." *HubSpot: INBOUND 2015 I&E*, November 12, 2015, https://www.youtube.com/watch?v=eoJ-RG5AqL0&t=363s

Sinek, Simon. *Start with Why: How Great Leaders Inspire Everyone to Take Action*. New York: Portfolio/Penguin, 2011.

Sjodin, Terri L. *Small Message, Big Impact: How to Put the Power of the Elevator Speech Effect to Work for You*. Austin, TX: Greenleaf Book Group Press, 2011.

"The State of American Jobs." *Pew Research Center Social and Demographics Trends*, October 6, 2016, http://www.pewsocialtrends.org/2016/10/06/the-state-of-american-jobs/

Stevenson, Doug. Talks at Google. "Doug Stevenson: 'The Power to Persuade—The Magic of Story.'" *YouTube*, August 4, 2014, https://youtu.be/sKUiE9DBkKcStone, Douglas, and Sheila Heen. *Thanks for the Feedback: The Science and Art of Receiving Feedback Well*. New York: Viking, 2014.

Stiggerpao. "Coca-Cola Classic Ad: Mean Joe Greene [Full Version] (1979)." *YouTube*, uploaded July 17, 2007, https://www.youtube.com/watch?v=xffOCZYX6F8

Sull, Donald, and Kathleen M. Eisenhardt. *Simple Rules: How to Thrive in a Complex World*. New York: Houghton Mifflin Harcourt, 2015.

Sutton, Robert I. "Karl Weick's Creativity." *Psychology Today*, May 29, 2010, https://www.psychologytoday.com/blog/work-matters/201005/karl-weicks-creativity

Team Tony. "The Making of 'Tony Robbins: I Am Not Your Guru': An Interview with Documentary Filmmaker Joe Berlinger." Robbins Research International (podcast audio), https://www.tonyrobbins.com/podcast/story-behind-tony-robbins-documentary/

Thiel, Peter. *Zero to One: Notes on Startups, or How to Build the Future*. New York: Crown Business, 2014.

Toobin, Jeffrey. *The Run of His Life: The People v. O. J. Simpson*. New York: Random House, 1996.

Trudeau, Justin [*see* CBC News].

Vaden, Rory. "Succeeding in the Speaking Industry with Brian Tracy." *Action Catalyst Podcast*, episode 163, October 12, 2016, http://roryvaden.com/blog/succeeding-speaking-industry-brian-tracy-action-catalyst-podcast/

Vaynerchuk, Gary. "Three Pieces of Advice to Build Confidence for Public Speaking." *Gary Vaynerchuk* (website), 2016, https://www.garyvaynerchuk.com/three-pieces-advice-build-confidence-public-speaking/

Webster, Tamsen. "Where Does the Red Thread Come From?" *Tamsen Webster* (website), episode 3, February 22, 2017, http://tamsenwebster.com/ep-003-red-thread-origins-right-path/

Weingarten, Gene. "Pearls before Breakfast: Can One of the Nation's Great Musicians Cut through the Fog of a D.C. Rush Hour? Let's Find Out." *Washington Post*, April 8, 2007, https://www.washingtonpost.com/lifestyle/magazine/pearls-before-breakfast-can-one-of-the-nations-great-musicians-cut-through-the-fog-of-a-dc-rush-hour-lets-find-out/2014/09/23/8a6d46da-4331-11e4-b47c-f5889e061e5f_story.html?utm_term=.12171d8bcd5b

Weiss, Joanna. "The Man Who Killed the SAT Essay." *Boston Globe*, March 14, 2014, https://www.bostonglobe.com/opinion/2014/03/13/the-man-who-killed-sat-essay/L9v3dbPXewKq8oAvOUqONM/story.html

Yale Law School Lillian Goldman Law Library Avalon Project. "Gettysburg Address," http://avalon.law.yale.edu/19th_century/gettyb.asp

"Yes, I'd Lie to You." *The Economist*, September 10, 2016, http://www.economist.com/news/briefing/21706498-dishonesty-politics-nothing-new-manner-which-some-politicians-now-lie-and

Yu, Howard. "What AlphaGo Means for Your Job." *Fortune*, March 21, 2016, http://fortune.com/2016/03/21/google-alphago-win-artificial-intelligence/

Zandan, Noah. "Wharton People Analytics Conference 2016: Panel on Methods." Wharton School. *YouTube*: 1:19 minute mark, August 5, 2016, https://youtu.be/NmOFGu3xw8w

Ziglar, Zig, narrated by Zig Ziglar. *See You at the Top: 25th Anniversary Edition*. Simon Schuster Audio/Nightingale-Conant, 2012, audible, 1 hour and 42 minutes.

Zito, Salena. "Taking Trump Seriously, Not Literally." *Atlantic*, September 23, 2016, https://www.theatlantic.com/politics/archive/2016/09/trump-makes-his-case-in-pittsburgh/501335/

Zyman, Sergio. *The End of Marketing As We Know It*. New York: Harper Business, 1999.

Notes

Preface

[1] Zeba Blay, "What the Viral Fame of the 'Cash Me Ousside' Girl Says about Us," *Huffington Post*, March 8, 2017, http://www.huffingtonpost.com/entry/what-the-viral-fame-of-the-cash-me-ousside-girl-says-about-us_us_58c01d90e4b0ed718268bea3?q630ykjqub22tvs4i&2

[2] Carmen Simon, *Impossible to Ignore: Creating Memorable Content to Influence Decisions* (New York: McGraw-Hill Education, 2016), Kindle edition, loc. 165.

Introduction

[1] Richard Burton, translator. *The Arabian Nights* (San Diego: Canterbury Classics, 2011), Kindle edition, loc. 137.

[2] Gene Simmons, *Me, Inc.: Build an Army of One, Unleash Your Inner Rock God, Win in Life and Business* (New York: HarperCollins, 2014), Kindle edition, loc. 23, https://www.safaribooksonline.com/library/view/me-inc-/9780062322623/Text/9780062322623_ch023.xhtml

[3] Darren Rovell, "Famed 'Be Like Mike' Gatorade Ad Debuted 25 Years Ago," *ESPN.com*, August 6, 2016, http://www.espn.com/nba/story/_/id/17246999/michael-jordan-famous-mike-gatorade-commercial-debuted-25-years-ago-monday

[4] James Rosebush, *True Reagan: What Made Ronald Reagan Great and Why It Matters* (New York: Center Street, 2016), Kindle edition, loc. 1650.

[5] Gregory Berns, *Iconoclast: A Neuroscientist Reveals How to Think Differently* (Boston: Harvard Business Press, 2008).

[6] Adam Grant, *Originals: How Non-Conformists Move the World* (New York: Viking, 2016), Kindle edition, loc. 3054.

[7] Jay Oza, *Speech Talk Live*, https://www.youtube.com/playlist?list=PLOySikLQ9FUg2tG4roh7l6R0URm3-yF_j

[8] Boris Johnson, *The Churchill Factor: How One Man Made History* (New York: Riverhead Books, 2014).

[9] Ed Umbao, "Miss Universe Top 3 Question & Answer (Q&A) Portion (Transcript & Video)," *Philippine News*, December 21, 2015, https://philnews.ph/2015/12/21/miss-universe-top-3-question-answer-qa-portion-transcript-video/

[10] Eric Schmidt and Jonathan Rosenberg, *How Google Works* (New York: Grand Central Publishing, 2014).

Chapter 1

[1] Drake Baer, "Warren Buffett Used to Throw Up Before Public Speaking—Here's How He Mastered It," *Business Insider*, December 12, 2014, http://www.businessinsider.com/how-warren-buffett-learned-public-speaking-2014-12

[2] Charles Duhigg, *The Power of Habit: Why We Do What We Do in Life and Business* (New York: Random House, 2012), Kindle edition, loc. 1557.

[3] Peter Bregman, "You Need to Practice Being Your Future Self," *Harvard Business Review*, March 28, 2016, https://hbr.org/2016/03/you-need-to-practice-being-your-future-self

4 Sally Hogshead, *How the World Sees You: Discover Your Highest Value through the Science of Fascination* (New York: HarperCollins, 2014), Kindle edition, loc. 83.

5 Robert Caro, *The Power Broker: Robert Moses and the Fall of New York* (New York: Vintage, 1975).

6 Gene Weingarten, "Pearls before Breakfast: Can One of the Nation's Great Musicians Cut through the Fog of a D.C. Rush Hour? Let's Find Out," *Washington Post*, April 8, 2007, https://www.washingtonpost.com/lifestyle/magazine/pearls-before-breakfast-can-one-of-the-nations-great-musicians-cut-through-the-fog-of-a-dc-rush-hour-lets-find-out/2014/09/23/8a6d46da-4331-11e4-b47c-f5889e061e5f_story.html?utm_term=.12171d8bcd5b

7 Frank MacCrory, George Westerman, and Erik Brynjolfsson of the MIT Sloan School, and Yousef Alhammadi of the Masdar Institute, "Racing with and against the Machine: Changes in Occupational Skill Composition in an Era of Rapid Technological Advance," *Thirty-Fifth International Conference on Information Systems*, Auckland, NZ, 2014, https://pdfs.semanticscholar.org/164e/93f0d99852a2b8474c9c0c902eb00807a379.pdf, cited in Martha E. Mangelsdorf, "The New World of Work," *MIT Sloan Management Review*, March 16, 2015, http://sloanreview.mit.edu/article/the-new-world-of-work/

8 Arjun Kharpal, "Mark Cuban: Robots Will 'Cause Unemployment and We Need to Prepare for It,'" *CNBC*, February, 20, 2017, https://www.technologyreview.com/s/545606/how-an-ai-algorithm-learned-to-write-political-speeches/

9 "How an AI Algorithm Learned to Write Political Speeches," *MIT Technology Review*, January, 19, 2016, https://www.cnbc.com/2017/02/20/mark-cuban-robots-unemployment-and-we-need-to-prepare-for-it.html

[10] David Z. Morris, "Google's AlphaGo AI Runs the Table on Asia's Go Champs," *Fortune*, January 7, 2017, http://fortune.com/2017/01/07/google-alphago-ai/

[11] Howard Yu, "What AlphaGo Means for Your Job," *Fortune*, March 21, 2016, http://fortune.com/2016/03/21/google-alphago-win-artificial-intelligence/

[12] Andrew McAfee and Erik Brynjolfsson, "Where Computers Defeat Humans, and Where They Can't," *New York Times*, March 16, 2016, https://www.nytimes.com/2016/03/16/opinion/where-computers-defeat-humans-and-where-they-cant.html

[13] Geoff Colvin, *Humans Are Underrated: What High Achievers Know That Brilliant Machines Never Will* (New York: Portfolio/Penguin, 2015).

[14] Colvin, "The Skills of Human Interaction Will Become Most Valuable in the Future," *New York Times*, March 9, 2016, http://www.nytimes.com/roomfordebate/2016/03/09/does-alphago-mean-artificial-intelligence-is-the-real-deal/the-skills-of-human-interaction-will-become-most-valuable-in-the-future

[15] Anand Giridharadas, "Donald Trump Breaks with Tradition, and It's Paying Off," *New York Times*, March 14, 2016, https://www.nytimes.com/2016/03/15/us/politics/donald-trump-surprise-over-substance.html

[16] Berkeley Lovelace Jr., "Cramer: Blankfein Uses Twitter to Prevent Others from Defining Goldman Sachs," *CNBC*, June 20, 2017, http://www.cnbc.com/2017/06/20/cramer-blankfein-tweets-to-prevent-others-from-defining-goldman-sachs.html

[17] Vicki Salemi, "Good Grades Are Meaningless in the Modern Workplace," *New York Post*, March 21, 2016, http://nypost.com/2016/03/21/good-grades-are-meaningless-in-the-modern-workplace/

[18] Francesca Levy and Christopher Cannon, "The Bloomberg's Job Skills Report 2016: What the Recruiters Want," *Bloomberg*, February 9, 2016, https://www.bloomberg.com/graphics/2016-job-skills-report/

[19] Erik Brynjolfsson and Andrew McAfee, "The Jobs That AI Can't Replace," *BBC News*, September 13, 2015, http://www.bbc.com/news/technology-34175290

[20] Thomas L. Friedman, "Owning Your Own Future," *New York Times*, May 10, 2017, https://www.nytimes.com/2017/05/10/opinion/owning-your-own-future.html?_r=0

[21] Ernest Hemingway, *The Sun Also Rises* (New York: Scribner, 2012), reprint edition.

[22] "The State of American Jobs," *Pew Research Center Social and Demographics Trends*, October 6, 2016, http://www.pewsocialtrends.org/2016/10/06/the-state-of-american-jobs/

[23] Mark Gimein, "The Fallacy of Job Insecurity," *New Yorker*, June 29, 2016, http://www.newyorker.com/business/currency/the-fallacy-of-job-insecurity

[24] Dacher Keltner, *The Power Paradox: How We Gain and Lose Influence* (New York: Penguin Press, 2016), Kindle edition, loc. 339.

[25] David Brooks, "A Nation of Healers," *New York Times*, June 21, 2016, https://www.nytimes.com/2016/06/21/opinion/a-nation-of-healers.html

[26] Thomas L. Friedman and Michael Mandelbaum, *That Used to Be Us: How America Fell Behind in the World It Invented and How We Can Come Back* (New York: Farrar, Straus and Giroux, 2011), pp. 137–138.

27 David De Cremer and Jason D. Shaw, "What China's Shift to a Service Economy Means for Its Managers," *Harvard Business Review,* July 26, 2016, https://hbr.org/2016/07/what-chinas-shift-to-a-service-economy-means-for-its-managers

28 Associated Press, "Obama Fires Up Democrats: 'I Want You to Argue with Them and Get in Their Face,'" September 18, 2008, http://www.nydailynews.com/news/politics/obama-fires-democrats-argue-face-article-1.323400

29 Michael Lewis, *Flash Boys: A Wall Street Revolt* (New York: W.W. Norton & Company, 2015), p. 209.

30 Carmen Simon, "The Neuroscience of Memorable Content," *HubSpot: INBOUND 2015 I&E,* November 12, 2015, https://www.youtube.com/watch?v=eoJ-RG5AqL0&t=363s

31 Keld Jensen, "Intelligence Is Overrated: What You Really Need to Succeed," *Forbes,* April 12, 2012, http://www.forbes.com/sites/keldjensen/2012/04/12/intelligence-is-overrated-what-you-really-need-to-succeed/#41a851096375

32 Danielle Ofri, "The Conversation Placebo," *New York Times,* January 19, 2017, https://www.nytimes.com/2017/01/19/opinion/sunday/the-conversation-placebo.html?_r=0

33 Nicholas Carlson, *Marissa Mayer and the Fight to Save Yahoo!* (New York: Twelve, 2015), Kindle edition, loc. 1877.

Chapter 2

1 Fox News Insider, "Megyn to Dr. Phil: This Advice from You Turned into My Life Philosophy," May 8, 2015, http://insider.foxnews.com/2015/05/08/dr-phil-all-things-wrong-life-can-be-made-right

2 Megyn Kelly, *Settle for More* (New York: HarperCollins, 2016).

3 Seth Godin, *Icarus Deception: How High Will You Fly?* (New York: Portfolio/Penguin, 2012), Kindle edition, loc. 2353.

4 Michael Port, "Seth Godin on Public Speaking and Performing during High Stakes Situations," *Steal the Show* (podcast audio), episode 57, http://stealtheshow.com/podcast/seth-godin-public-speaking/

5 Mike Brooks and Dino Dogan, "How Bryan Kramer Went from Reinventing Himself to TED," *Road to TED* (podcast audio), July 1, 2015, http://roadtoted.com/how-bryan-kramer-went-from-reinventing-himself-to-ted/

6 Michael Beer, Magnus Finnström, and Derek Schrader, "Why Leadership Training Fails—and What to Do about It," *Harvard Business Review*, October 2016, https://hbr.org/2016/10/why-leadership-training-fails-and-what-to-do-about-it

7 Charles Duhigg, *Smarter Faster Better: The Secrets of Being Productive in Life and Business* (New York: Random House, 2016), Kindle edition, loc. 3296.

8 Peter Thiel, *Zero to One: Notes on Startups, or How to Build the Future* (New York: Crown Business, 2014), Kindle edition, loc. 73.

9 Ibid., loc. 75.

10 Niccolò Machiavelli, *The Prince*, translated by W. K. Marriott (Ballingslöv, Sweden: Wisehouse Classics, 2015), Kindle edition, loc. 1128.

11 Nancy Duarte and Patti Sanchez, "Illuminate," *Talks at Google*, July 14, 2016, https://youtu.be/iUoiKidIbxU

12 Apollo Robbins, "The Art of Misdirection," *TED*, September 13, 2013, https://youtu.be/GZGY0wPAnus

13 Stephen Hawking, *A Brief History of Time* (New York: Bantam Books, 1988).

Chapter 3

[1] Jennifer Rubin, "Who Flunks—and Who Passes—the Beer Test?" *Washington Post*, April 15, 2015, https://www.washingtonpost.com/blogs/right-turn/wp/2015/04/15/who-flunks-and-who-passes-the-beer-test/?utm_term=.0de009b175a3

[2] Tim Sanders, *The Likeability Factor: How to Boost Your L-Factor and Achieve Your Life's Dreams* (New York: Crown Publishers, 2005), p. 33.

[3] Ibid., p. 100.

[4] Ibid., p. 108.

[5] Ibid., p. 115.

[6] Ibid., p. 124.

[7] Michael Port, "Creative Path to Successful Speaking with Mitch Joel," *Steal the Show* (podcast audio), episode 67, http://stealtheshow.com/podcast/creative-path-to-successful-speaking-mitch-joel/

[8] Dan Pink, *To Sell Is Human: The Surprising Truth about Moving Others* (New York: Riverhead Books, 2012), Kindle edition, loc. 68.

[9] Timothy Egan, "The Eight-Second Attention Span," *New York Times*, January, 22, 2016, https://www.nytimes.com/2016/01/22/opinion/the-eight-second-attention-span.html

[10] Tyler Cowen, *Average Is Over: Powering America beyond the Age of the Great Stagnation* (New York: Dutton, 2013), Kindle edition, loc. 312.

[11] Eric Bradner, "Conway: Trump White House Offered 'Alternative Facts' on Crowd Size," *CNN politics*, January 23, 2017, http://www.cnn.com/2017/01/22/politics/kellyanne-conway-alternative-facts/

[12] "Art of the Lie," *The Economist*, September 10, 2016, http://www.economist.com/news/leaders/21706525-politicians-have-always-lied-does-it-matter-if-they-leave-truth-behind-entirely-art

[13] "Yes, I'd Lie to You," *The Economist*, September 10, 2016, http://www.economist.com/news/briefing/21706498-dishonesty-politics-nothing-new-manner-which-some-politicians-now-lie-and

[14] Erik Wemple, "The Brian Williams Scandal Is an *NBC News*–wide Scandal," *Washington Post*, February 5, 2015, https://www.washingtonpost.com/blogs/erik-wemple/wp/2015/02/05/the-brian-williams-scandal-is-an-nbc-news-wide-scandal/?utm_term=.da3f0079dfcd

[15] Jeffrey Pfeffer, *Leadership BS: Fixing Workplaces and Careers One Truth at a Time* (New York: HarperCollins, 2015), Kindle edition, loc. 1721.

[16] Peter Bregman, "Jeff Pfeffer—*Leadership BS*," *The Bregman Leadership Podcast* (podcast audio), episode 23, May 23, 2016, http://peterbregman.com/podcast/jeff-pfeffer-leadership-bs/#.WLNAdPnythE

[17] CNN, All Politics, "Mondale's Acceptance Speech, 1984: Walter Mondale Throws Down Gauntlet in Run against Reagan," *Chicago 96 Facts*, http://www.cnn.com/ALLPOLITICS/1996/conventions/chicago/facts/famous.speeches/mondale.84.shtml

[18] Sydney Finkelstein, *Superbosses: How Exceptional Leaders Master the Flow of Talent* (New York: Portfolio/Penguin, 2016), Kindle edition, loc. 1987.

[19] Democratic National Convention, "President Bill Clinton at the 2012 Democratic National Convention," September 6, 2012, https://youtu.be/lFUtEyh20Ok

[20] E News Tonight, "'When They Go Low, We Go High'—Hillary Clinton Slams Donald J. Trump over His 'Birther' Claims," September 26, 2016, https://youtu.be/qNpAJrRz6uY

[21] Jeffrey Toobin, *The Run of His Life: The People v. O. J. Simpson* (New York: Random House, 1996), pp. 10–11.

[22] Alan Dershowitz, *The Best Defense: The Courtroom Confrontations of America's Most Outspoken Lawyer of Last Resort—The Lawyer Who Won the Claus von Bulow Appeal* (New York: Vintage, 2011).

[23] NPR Special Series: Echoes of 1968, "Robert Kennedy: Delivering News of King's Death," April 4, 2008, http://www.npr.org/2008/04/04/89365887/robert-kennedy-delivering-news-of-kings-death

[24] Ian Christopher McCaleb, "Bush Tours Ground Zero in Lower Manhattan," *CNN.com/U.S.*, September 14, 2001, http://edition.cnn.com/2001/US/09/14/bush.terrorism/

Chapter 4

[1] Seth Godin, *Linchpin: Are You Indispensable?* (New York: Portfolio, 2010), Kindle edition, loc. 3765.

[2] Tomas Chamorro-Premuzic, *Confidence: How Much You Really Need and How to Get It* (New York: Hudson Street Press, 2013), Kindle edition, loc. 469.

[3] Nick Morgan, *Power Cues: The Subtle Science of Leading Groups, Persuading Others, and Maximizing Your Personal Impact* (Boston: Harvard Business Review Press, 2014).

[4] Sheryl Sandberg with Nell Scovell, *Lean In: Women, Work, and the Will to Lead* (New York: Alfred A. Knopf, 2013), Kindle edition, loc. 1017.

[5] Ibid., loc. 1020.

Chapter 5

[1] Scott Adams, *How to Fail at Almost Everything and Still Win Big: Kind of the Story of My Life* (New York: Portfolio/Penguin, 2013), Kindle edition, loc. 584.

[2] Ashley Feinstein, "Why You Should Be Writing Down Your Goals," *Forbes*, April 8, 2014, http://www.forbes.com/sites/ellevate/2014/04/08/why-you-should-be-writing-down-your-goals/#60f2fe7e2f14

[3] Duhigg, *Smarter Faster Better*, Kindle edition, loc. 1827.

[4] MIT Human Resources: Performance Development, "SMART Goals," http://hrweb.mit.edu/performance-development/goal-setting-developmental-planning/smart-goals

[5] Amy Chua, *Battle Hymn of the Tiger Mother* (New York: Penguin Books, 2011), p. 29.

[6] Angela Duckworth, *Grit: The Power of Passion and Perseverance* (New York: Scribner, 2016), Kindle edition, loc. 956.

[7] Sir Isaiah Berlin, *The Hedgehog and the Fox: An Essay on Tolstoy's View of History* (London: Weidenfeld & Nicolson, 1953; New York: Simon & Schuster, 1957; New York: New American Library, 1986), excerpted by Dr. Erik K. Antonsson at California Institute of Technology Engineering Design Research Laboratory, http://www.design.caltech.edu/erik/Misc/Fox_Hedgehog.html

Chapter 6

[1] Stephen R. Covey, *The 7 Habits of Highly Effective People: Powerful Lessons in Personal Change* (New York: Fireside, 1989), p. 98.

[2] Jay Oza, "My First Blog Post: It Starts Today," *5ToolGroup*, August 2, 2011, http://www.5toolgroup.com/blogs/first-post

3 Andrew M. Lane, Peter Totterdell, Ian MacDonald, Tracey J. Devonport, Andrew P. Friesen, Christopher J. Beedie, Damian Stanley, and Alan Nevill, "Brief Online Training Enhances Competitive Performance: Findings of the BBC Lab UK Psychological Skills Intervention Study," *Frontiers in Psychology*, March 30, 2016, http://journal.frontiersin.org/article/10.3389/fpsyg.2016.00413/full

4 James Altucher, "What I Learned from Spanx Founder Sara Blakely: How to Get a Billion Dollar Idea," *The James Altucher Show* (podcast audio), episode 211, http://www.jamesaltucher.com/2017/02/sara-blakely/

Chapter 7

1 Steven Pressfield, *The War of Art: Break through the Blocks and Win Your Inner Creative Battles* (New York: Black Irish Entertainment, 2002), Kindle edition, loc. 1113.

2 Eric Ries, *The Lean Startup: How Today's Entrepreneurs Use Continuous Innovation to Create Radically Successful Businesses* (New York: Crown Business, 2011).

3 Dave Paradi, "Are We Wasting $250 Million per Day Due to Bad PowerPoint?" *Think outside the Slide*, http://www.thinkoutsidetheslide.com/are-we-wasting-250-million-per-day-due-to-bad-powerpoint/

4 Donald Sull and Kathleen M. Eisenhardt, *Simple Rules: How to Thrive in a Complex World* (New York: Houghton Mifflin Harcourt, 2015), Kindle edition, loc. 954.

5 Ibid., loc. 958.

6 Herminia Ibarra, *Act Like a Leader, Think Like a Leader* (Boston: Harvard Business Review Press, 2015), Kindle edition, loc. 140.

[7] Noah Charney, "Jodi Picoult on Writing, Publishing, and What She's Reading," *The Daily Beast*, April 3, 2012, http://www.thedailybeast.com/articles/2012/04/03/jodi-picoult-on-writing-publishing-and-what-she-s-reading.html

[8] Matt Abrahams, "Tips and Techniques for More Confident and Compelling Presentations," *Stanford Business*, March 2, 2015, https://www.gsb.stanford.edu/insights/matt-abrahams-tips-techniques-more-confident-compelling-presentations

[9] Mark Levy, *Accidental Genius* (San Francisco: Berrett-Koehler Publishers, 2010).

[10] Josh Bernoff, "Your Outlines Are Useless. You Need a Fat Outline," *Without Bullshit*, November 24, 2015, https://withoutbullshit.com/blog/fat-outline

[11] James Clear, "The Ivy Lee Method: The Daily Routine Experts Recommend for Peak Productivity," *Huffington Post*, June 2, 2016, http://www.huffingtonpost.com/james-clear/the-ivy-lee-method-the-da_b_10257938.html

[12] Mattan Griffel, "If You're Not Embarrassed by Your Startup, You've Launched Too Late," *One Month*, May 5, 2015, http://learn.onemonth.com/if-youre-not-embarrassed-by-your-startup-you-launched-too-late

[13] Ben Parr, "The 'Iterate Fast and Release Often' Philosophy of Entrepreneurship," *American Express OPEN Forum*, November 12, 2009, https://www.americanexpress.com/us/small-business/openforum/articles/the-iterate-fast-and-release-often-philosophy-of-entrepreneurship-1/

Chapter 8

[1] Jia Jiang, *Rejection Proof: How I Beat Fear and Became Invincible One Rejection at a Time* (New York: Harmony, 2015).

Chapter 9

[1] Grant Baldwin, "Heroic Public Speaking, with Michael Port," *The Speaker Lab with Grant Baldwin// Public Speaking/ Motivational Speaking/ Entrepreneurship* (podcast audio), episode 7, January, 19, 2016, http://thespeakerlab.libsyn.com/007-heroic-public-speaking-with-michael-port

[2] Dominique Mosbergen, "South African CEO's 'Bitch-Switch' Comment Prompts Firestorm," *Huffington Post*, April 28, 2016, http://www.huffingtonpost.com/entry/south-africa-ceo-women-bitch-switch_us_57218b15e4b0b49df6aa3452

[3] Huffington Post Canada, "Chip Wilson, Lululemon Founder: 'Some Women's Bodies' Not Right for Our Pants," November 6, 2013, http://www.huffingtonpost.com/2013/11/06/lululemon-chip-wilson-womens-bodies_n_4228113.html

[4] Tom LoBianco, "VA's McDonald Apologizes for Disney Waiting Line Comparison," *CNN politics*, May 24, 2016, http://www.cnn.com/2016/05/24/politics/bob-mcdonald-veterans-affairs-disney/

[5] CBC News, "Canadian Prime Minister Justin Trudeau Schools Reporter on Quantum Computing during Press Conference," *YouTube*, April 15, 2016, https://www.youtube.com/watch?v=Eak_ogYMprk

Chapter 10

[1] Tamsen Webster, "Where Does the Red Thread Come From?" *Tamsen Webster* (website), episode 3, February 22, 2017, http://tamsenwebster.com/ep-003-red-thread-origins-right-path/

[2] Frank Luntz, *Words That Work: It's Not What You Say, It's What People Hear* (New York: Hyperion, 2007).

[3] Maurice Saatchi, "The Strange Death of Modern Advertising," *Financial Times*, June 22, 2006,

http://www.ft.com/cms/s/0/abd93fe6-018a-11db-af16-
0000779e2340.html?ft_site=falcon&desktop=true#axzz4dzDtskC9
4 FoxNews.com, "Spicer Says 'Trust' Issues Triggered Flynn
Ouster, Downplays Legal Questions," February 14, 2017,
http://www.foxnews.com/politics/2017/02/14/spicer-says-
trust-issues-triggered-flynn-ouster-downplays-legal-questions.html
5 Altucher, "What I Learned from Spanx Founder Sara Blakely,"
http://www.jamesaltucher.com/2017/02/sara-blakely/
6 David McCollough, *The Path between the Seas: The Creation of the
Panama Canal, 1870–1914* (New York: Simon & Schuster, 2001),
Kindle edition, loc. 5090.
7 Walter Isaacson, *Steve Jobs* (New York: Simon & Schuster, 2011),
Kindle edition, loc. 5756.
8 Roger Ailes with Jon Kraushar, *You Are the Message: Getting What
You Want by Being Who You Are* (New York: Currency and
Doubleday, 1988), Kindle edition, loc. 277.
9 James C. Humes, *The Sir Winston Method: The Five Secrets of
Speaking the Language of Leadership* (New York: William Morrow
and Company, 1991), p. 45.
10 Wikipedia, "Log Line," https://en.wikipedia.org/wiki/Log_line
11 Ricardo Bellino, *You Have Three Minutes! Learn the Secret of the
Pitch from Trump's Original Apprentice* (New York: McGraw-Hill,
2006), p. ix.
12 Todd Benson, "Trump Takes a Meeting, Now Backs a Resort
in Brazil," *New York Times*, May 19, 2004,
http://www.nytimes.com/2004/05/19/business/trump-takes-a-
meeting-now-backs-a-resort-in-brazil.html
13 Bellino, *You Have Three Minutes!* p. 68.
14 Chip Heath and Dan Heath, *Made to Stick: Why Some Ideas Survive
and Others Die* (New York: Random House, 2007), Kindle edition,
loc. 297.

[15] Ibid., loc. 348.

[16] Callaway Live, "The Origins of Herm Edward's 'Hello! You Play to Win the Game!' Rant" (*YouTube*), September 1, 2016, https://youtu.be/N3rPrmhsVV4

[17] Terri L. Sjodin, *Small Message, Big Impact: How to Put the Power of the Elevator Speech Effect to Work for You* (Austin, TX: Greenleaf Book Group Press, 2011), Kindle edition, loc. 1769.

[18] Amy Chua and Jed Rubenfeld, *The Triple Package: How Three Unlikely Traits Explain the Rise and Fall of Cultural Groups in America* (New York: The Penguin Press, 2014), Kindle edition, loc. 120.

[19] Salena Zito, "Taking Trump Seriously, Not Literally," *Atlantic*, September 23, 2016, https://www.theatlantic.com/politics/archive/2016/09/trump-makes-his-case-in-pittsburgh/501335/

[20] Lauren Carroll, "Fact-Checking Trump's Claim That Thousands in New Jersey Cheered When World Trade Center Tumbled," *Politifact*, November, 22, 2015, http://www.politifact.com/truth-o-meter/statements/2015/nov/22/donald-trump/fact-checking-trumps-claim-thousands-new-jersey-ch/

Chapter 11

[1] Thomas L. Friedman, *Thank You for Being Late: An Optimist's Guide to Thriving in the Age of Accelerations* (New York: Farrar, Straus and Giroux, 2016), Kindle edition, loc. 193.

[2] David Carnoy, "Watch Steve Jobs Introduce the iPhone 10 Years Ago Today," *CNET, The Verge*, January 9, 2017, https://www.cnet.com/news/watch-steve-jobs-introduce-the-original-iphone-10-years-ago-today/

³ TEDxEast Interconnectivity, "Nancy Duarte Uncovers Common Structure of Greatest Communicators" (Ted Talk on *YouTube*), November 11, 2010 (uploaded December 10, 2010), https://www.youtube.com/watch?v=1nYFpuc2Umk

⁴ Rory Vaden, "Succeeding in the Speaking Industry with Brian Tracy," *Action Catalyst Podcast*, episode 163, October 12, 2016, http://roryvaden.com/blog/succeeding-speaking-industry-brian-tracy-action-catalyst-podcast/

Chapter 12

¹ Matt McGarrity, "Introduction to Public Speaking," University of Washington Coursera course, https://www.coursera.org/learn/public-speaking

² Samuel Beckett, *The Unnamable* [originally in French: *L'Innommable*], trans. Samuel Beckett (Paris: Les Éditions de Minuit, 1953; New York: Grove Press, 1958), discussed by Tom Clark, "Samuel Beckett: Aporia," *Beyond the Pale* [blog], April 3, 2010, http://tomclarkblog.blogspot.com/2010/04/samuel-beckett-aporia.html

³ Georgetown University Berkeley Center for Religion, Peace & World Affairs, "Bill Clinton on Overcoming Evil in Oklahoma City Bombing Memorial Speech," April 23, 1995, https://berkleycenter.georgetown.edu/quotes/bill-clinton-on-overcoming-evil-in-oklahoma-city-bombing-memorial-speech

⁴ Benjamin Franklin, *Poor Richard's Almanack* (Philadelphia: New Printing Office, 1755), 5.471.

⁵ The History Place: Great Speeches Collection, "Ronald Reagan, 'Tear Down This Wall,'" http://www.historyplace.com/speeches/reagan-tear-down.htm

[6] American Rhetoric: Top 100 Speeches, "Martin Luther King Jr. 'I Have a Dream,'" http://www.americanrhetoric.com/speeches/mlkihaveadream.htm

Chapter 13

[1] William Shakespeare, *As You Like It* (Act 2, Scene 7), public domain book, 2012, Kindle edition, loc. 556.

[2] Chancellor Agard, "Seinfeld, Rock, Chappelle, Schumer, and Ansari Share 'Night to Remember,'" *Entertainment*, January 12, 2017, http://ew.com/tv/2017/01/12/seinfeld-rock-chappelle-schumer-ansari-comedy-cellar/

[3] Sridhar Pappu, "Aziz Ansari Is Still Searching," New York Times, June 8, 2017, https://www.nytimes.com/2017/06/08/fashion/aziz-ansari-master-of-none.html?_r=0

[4] Michael Port, *Steal the Show: From Speeches to Job Interviews to Deal-Closing Pitches, How to Guarantee a Standing Ovation for All the Performances in Your Life* (New York: Houghton Mifflin Harcourt, 2015), Kindle edition, locs. 52, 55.

[5] Anne Lamott, *Bird by Bird: Some Instructions on Writing and Life* (New York: Anchor Books, 1994), Kindle edition, loc. 518.

[6] Edward Dwight Easty, *On Method Acting: The Classic Actor's Guide to the Stanislavsky Technique as Practiced at the Actors Studio* (New York: Ivy Books, 1981), Kindle edition, loc. 241.

[7] Ibid., loc. 250.

[8] Team Tony, "The Making of 'Tony Robbins: I Am Not Your Guru': An Interview with Documentary Filmmaker Joe Berlinger," Robbins Research International (podcast audio), https://www.tonyrobbins.com/podcast/story-behind-tony-robbins-documentary/

[9] TED Talks (One of 1,000+ TED Talks), "Your Body Language Shapes Who You Are | Amy Cuddy," *YouTube*, October 1, 2012, https://youtu.be/Ks-_Mh1QhMc

[10] R.I.N. Dunbar, Neocortex Size As a Constraint on Group Size in Primates, *Journal of Human Evolution* 22 (6), June 1992, 469–93, abstract at http://www.sciencedirect.com/science/article/pii/004724849290081J

[11] Kelly Leonard and Tom Yorton, *Yes, And: How Improvisation Reverses "No, But" Thinking and Improves Creativity and Collaboration—Lessons from* The Second City (New York: Harper Collins, 2015), Kindle edition, loc. 177.

[12] AP Archive, "President Ronald Reagan Address an Adoring Crowd at the [1988] Republican National Convention), *YouTube*: 2:44 minute mark, July 31, 2015, https://youtu.be/j0-PuZDfiuc

[13] Neel Doshi and Lindsay McGregor, *Primed to Perform: How to Build the Highest Performing Cultures through the Science of Total Motivation* (New York: Harper Business, 2015).

[14] Drew Hansen, "Mahalia Jackson, and King's Improvisation," *New York Times*, August 27, 2013, http://www.nytimes.com/2013/08/28/opinion/mahalia-jackson-and-kings-rhetorical-improvisation.html

[15] Gina Dalfonzo, "Remember When Actors Wanted to Be Versatile? Benedict Cumberbatch Does," *Atlantic*, May 21, 2013, https://www.theatlantic.com/entertainment/archive/2013/05/remember-when-actors-wanted-to-be-versatile-benedict-cumberbatch-does/276061/

[16] *Face the Nation*, "Ronald Reagan at 1980 GOP Debate: 'I Am Paying for This Microphone,'" *YouTube*, February 11, 2016, https://youtu.be/KVHlHR5RcSg

Chapter 14

[1] Tony Robbins, "Why We Do What We Do," *TED Ideas Worth Spreading* (subtitles and transcript) posted June 2006, https://www.ted.com/talks/tony_robbins_asks_why_we_do_ what_we_do/transcript?language=en

[2] Chip Heath and Dan Heath, "The Curse of Knowledge," *Harvard Business Review*, December 2006, https://hbr.org/2006/12/the-curse-of-knowledge

[3] Wikipedia, "Albert Mehrabian," https://en.wikipedia.org/wiki/Albert_Mehrabian

[4] Michael Port, "The Business of Speaking for Women, Business Models for Speakers, and Much More with Neen James," *Steal the Show* (audio podcast), episode 70, http://stealtheshow.com/podcast/business-of-speaking-for-women-neen-james/

[5] Zig Ziglar, narrated by Zig Ziglar, *See You at the Top: 25th Anniversary Edition* (Simon Schuster Audio/Nightingale-Conant, 2012), audible, 1 hour and 42 minutes.

[6] Rosebush, *True Reagan*, Kindle edition, loc. 248.

[7] Amy Cuddy, *Presence: Bringing Your Boldest Self to Your Biggest Challenges* (New York: Little, Brown and Company, 2015), Kindle edition, loc. 237.

[8] Heath and Heath, *Made to Stick*, Kindle edition, loc. 2775.

[9] Scott McKain, *ALL Business Is STILL Show Business: Create Distinction and Earn Standing Ovations from Customers in a Hyper-Competitive Marketplace* (Las Vegas, NV: Distinction Press, 2017), Kindle edition, loc. 2685.

[10] Colonial Williamsburg Foundation Center for History and Citizenship, "Give Me Liberty or Give Me Death," http://www.history.org/almanack/life/politics/giveme.cfm

[11] Yale Law School Lillian Goldman Law Library Avalon Project, "Gettysburg Address," http://avalon.law.yale.edu/19th_century/gettyb.asp

[12] Peggy Noonan, *Simply Speaking: How to Communicate Your Ideas with Style, Substance, and Clarity* (New York: HarperCollins, 1998), p. 65.

[13] Ibid., taken from Paul Revere Frothingham, *Edward Everett, Orator and Statesman* (Boston: Houghton Mifflin, 1925), pp. 454–58.

[14] American Rhetoric, Top 100 Speeches, "Martin Luther King, Jr., 'I Have a Dream,'" http://www.americanrhetoric.com/speeches/mlkihaveadream.htm and for just the "dream" part in real time: Ilya Gokadze. "Martin Luther King, Jr., I Have a Dream Speech," *YouTube*, published August 28, 2013, https://www.youtube.com/watch?v=3vDWWy4CMhE

Chapter 15

[1] Simon, *Impossible to Ignore: Creating Memorable Content to Influence Decisions*, Kindle edition, loc. 688.

[2] C. Peter Giuliano, "What Made Ronald Reagan 'the Great Communicator,'" *The Public Relations Strategist*, Summer 2004, http://ecgcoaching.com/library/Strategist_S04.pdf

[3] Ronald Reagan, "Remarks at the Annual Conference of the Council of the Americas," May 21, 1985, *The American Presidency Project*, http://www.presidency.ucsb.edu/ws/?pid=38669

[4] Stiggerpao, "Coca-Cola Classic Ad: Mean Joe Greene [Full Version] (1979)," *YouTube*, uploaded July 17, 2007, https://www.youtube.com/watch?v=xffOCZYX6F8

[5] Sergio Zyman, *The End of Marketing As We Know It* (New York: Harper Business, 1999), p. 3.

6 Antisubliminal, "Apple—1984," *YouTube*, uploaded June 19, 2006, https://www.youtube.com/watch?v=R706isyDrqI

7 Jay Oza, "Conversation with Thom Winninger," *Speech Talk Live*, episode 61, *YouTube*, uploaded January 20, 2017, https://youtu.be/fKUC7m1tLAU?list=PLOySikLQ9FUgOrojDa Z_zIxjlwjF1xhJN

8 Simon, *Impossible to Ignore: Creating Memorable Content to Influence Decisions*, Kindle edition, loc. 2598.

9 Reagan Foundation, "Moscow State University: President Reagan's Address at Moscow State University—5/31/88," *YouTube*, uploaded April 21, 2009, https://youtu.be/1lutYGxMWeA

10 NASA.gov Video, "President Kennedy's Speech at Rice University," September 12, 1962, *YouTube*, published May 18, 2013, https://youtu.be/WZyRbnpGyzQ

11 Rosebush, *True Reagan*, Kindle edition, loc. 214.

12 Joanna Weiss, "The Man Who Killed the SAT Essay," *Boston Globe*, March 14, 2014, https://www.bostonglobe.com/opinion/2014/03/13/the-man-who-killed-sat-essay/L9v3dbPXewKq8oAvOUqONM/story.html

13 Democratic National Convention, "Senator Tim Kaine at DNC 2016," *YouTube*, July 28, 2016, https://youtu.be/Fis6X19Y6eU

14 Democratic National Convention, "Khizr Khan at DNC 2016," *YouTube*, July 28, 2016, https://youtu.be/Ery-Zgo5ALs

15 Larry J. Sabato, Kyle Kondik, and Geoffrey Skelley, "Romney, Ryan, Republicans and… Eastwood?" *University of Virginia Center for Politics: Sabato's Crystal Ball*, August 31, 2012, http://www.centerforpolitics.org/crystalball/articles/romney-ryan-republicans-and-eastwood/

16 Ailes and Kraushar, *You Are the Message*, Kindle edition, loc. 589.

[17] Ibid., loc. 601.

[18] Ibid., loc. 638.

[19] Decker Communications, "Mark McGwire Testifying to Congress (Poorly)," C-SPAN recording of U.S. House of Representatives Government Reform Committee, March 17, 2005, *YouTube*, uploaded October 19, 2009, https://youtu.be/up_eQUuiDN0

Chapter 16

[1] Matthew Dixon and Brent Adamson, *The Challenger Sale: Taking Control of the Customer Conversation* (New York: Portfolio/Penguin, 2011).

[2] Sandberg and Scovell, *Lean In*, Kindle edition, loc. 865.

[3] Peter Guber, *Tell to Win: Connect, Persuade, and Triumph with the Hidden Power of Story* (New York: Crown Business, 2011), Kindle edition, loc. 2041.

[4] Isaacson, *Steve Jobs*, Kindle edition, loc. 2838.

[5] Jonathan Martin and Amie Parnes, "Obama Not an Arab, Crowd Boos," *Politico*, October 10, 2008, http://www.politico.com/story/2008/10/mccain-obama-not-an-arab-crowd-boos-014479 and Associated Press, "McCain Counters Obama 'Arab' Question," *YouTube*, October 11, 2008, https://youtu.be/jrnRU3ocIH4

[6] Jason La Canfora, "Super Bowl 49: Pete Carroll's Decision Astonishing, Explanation Perplexing," *CBS Sports*, February 2, 2015, http://www.cbssports.com/nfl/news/super-bowl-49-pete-carrolls-decision-astonishing-explanation-perplexing/

[7] Gordievsky, "Iverson Practice!" *YouTube*, uploaded April 15, 2006, https://www.youtube.com/watch?v=eGDBR2L5kzI

[8] National Baseball Hall of Fame, "Luckiest Man," http://baseballhall.org/discover/lou-gehrig-luckiest-man

Chapter 17

[1] Tom Friedman, *NBC News: Meet the Press*, January 29, 2017, http://www.nbcnews.com/meet-the-press/meet-press-01-29-17-n713751

[2] Talks at Google, "Doug Stevenson: 'The Power to Persuade—The Magic of Story,'" *YouTube*, August 4, 2014, https://youtu.be/sKUiE9DBkKc

[3] John Rampton, "The Secrets to Building a Product Roadmap," *Inc.*, May 1, 2015, http://www.inc.com/john-rampton/secrets-to-building-a-product-roadmap.html

[4] TED Talks (One of 1,000+ TED Talks), "Your Body Language Shapes Who You Are | Amy Cuddy," *YouTube*, October 1, 2012, https://youtu.be/Ks-_Mh1QhMc

[5] Stanford University, "Steve Jobs' 2005 Stanford Commencement Address," *YouTube*, May 7, 2008, https://youtu.be/UF8uR6Z6KLc

[6] Isaacson, *Steve Jobs*, Kindle edition, loc. 7896.

[7] TED Talks, "Why We Have Too Few Women Leaders | Sheryl Sandberg," *YouTube*, December 21, 2010, https://youtu.be/18uDutylDa4

Chapter 18

[1] The First Round Review, "Radical Candor—The Surprising Secret to Being a Good Boss," http://firstround.com/review/radical-candor-the-surprising-secret-to-being-a-good-boss/

[2] Douglas Stone and Sheila Heen, *Thanks for the Feedback: The Science and Art of Receiving Feedback Well* (New York: Viking, 2014), Kindle edition, loc. 502.

[3] Chamorro-Premuzic, *Confidence*, Kindle edition, loc. 514.

4 François-Marie Arouet (Voltaire), *"Art dramatique," Dictionaire philosophique*, 1770.

5 Robert I. Sutton, "Karl Weick's Creativity: Why Specialists Are Grumpy and Generalists Are Happy," *Psychology Today*, May 29, 2010, https://www.psychologytoday.com/blog/work-matters/201005/karl-weicks-creativity

6 Charney, "Jodi Picoult."

7 TED Talks, "The Mind behind Tesla, SpaceX, SolarCity… | Elon Musk," *YouTube*, March 19, 2013, https://youtu.be/IgKWPdJWuBQ

8 Kevin Kruse, "How to Receive Feedback and Criticism," *Forbes*, August 12, 2014, https://www.forbes.com/sites/kevinkruse/2014/08/12/how-to-receive-feedback-and-criticism/#691f41dd7c3f

9 Francesco Gino, "Research: We Drop People Who Give Us Critical Feedback," *Harvard Business Review*, September 16, 2016, https://hbr.org/2016/09/research-we-drop-people-who-give-us-critical-feedback

Chapter 19

1 Cuddy, *Presence*, Kindle edition, loc. 198.

2 Atul Gawande, *Checklist Manifesto: How to Get Things Right* (New York: Henry Holt and Company, 2009).

3 Chris Vander Mey, *Shipping Greatness: Practical Lessons on Building and Launching Outstanding Software, Learned on the Job at Google and Amazon* (Sebastopol, CA: O'Reilly Media, 2012).

4 Ray Edwards, *How to Write Copy That Sells: The Step-by-Step System for More Sales, to More Customers, More Often* (New York: Morgan James, 2016), Kindle edition, loc. 439.

[5] Clayton M. Christensen, Taddy Hall, Karen Dillon, and David S. Duncan, *Competing against Luck: The Story of Innovation and Customer Choice* (New York: Harper Business, 2016).

[6] Simon Sinek, *Start with Why: How Great Leaders Inspire Everyone to Take Action* (New York: Portfolio/Penguin, 2011).

[7] Gary Vaynerchuk, "Three Pieces of Advice to Build Confidence for Public Speaking," *Gary Vaynerchuk* (website), 2016, https://www.garyvaynerchuk.com/three-pieces-advice-build-confidence-public-speaking/

[8] Vaden, "Succeeding in the Speaking Industry with Brian Tracy."

[9] Theodore H, White, *Making of the President: 1960* (New York: HarperCollins, 2009), Kindle edition, loc. 3769.

Chapter 20

[1] Pink, *To Sell Is Human*, Kindle edition, loc. 67.

[2] "The Highest-Paid Show Hosts of All Time," *Forbes*, 2017, https://www.forbes.com/pictures/gjdm45eded/the-highest-paid-show-ho/#1f992c715992

Conclusion

[1] Brad Kallet, "Eighteen Years Later, Lučić-Baroni Returns to a Major Quarterfinal, *Tennis*, January 23, 2017, http://www.tennis.com/pro-game/2017/01/mirjana-lucic-baroni-australian-open-wta-tennis/63604/

Appendix A

[1] Dan Roam, *Draw to Win: A Crash Course on How to Lead, Sell, and Innovate with Your Visual Mind* (New York: Portfolio/Penguin, 2016), p. 14.

Appendix B

[1] Noah Zandan, "Wharton People Analytics Conference 2016: Panel on Methods," Wharton School, *YouTube*: 1:19 minute mark, August 5, 2016, https://youtu.be/NmOFGu3xw8w

[2] Robert B. Miller, Gary A. Williams, and Alden M. Hayashi, *The 5 Paths to Persuasion: The Art of Selling Your Message* (New York: Hachette Book Group, 2004).

[3] Oren Klaff, *Pitch Anything: An Innovative Method for Presenting, Persuading, and Winning the Deal* (New York: McGraw-Hill Education, 2011).

Index

Index

223, 231

158, 171, 256

not mingling with, 256

nothing else matters, 51

part of performance, 217, 228

processing more important than
what you say, 168

questioning your, 223, 330

regarding as customers, 290

reinforcing beliefs of, 217

resonating with. *See* connecting
with the audience

surprising your, 257, 283

tailoring your speech to, 198, 274,
327, 328

trust of. *See* authenticity; credibility;
message, being the

viewing as though venture
capitalists, 246

wasting time of, 54, 123, 282

won't know what you leave out,
202, 331

wowing your, 283–300

authenticity, 235

avoiding exaggeration, 73, 76

believing in your message, 259,
328, 329, 357

consequences of truth telling, 77,
278

importance of, 67, 246

See also credibility

author's background, 11, 359, 366

automation, insurance against, 32–36,
218, 236

B

backup plan, 225
rehearsing, 223, 226

Bacon, Francis, on the power of
knowledge, 58

bad breath, avoiding, 332

Balachandra, Lakschmi, on
enthusiasm and confidence more
important than credentials, 243

beauty pageant metaphor for life, 15–18

beer test, to gauge likability, 66, 285

Beethoven's Fifth Symphony,
importance of first few seconds,
174

believability. *See* authenticity;
credibility; message, being the

Bell, Joshua, playing incognito, 32

Bellino, Ricardo R., on principles of
pitching, 179

Belsky, Scott, on method consistency,
56

Berlin, Sir Isaiah, on prioritizing, 107

Bernard, Claude, on knowledge
impeding learning, 303

Bernoff, Josh, on outlining, 131

Berns, Gregory, on fear of public
speaking, 8

Bezos, Jeff
on brands and reputation, 351
on interviewing, 38
on long-term success, 47
on making money, 70

"big league" speakers, 227, 335–41

Blakely, Sara
on importance of single word, 170
on setting a long-term goal, 117

Blankfein, Lloyd, on social media, 37

blog post
author's first, 114
converting video into, 120
writing them can repurpose into a
speech, 358

blunders in public speaking, 154–55

bobbing, weaving, and swaying during
speech. *See* body language

421

Index

D

dating, communication important for, 46–47, 285

debate
high-stakes speaking in, 77, 154, 156, 158, 167, 246, 269
message hack useful for, 166

defining moment. *See* signature moment

delivery
bobbing, weaving, and swaying during. *See* body movement
business presentation, 351–56
checklist for, 323–34
displaying power during, 333, 357
enjoying yourself during, 15, 118, 151, 232, 327, 330, 332, 333
following up on, 333
football compared with, 257, 279, 282
Jobs, Steve, effective, 200
lowering expectations during, 118, 232, 327
pausing in your, 241, 333
relaxation activities before, 333
repeating your BIG idea during, 268, 329
short checklist for, when time-constrained, 326–27
smash-mouth approach in, 279
surprises in, rehearsing, 258
warming up before, 333
working with your body language, 241
working with your voice, 239
See also performance; structure of speech

Dershowitz, Alan, on winning at any cost, 82

details
less important than themes, 270
providing after the speech, 274, 352, 355

See also words

DiMaggio, Joe, on playing so hard, 323

distractions, xi
See also attention of audience, short span of

Dixon, Matthew, and Brent Adamson, on teaching, tailoring, and taking control, 274

dos Santos, José, public speaking gaffe of, 154

Doshi, Neel, and Lindsay McGregor, on tactical, adaptive, and maladaptive performance, 224

Dr. Phil, on not settling for less, 53

dream goals. *See* stretch goals

dressing appropriately, 330, 332

Duarte, Nancy, analyzing the "I Have a Dream" speech, 201

Duckworth, Angela, on hierarchy of goals, 107

Duhigg, Charles
on goal setting, 101
on old versus new information, 59
on the keystone habit, 26

Dunbar, Robin, on being social to survive, 218

E

Eastwood, Clint, unfortunate memorable moment of, 269

education. *See* coaching; training

Einstein, Albert, on explaining to a six-year-old, 347

Eisenhardt, Kathleen, and Donald Sull, how-to rules of, 125

Emerson, Ralph Waldo
on improvement, vi
on power of speech, 23

emotions
capturing audience attention with, 58
controlled, 243–46

Guber, Peter, on Bill Clinton's
signature moment to get funding,
277

H

hack
building a speech, steps for, 130–
33
content. *See* content hack
definition of, 11–12, 122
getting a speech started with a, 122
integrating all three hacks, 284
learning with the 60/30/10 rule,
117
message. *See* message hack
mitigating speech failures with a,
123
"one shot" method for building a
speech, 137
performance. *See* performance hack
simplifying speech development
with a, 125–28
See also minimum viable speech
(MVS)
hand gestures. *See* body language
Heath, Chip and Dan
on the difficulty of conveying
content, 233
on the strength of emotional
appeal, 244
SUCCES model of, 182
Heen, Sheila, and Douglas Stone, on
feedback, 305
helping people more important than
job title, 92–93
Henry, Patrick, historic speech of, 250
high-stakes speaking
becoming good to great at, 161–
300, 339, 357–58
business presentation, in a, 354
checklist for, 323–34
closing the deal with a defining
moment, 276

consider all public speaking as, 14
debate, in a, 77, 154, 156, 158, 167,
246, 269
example of, 1–2, 79, 84, 250, 252,
253
factors for winning at, 51, 204–10,
280
focus of this book, 11, 343
importance of, 2, 4, 26, 80–81
introducing yourself, 87–95
job interview, in a, 325
Jobs, Steve, doing, 199–200
method for, 96–100
performance hack advised for, 299
recording goals for, 114
seminar or workshop in, 361
short checklist for, when time-
constrained, 326–27
vulnerability and, 238
work in progress, 99
historic speeches
Clinton, Bill, 79
Henry, Patrick, 250
Kennedy, John F., 183
Kennedy, Robert F., 84
King Jr., Martin Luther, 253
Lincoln, Abraham, 252
Mondale, Walter, 77
Reagan, Ronald, 209, 269–71
simple logic in, 248
Hoffman, Reid, on being embarrassed
by version 0, 132
Hogshead, Sally, on visibilty, 30
hostility of audience, dealing with, 75,
207, 329
humor
cautions about, 265
Cuddy, Amy, use of, 294
making informative speech
interesting with, 195
rehearsing, 93
self-deprecating, 239, 265
simple logic more important than,
248, 249, 282

O

P

Q

success (*continued*)
  setting goals necessary for, 100–
    108
  short checklist for, when time-
    constrained, 326–27
  zone of speech, 222
Sull, Donald, and Kathleen
  Eisenhardt, how-to rules of, 125
Super Bowl ads containing ineffective
  stories, 262
Sweeney, Paul, on success, 7
symploce stylistic technique, 208
system. *See* method

T

tactical performance, 224
tagline. *See* slogan
teaching, importance of, 78–80, 274
"Tear Down This Wall" speech,
  maxim stylistic technique in, 209
TED Talk
  Cuddy, Amy, 291
  long-term effect of, 250
  preparing for a, 55
  Sandberg, Sheryl, 297
tell them, tell them, tell them
  structure. *See* Aristotelian speech
  structure
testing your speech
  different arguments, 140
  different venues for, 213
  ensuring an effective message, 164
  improvement from, 12, 121, 127,
    166, 188, 287
  See also feedback; iteration
Thatcher, Margaret, on fear of public
  speaking, 8
themes more important than details,
  270
Theseus and Ariadne myth, relevance
  to developing a message, 164
Thiel, Peter, on manipulation, 59

thinking on your feet. *See* winging a
  speech
third-party actor, first-party
  performer, 220
third-party actor, third-party
  performer, 220
thought leader, being seen as a, 288
time
  budgeting your, 331, 354
  needed to prepare, 55–56, 125, 299,
    324
  reducing the speech's overall, 136,
    331, 353
  time-bound goals, 101–3
time takes in content hack, 136
Toastmasters International,
  overcoming fear with, 7
topic, selecting a, 130
top-level goals, 103–8
Tracy, Brian, speaking tips of, 202,
  331
training
  courses, ineffectiveness of short,
    57, 143
  customized, 361
  importance of, 1, 40
  See also coaching; communication
  skills
transitions in speech, 201, 329
Trudeau, Justin, deflecting surprise
  question, 156
Trump, Donald J.
  audience appeal of, 15
  communication power of, xii–xiii,
    36–37, 288
  endorsing project of Ricardo
    Bellino after 3-minute speech,
    179
  entertaining his audience, 224
  example of maladaptive
    performance, 225
  a great public speaker?, 229
  resonating message of, 192–93

winning speech moment (*continued*)
  celebrating after creating, 334
  checklist for, 323–34
  creating the right, 83–86
  definition of, x
  integrating the parts of, xiv
  mindset for, developing the, xiv, 19, 112, 283
  most effective near the end of the speech, 279
  people remember a, xii, 257–72
  power of, xii, 230
  practice, importance of in developing, xiv, 106, 230, 339, 341
  short checklist for, when time-constrained, 326–27
  simple, memorable, repeatable, 14–15
  teaching, tailoring, and taking control, 274
  time needed to create, 299, 324
  See also job interview; memorable moment; performance hack; presentation moment; signature moment
Winninger, Thom, on levels of story, 264
Wooden, John, on preparation, 55
words
  less important than visual and vocal aspects, 236, 354
  one word first step in message hack, 168–71
  overuse of, xiii, 18, 119, 157, 159, 202, 205, 260, 331
  showing you are having fun with your, 333
  speech without message is just, 164
  See also content; message
workplace, speaking at the
  importance of, 35, 38–40
  making a business presentation, 351–56

usefulness of this book for, 11
  See also job interview
wowing the audience, 283–300
  not always the most important objective, 5
writing compared with public speaking, 234

Y

"Yes We Can!" slogan, 172, 229
YouTube
  Cuddy, Amy, TED Talk of, 291
  evaluating a speech on, 300
  examples of speeches, 25, 291, 295, 297
  getting feedback from, 120, 125
  Jobs, Steve, commencement address of, 295
  perfection, eschewing, 137
  producing for, 139, 140, 145, 320, 332, 337
  Sandberg, Sheryl, TED Talk of, 297
  See also 3/30 Challenge; recording your speech; *Speech Talk Live*; video

Z

Zandan, Noah, on what business leaders focus on, 354
Ziglar, Zig
  on taking the first step, 111
  vocal techniques of, 240
Zito, Salena, on Donald Trump, 193
Zyman, Sergio, on ineffective story, 263

www.ingramcontent.com/pod-product-compliance
Lightning Source LLC
Chambersburg PA
CBHW062355090426
42740CB00010B/1286